Easy
Internet
troubleshooting

Other Computer Titles

by

Robert Penfold

Other Titles of Interest

Easy Internet troubleshooting

Robert Penfold

Bernard Babani (publishing) Ltd
The Grampians
Shepherds Bush Road
London W6 7NF
England
www.babanibooks.com

Please note

Although every care has been taken with the production of this book to ensure that any projects, designs, modifications, and/or programs, etc., contained herewith, operate in a correct and safe manner and also that any components specified are normally available in Great Britain, the Publisher and Author do not accept responsibility in any way for the failure (including fault in design) of any projects, design, modification, or program to work correctly or to cause damage to any equipment that it may be connected to or used in conjunction with, or in respect of any other damage or injury that may be caused, nor do the Publishers accept responsibility in any way for the failure to obtain specified components.

Notice is also given that if any equipment that is still under warranty is modified in any way or used or connected with home-built equipment then that warranty may be void.

First Published - October 2001

British Library Cataloguing in Publication Data

A catalogue record for this book is available from the British Library

ISBN   0 85934 507 6

Cover Design by Gregor Arthur

Printed and bound in Great Britain by Cox & Wyman

Preface

The Internet has developed from the days when it was strictly the domain of real computer experts, and it is now possible for anyone to buy a computer and get online. Once online you have access to a huge resource that was in the realms of science fiction not all that long ago. Although the Internet is now usable by the "man and woman in the street", the technology behind it is still very advanced. In fact it is more advanced now than in the days when it was the realm of computer "nerds" and "geeks". The difference is that advanced technology is, as far as possible, hidden from the user. This makes it possible to sign up for an Internet access account in a couple of minutes rather than the couple of hours of intense effort that it took at one stage.

Unfortunately, the fact that it is easier to get your PC connected to the Internet does not mean that everything will always work perfectly. The huge complexity hidden away in the background gives plenty of scope for things to go wrong. There can still be difficulties in getting connected to the Internet in the first place, or the information super-highway may grind along very slowly once you are connected. The sheer quantity of information available can also create problems. It is easy to carry out searches that provide information on almost everything under the sun, but somehow manage to miss the information you are actually looking for. Having sought out a music file or a video, will you actually be able to play it on your PC? By enabling huge numbers of people to exchange almost limitless amounts of information, security becomes an important issue. How do you keep your PC safe from attack, and what do you do if a virus should strike?

With the aid of this book you can tackle connection problems, slow connection speeds, problems with Emails, multimedia, search engines, downloads, and security, plus a great deal else. A wide range of difficulties and annoyances are covered. These range from the removal of irksome branding that some Internet service providers insist on adding to Internet Explorer and Outlook Express, to reinstalling Windows after a serious attack from a virus. Virtually all aspects of using the Internet are covered.

You do not have to be a computer expert in order to follow the procedures detailed in this book, but you do have to be familiar with the basics of using the Windows user interface. None of the suggestions should be beyond someone having at least a few months experience with Windows. You need to be someone who is reasonably practical in order to deal with the few procedures that involve the computer's hardware, but again, you by no means need to be an expert.

Robert Penfold

Trademarks

Microsoft, Windows, Windows Me, Windows 98 and Windows 95 are either registered trademarks or trademarks of Microsoft Corporation.

All other brand and product names used in this book are recognised trademarks, or registered trademarks of their respective companies. There is no intent to use any trademarks generically and readers should investigate ownership of a trademark before using it for any purpose.

Contents

3

Download managers 97

4

Browser problems 123

5

Email problems 181

6

Multimedia problems 223

7

Search problems 257

8

Security matters 289

Getting connected

What modem?

When you are having connection difficulties the obvious starting point is to check that the modem is installed correctly. It is definitely the first thing to check if you get any error messages along the lines of "modem not detected". If the modem is newly installed or the computer itself is new, it might be worthwhile opening up the PC to check that the modem card is properly fitted into its expansion slot. It should be like Figure 1.1, with the connector on the card fully pushed down into the expansion slot. Sometimes the card fits properly into place initially, but then goes out of position when its mounting bracket is bolted to the chassis of the computer. The card pulls out slightly and goes at an angle to the expansion slot (Figure 1.2). The top of the mounting bracket being at something other than a true right angle usually causes this, and a little adjustment here should cure the problem.

External problems

If the modem is an external type check that the connectors all fit together properly and that everything is wired up correctly. USB modems are normally powered from the USB port, but serial types have their own power supply. This can be an internal mains power supply unit, an external power supply, or batteries, depending on the make and model of the modem. Whatever type of power source is used, is it all present and correct. Frantically searching for the cause of a fault when the only problem is that the "faulty" unit has not been switched on is not exactly a rare occurrence.

Ports that are provided by a PC's motherboard are normally switched on by default, but I have encountered problems with peripherals that were caused by the relevant port being deactivated. First check to see if the

Fig.1.1 A correctly installed PCI modem card

port used for the modem has been recognised by Windows. In order to do this you must go to the Windows Device Manager. One route to Device Manager is to select Settings from the Start window and then double-click on the System icon in the new window that appears. Alternatively, right-click on the My Computer icon on the Windows desktop to produce the popup menu of Figure 1.3, and then select the Properties option. Either way, the System Properties window will appear, and operating the Device Manager tab will produce something like Figure 1.4.

Practically all of the hardware in the PC system will be listed in Device Manager. In this case it is the ports that are of interest, so double-click on the Ports entry in the list to expand it and show the available ports (Figure 1.5). There will usually be a minimum of one parallel (LPT) and two serial (COM) ports, and an external serial modem will therefore connect to COM1 or COM2. Incidentally, internal modems usually connect to a notional COM3 or COM4, but as they do not use conventional serial port hardware these ports are not usually listed in the Ports section of Device Manager. If one of the ports has a problem there will be a

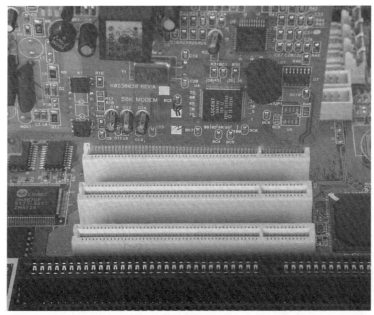

Fig.1.2 This modem card is not fitted into the slot correctly

yellow exclamation mark against its entry. Double clicking on an entry for a port will produce its Properties Window (Figure 1.6), and this will either state that the port is functioning correctly or give basic details of any problem.

As serial port hardware is usually part of the motherboard and the device drivers are standard Windows drivers, a problem here probably indicates a serious hardware fault. A problem with the Windows installation is also possible. Reinstalling Windows is covered in chapter 8.

A detailed discussion of hardware faultfinding goes beyond the scope of this book and in most cases the PC will require a visit to

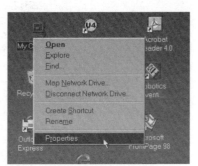

Fig.1.3 Launching the System Properties window

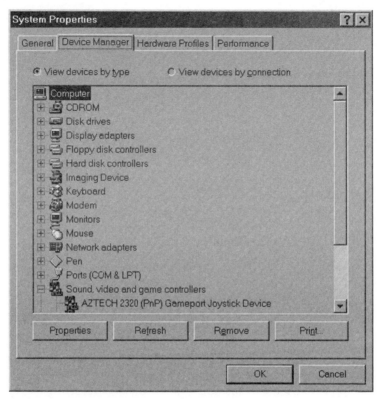

Fig.1.4 The list of installed hardware in Device Manager

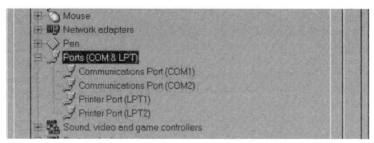

*Fig.1.5 An entry can be expanded to show the individual items of
hardware (in this case the serial and parallel ports)*

a proper servicing facility. Before resorting to professional help there is a useful ploy that can be tried with the problematic hardware. First delete its entry from the list in Device Manager and then reboot the computer. To delete an item first left-click on its entry to select it, and then operate the Remove button. This will produce a warning message like the one in Figure 1.7. Operate the OK button to go ahead and remove the item. When the computer is rebooted, Windows will detect the port hardware and reinstall the device drivers. Device Manager can then be used to determine whether or not the reinstallation has cleared the fault.

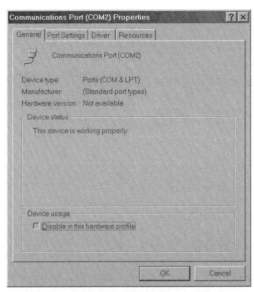

Fig.1.6 The Properties window for a serial port

Fig.1.7 Operate the OK button in order to go ahead and delete the device

Port settings

Left clicking on the Port Settings tab in the Properties Window produces a window like the one in Figure 1.8. The various port settings control the speed at which data is transferred via the port, and the various protocols used for data exchanges. A modern modem is unlikely to require the default settings, and the speed setting normally has to be set at its

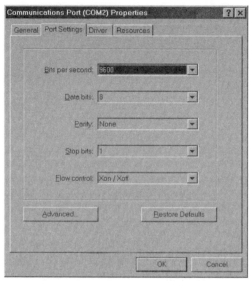

maximum. This is usually 115200 bits per second. The settings might be made by the Setup program on the disc provided with the modem. If not, they have to be changed manually. The modem's instruction manual should give instructions on getting the port set up correctly.

Fig.1.8 The Port Settings window

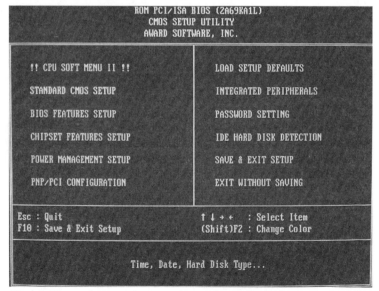

Fig.1.9 The main menu for a version of the Award BIOS Setup program

What port?

If one of the serial ports on the motherboard is absent from the list of ports in Device Manager it is likely that there is a hardware fault. However, as pointed out previously, there is a chance that the port has simply been deactivated. In the past it was common for the ports to be controlled by switches or jumpers on the motherboard, but these days the BIOS is invariably used to control this type of thing. The manual for your PC or its motherboard should have some basic information about the BIOS Setup program, which you must enter to check the port settings.

The first thing you need to know is how to enter the Setup program. This is not usually possible from within Windows, and is normally achieved early in the boot process. In fact the Setup program is normally entered before Windows starts to boot and the BIOS is still performing the usual start up checks. The most common method is to press the Delete key during the BIOS start up routine, but other keys such as Escape and the F1 function key are used. The instruction manual for your computer should explain the correct method. In most cases a message telling you which key or keys to press will be included on one of the BIOS start-up screens.

In early PCs the BIOS Setup program was only used to control a few basic functions such as the time setting of the PC's clock, details of the disc drives fitted, and the amount of memory. With modern PCs it controls a huge range of settings, and it is usually divided into about six pages. Each page controls all the settings of a general type, and all the pages are accessed via the main menu. This menu should appear on entering the program. There are several BIOS programs in common use, and each one is tailored to suit individual makes and models of motherboard. Consequently it is only possible to deal with the subject in fairly broad terms here. Anyway, Figure 1.9 shows the main page for a version of the Award BIOS.

The page that controls the ports will have a name such as Integrated Peripherals or Onboard Peripherals. Use the cursor keys to highlight the correct page in the menu system and then press the Return key to enter the page (Figure 1.10). Look for entries that govern the serial ports, and in this example there are two. These are the Onboard Serial Port 1 and Onboard Serial Port 2 settings. In Figure 1.10 these are at the normal settings of 3F8/IRQ4 for port 1, and 2F8/IRQ3 for port 2. Other address and interrupt numbers are usually available, but are only used if there are conflicts between the onboard ports and hardware added to one of the expansion ports. You only need to change things if the setting is

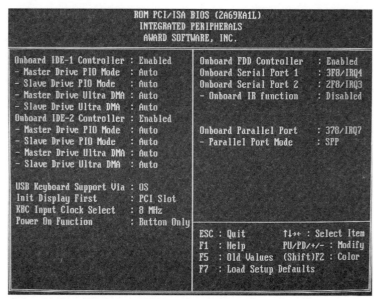

```
                    ROM PCI/ISA BIOS (2A69KA1L)
                       INTEGRATED PERIPHERALS
                       AWARD SOFTWARE, INC.

Onboard IDE-1 Controller : Enabled      Onboard FDD Controller    : Enabled
- Master Drive PIO Mode   : Auto        Onboard Serial Port 1     : 3F8/IRQ4
- Slave Drive PIO Mode    : Auto        Onboard Serial Port 2     : 2F8/IRQ3
- Master Drive Ultra DMA  : Auto        - Onboard IR function     : Disabled
- Slave Drive Ultra DMA   : Auto
Onboard IDE-2 Controller : Enabled
- Master Drive PIO Mode   : Auto        Onboard Parallel Port     : 378/IRQ7
- Slave Drive PIO Mode    : Auto        - Parallel Port Mode      : SPP
- Master Drive Ultra DMA  : Auto
- Slave Drive Ultra DMA   : Auto

USB Keyboard Support Via : OS
Init Display First       : PCI Slot
KBC Input Clock Select   : 8 MHz
Power On Function        : Button Only
                                        ESC : Quit          ↑↓→← : Select Item
                                        F1  : Help          PU/PD/+/- : Modify
                                        F5  : Old Values  (Shift)F2 : Color
                                        F7  : Load Setup Defaults
```

Fig.1.10 The page of the BIOS Setup program that controls the port settings

something like Disabled or Off. The settings should then be changed to match those in Figure 1.10, or the Auto setting can be used if there is one.

Having made any necessary changes to the settings, press the Escape key to Return to the main menu. Then select the Save And Exit option and press the Return key. You will be asked to confirm that you wish to save the changes, and having confirmed that you do the PC will start to reboot. During the reboot process Windows should discover the newly activated port or ports and install the drivers for them. A check using Device Manager should then confirm that the ports are "up and running".

It is only fair to point out here that messing around with the BIOS settings is not a good idea. Only make a change if you are sure you know what you are doing and the change is necessary. It is unlikely that using inappropriate settings could cause any damage, but it is certainly possible to render the PC unreliable or even unusable until suitable settings have been restored. If you think that you might have accidentally altered a setting, use the Exit Without Saving option to go out of the BIOS Setup program without implementing any changes. You can then re-enter the BIOS and try again. It is not necessarily too serious if you should

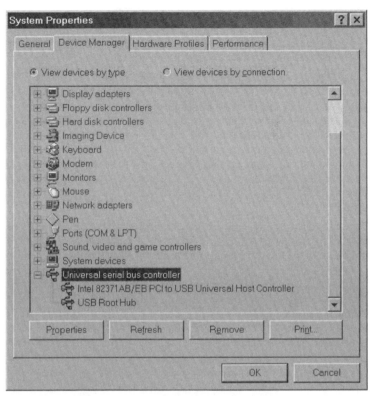

Fig.1.11   Checking the USB ports in Device Manager

somehow manage to make a mess of the BIOS settings. The BIOS Setup program will almost certainly have an option for using sensible default settings or returning to a previous set. Using either of these should get the computer back into working order.

USB Modems

Windows should detect a USB modem during the boot up sequence, or when it is first switched on and connected to the PC if the PC is running at the time. Either way the installation disc supplied with the modem will be requested, and after the usual Windows style installation procedure the modem should be ready for use. If Windows fails to detect the modem there is probably a hardware fault or something is not connected properly. If a check shows that everything is wired up correctly, go to Device Manager and look at the entry for the USB ports. Note that the USB ports have an entry of their own (Figure 1.11) and are not included in Ports section.

If the ports are absent it is likely that there is a major hardware fault or the ports are not switched on in the BIOS. Modern PCs are invariably supplied with at least two active USB ports, but some older PCs were supplied with the USB ports disabled. This was presumably due to the lack of proper operating system support at the time. Where there is a setting for switching the USB ports on and off it will probably be in the Integrated Peripherals or Chipset Features section of the BIOS Setup program. Note though, that this feature is not present on all PCs, and it is often absent on modern PCs.

If you are using an old operating system a lack of proper support can still cause problems with USB ports. Using Windows 98 or later it is unlikely that there will be any installation problems, but the situation is very different with Windows 95. USB ports were never properly supported by the early versions of this operating system, and there can also be problems with the final version (OSR2). With the earlier versions USB device drivers may be installed, but there will be yellow exclamation marks against the entries for the ports in Device Manager. With the final version of Windows 95 there should be no problems with the dreaded exclamation marks, but in practice the ports might not work properly. If you are going to use the USB ports with any type of peripheral device it is advisable to use Windows 98 or a later version of the Windows operating system.

Modem drivers

If there are no problems with the ports, the settings for the modem itself should be checked. First look in Device Manager to see if there are any yellow exclamation marks against the entry for the modem. Where a problem is indicated it is a good idea to try reinstalling the device drivers. The easiest way of doing this is to delete the modem's entry from Device Manager. You can not remove a category from Device Manager, only individual items. Double-click on the modem's entry to expand it, and then left-click on the modem's entry to select it. Then operate the Remove button followed by the Yes button when you are asked if you are sure that you wish to remove the modem. The modem's entry in Device Manager will then disappear, as will the Modem category if only one modem was installed.

If at first...

On rebooting the computer the modem can be reinstalled, following the manufacturer's installation instructions. It is possible that things will not go any better at the second attempt, but it is worth trying again. This time close down and switch off the computer once the modem has been removed from Device Manager. Physically remove the modem from the PC, and then reboot without it. Check that the modem is still absent from Device Manager, and if necessary remove it and reboot the PC again. Once you have established that the modem has been properly uninstalled from Windows, close down Windows and switch off the computer. Refit the modem, switch the computer back on again, and then reinstall the driver software. This should avoid having the old and non-working drivers reactivated. With the device drivers installed from scratch there is a better chance of the reinstallation being successful.

Resources

A PC can accommodate a fair amount of hardware, but there are limits to the number of gadgets that can be used in expansion slots. One of the reasons for USB being introduced is that it enables a PC to be used with an almost endless range of peripherals without any danger of two devices trying to use the same hardware resources. In this respect both serial and USB modems are better than any form of internal modem, because they normally use the existing ports and resources of the PC. With an internal modem you can check to see if there

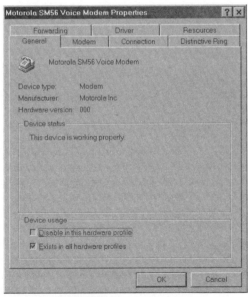

Fig.1.12 The Modem Properties window

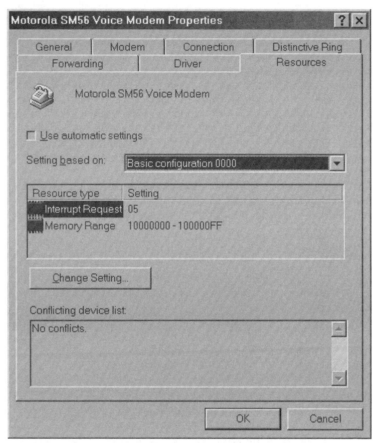

Fig.1.13 Checking for problems in the resource settings

are any problems with hardware conflicts by first going to Device Manager and double clicking on the modem's entry. This brings up a window like the one in Figure 1.12. Left click on the Resources tab to produce a window like the one of Figure 1.13.

In this example all is well, and near the bottom of the screen it indicates that there are no conflicts. If there is a conflict, this will be pointed out and some technical details will be provided. Sorting out hardware conflicts is a somewhat involved process, with no guarantee of success. Some items of hardware are simply incompatible and can not be used in

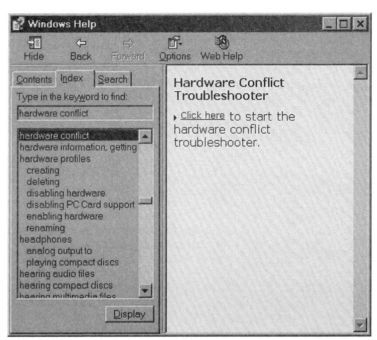

Fig.1.14 Using the Windows Troubleshooter to help resolve problems with hardware conflicts

the same PC. For those lacking expertise at sorting out this type of thing there is some built-in help available from Windows. Select Help from the Start menu, enter "hardware conflict" into the text box, and then double-click on the entry of the same name that appears in the list below the textbox.

This should produce something like Figure 1.14. Left-click where it says, "click here" in the right-hand side of the window to start the Hardware Troubleshooter. This produces a screen like the one of Figure 1.15, and it is then a matter of going through various screens so that Windows can be fed the information it requires. It is normally necessary to do some delving with Device Manager in order to come up with the right answers, but detailed instructions are provided. With luck, at the end of the process you will have a solution to the problem.

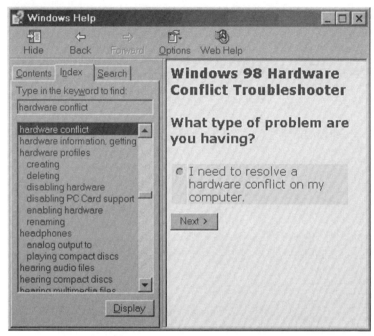

Fig.1.15 Using the Troubleshooter is largely a matter of running checks when prompted and supplying answers

All change

Probably the most common cause of a hardware conflict when using a modem is the modem and the mouse trying to use the same interrupt request (IRQ) number. This usually manifests itself in the form of the mouse operating either erratically or not at all. Where possible, the simplest solution is to move the mouse to the other serial port. If this port is already in use this option is not available, and the only way to avoid the conflict might be to change the modem's settings. However, it is usually worthwhile swapping over the two items on the serial ports. This port swapping is a useful ploy whenever problems arise with serial devices, and has even been known to work with USB equipment.

Fig.1.16 The Windows Control Panel. There may be more or fewer icons depending on the set-up of your PC

Dialling set-up

Having established that the hardware is present and correct, the next step is to check the dialling set-up for any obvious errors. First select Settings from the Start menu, which will bring up the Control Panel (Figure 1.16). This may have two modem icons, as in Figure 1.16. One is the general modem icon that gives access to the standard Windows facilities, and the other is specific to the particular modem that is installed. This second icon and the facilities it provides are added when the device drivers are installed. It might be worthwhile looking at the settings available via this second icon, but the facilities available here vary from one modem to another. The standard modem settings are more important, so double-click on this icon to launch the Modem Properties window (Figure 1.17).

The modems installed in the computer will be listed, and there will presumably just be the one. Sometimes the Windows plug and play system glitches and a device that is already installed is installed a second

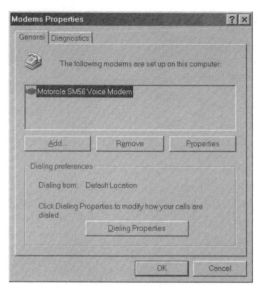

Fig.1.17 The Modem Properties window

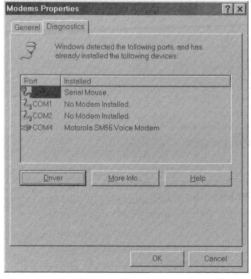

Fig.1.18 Checking the Diagnostics section

time. If this happens with the modem there will be two entries for the same hardware in the Modem Properties window and in Device Manager. When this doubling-up occurs it is "par for the course" if neither installation works. The solution is to remove both in Device Manager and then reinstall the modem.

Assuming one modem is installed and one entry is shown in the Modem Properties window, left-click the Diagnostics tab to produce a window like the one in Figure 1.18. This shows a list of the serial ports and indicates which one the modem is connected to. Select the modem's port and then operate the More Info button. A message will appear on the screen explaining that the program is trying to communicate with the modem. Then an additional window will be produced

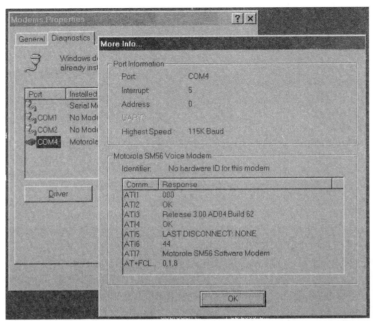

Fig.1.19 Test results for the modem, and everything seems to be in order. There is a problem if "garbage" or an error message is produced

(Figure 1.19). The bottom section of this window shows the codes sent to the modem and the responses obtained. In the example of Figure 1.19 the modem is clearly being contacted correctly and it is providing sensible responses.

When an internal modem appears to be installed correctly, but this test produces either no response or garbled results, the most likely cause of the problem is a hardware fault, probably with the modem itself. This can also be indicative of a hardware fault if the modem is an external type, or it could just be that the modem is not connected properly or is switched off! In the case of an external serial modem it is worth checking the cable for signs of damage and trying a new one if possible. There is more than one type of serial connection lead, and two leads that look the same do not necessarily have the connectors wired together in the same way. An external serial modem is normally supplied complete with a suitable connecting cable, and it is advisable to use this lead to connect the unit to the PC.

No dialling tone

An error message along the lines of "no dialling tone detected" is not an uncommon problem. Obviously this can occur because there is genuinely no dialling tone present, and this problem is one that is covered later in this chapter. It is easy to check this point by picking up the telephone and listening for the usual dialling tone. If the dialling tone is present and correct there is probably a minor problem with the lead from the modem to the telephone wall socket. Try disconnecting and reconnecting the lead both at the modem and the telephone socket. If an extension lead is in use, disconnect and reconnect this as well. Make sure that all the plugs are properly locked into the sockets. The connectors used for telephones and modems are quick and easy to use, but they are not the toughest of components. Leads tend to get kicked around and tripped over, and the connectors are damaged occasionally. Look carefully at all the connectors and replace any leads that have a seriously damaged plug or socket.

The connection to the telephone socket is via a standard BT plug, but the connection to the modem is by way of a smaller American style telephone plug. Both types of plug are shown in Figure 1.20. The

American style plugs and sockets seem to be something less than rigidly standardised. Some plugs do not lock into the sockets properly, while others are difficult to fit into place at all. Unfortunately, a few seem to fit into place perfectly but do not make reliable connections. When installing a new modem or PC it is normal to use the

Fig.1.20 The two styles of telephone plug

existing lead to connect the modem to the telephone socket. However, this can give problems and it is safer to make the connection to the modem via the lead supplied with the modem or PC. This should be a good and reliable match for the socket fitted to the modem.

A faulty modem can sometimes result in the telephones on the system failing to work properly. Typically, as soon as the modem is plugged into the wall socket the telephones on the same circuit ring until the modem is disconnected again. This can also be caused by a faulty cable or one of the wrong type. A cable of the so-called American variety will not give the correct set of connections between the modem and socket and will usually produce this fault. Once again, it is a matter of using the cable provided with the modem wherever possible and making sure that any extension cables are of the correct type.

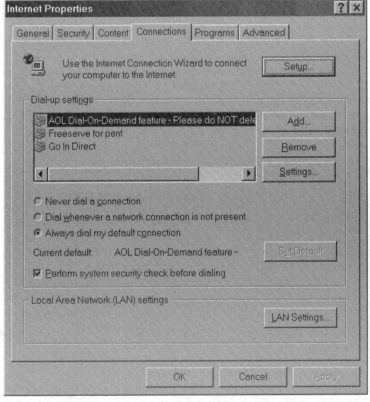

Fig.1.21 The Connections section of the Internet Properties window

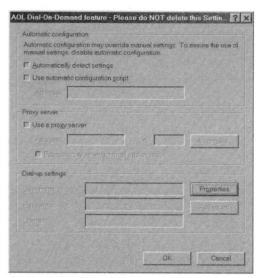

Fig.1.22 Checking the settings for an ISP

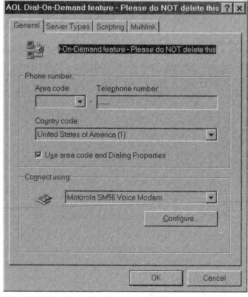

Fig.1.23 Is the telephone number correct?

More settings

If you have progressed this far and the problem has not been found, there are still some settings that can be checked. Provided you have signed on to at least one Internet service there should be a default provider for the PC to dial. To check this, go to the Control Panel and double-click on the Internet Options icon and then operate the Connections tab on the window that appears. This should give something like Figure 1.21. To set an entry in the "Dial-up settings" list as the default it is first selected by left clicking on its entry. Then operate the Set Default button, which should become active when an entry other than the current default is selected.

To check that an entry in the list is set up correctly, select the appropriate entry in the list and then operate the Settings button. This brings up the window of Figure 1.22, where the Properties button is left clicked in order to produce a window like the one in Figure 1.23. The top section of the window should contain the telephone number of the Internet service provider, and in Figure 1.23 this information is clearly absent. This may look like an error, but in this case it is actually correct. The Internet service provider in this

Fig.1.24 With most ISPs the telephone number will be included here

instance is AOL, and this company uses software that has its own database of telephone numbers. Hence no number is needed here, but in most cases the relevant fields of this window should be filled in correctly, as in the example of Figure 1.24. If the number includes an area code that is required from you dialling area, make sure that the checkbox is ticked. Also make sure that the correct modem is selected in the menu near the bottom of the window.

Next try operating the Server Types tab to switch the window to one like Figure 1.25. Using Windows ME these settings are available by selecting the Networking tab incidentally. The type of dial-up server should be PPP, and TCP/IP should be selected as the only allowed network protocol. The checkbox that enables software compression is normally checked, but you can try turning off this feature to see if it improves matters.

Windows ME has a Security tab, and left clicking on this one produces a window like the one in Figure 1.26. This is another case of AOL doing things its own way, so the User name and Password fields are blank in this example. With most Internet service providers the appropriate user

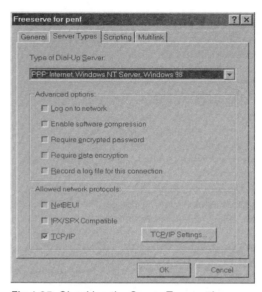

Fig.1.25 Checking the Server Type settings

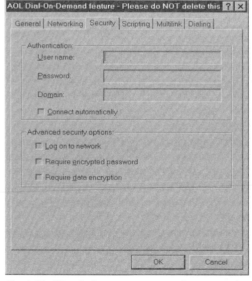

Fig.1.26 Check the user name and password

name will be shown, but the password field will of course show a series of asterisks rather than the password. If necessary the user name can be edited, and the password can be re-entered if you think that it might be wrong. Note that these are the user name and password issued by your Internet service provider during the sign-up process. They are not any special name and password used to gain initial entry to the system so that the sign-up process can commence. These are only required the first time you access the system and are not needed thereafter.

Lost connections

Sometimes the problem is not one of getting connected to the Internet, but one of staying connected. Bear in mind that most of the unmetered Internet service providers will cut your Internet connection if there is more than about 10 or 20 minutes of inactivity. Also, many have a cut off period of about two hours that comes into operation even if the connection is in use.

In addition to these enforced cuts in connection, there will inevitably be the occasional glitch on the line that results in the connection to the server being lost. If the connection is frequently lost for no apparent reason it could be that there is an intermittent fault on the line. If voice communication via your telephone is a bit noisy and unreliable there is little chance of reliable Internet operation with good connection speeds. The relevant telephone company should be prepared to investigate if the line consistently provides bad results.

Stuck online

A problem I have encountered several times is that of a connection not being cut off at the end of a session. This seems to occur mainly when using an Internet service provider that has its own Internet software. Usually everything seems to shut down correctly, but the modem has not hung up and it is still connected to the host. You generally remain oblivious to the problem until you pick up the telephone handset and here the signals from the modems, or an error message is produced when you shut down Windows.

When using an unmetered service it is not the end of the world if the connection fails to terminate, since the extra time connected to the system will not cost anything. It is undesirable to have the telephone line tied up unnecessarily, but the Internet service provider will probably cut off the call after about 20 or 30 minutes of inactivity. It is clearly more serious if you are paying for a peak rate call, even if it is only at the local peak rate. If you are lucky, the Internet service provider will cut off the connection after 20 or 30 minutes so that cost of the fault is minimised. If not, the call could be quite expensive.

If you find that the connection has not terminated correctly the first task is to cut the connection. Shutting down Windows and switching off is one way of getting offline. Simply unplugging the telephone cable from the modem or telephone socket is another way. Lifting and lowering the handset a few times is usually sufficient to disrupt communications and cut off the connection. To minimise the damage if the same thing should happen again it is a good idea to alter one of the dialup settings. Launch Internet Explorer and choose Internet Options from the Tools menu.

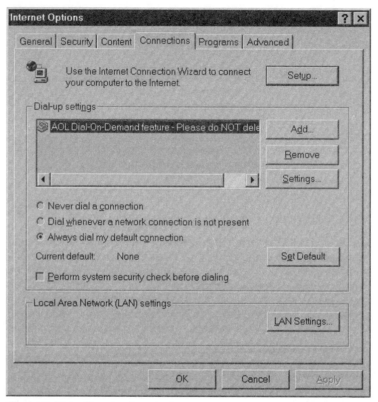

Fig.1.27 Operating the Connections tab produces a window like this

Alternatively, choose Settings from the Start menu to launch the Windows Control Panel and then double-click on the Internet Options icon.

Now left-click on the Connections tab to produce a window like Figure 1.27 and then on the Settings button in the new version of the window. This should produce something like Figure 1.28. Next operate the Properties button followed by the Dialling tab on the new window that appears. This should give a window like the one in Figure 1.29. Make sure that the checkbox labelled "Enable idle disconnect" is ticked. The required time can then be added in the appropriate textbox. The time used here has to be something of a compromise. It is obviously desirable to have the connection disconnected as soon as possible if things go wrong, but you must avoid having the connection terminated during

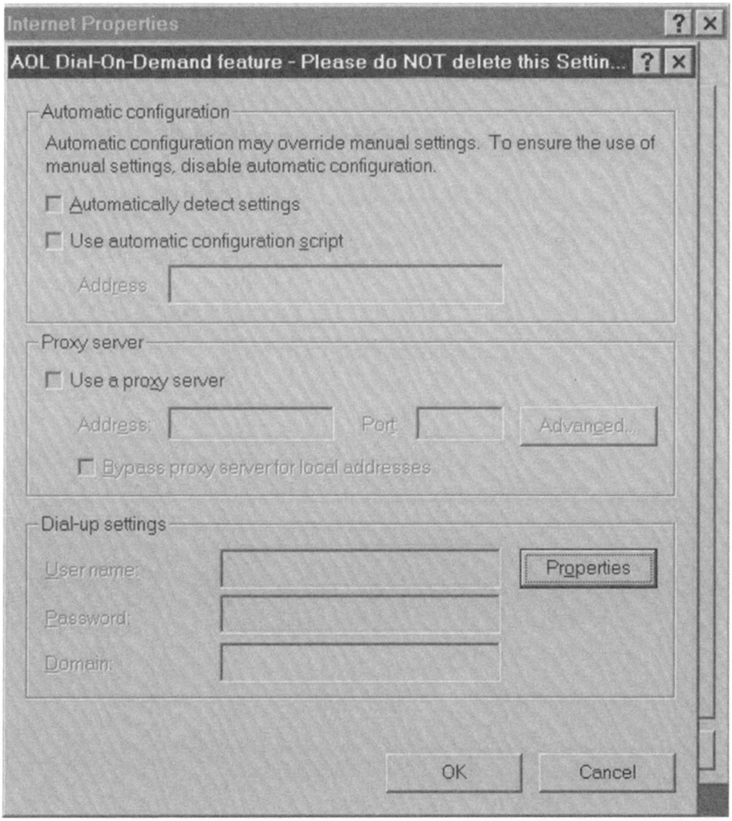

Fig.1.28 Operate the Properties button to check the ISPs dial-up settings

normal use. It could take a few minutes to answer the door, or to read a large Internet page. The default value is 20 minutes, but a 10-minute cut-off time is more than adequate for most users. Note that inactivity in this case means some sort of data transfer between your PC and the host. Things like mouse and keyboard operations count as inactivity unless they result in something being uploaded or downloaded. Tick the "Don't prompt before disconnecting" checkbox if you prefer to have the connection terminated without warning. It is probably best not to do this, as it could leave you unaware that there is a continuing problem.

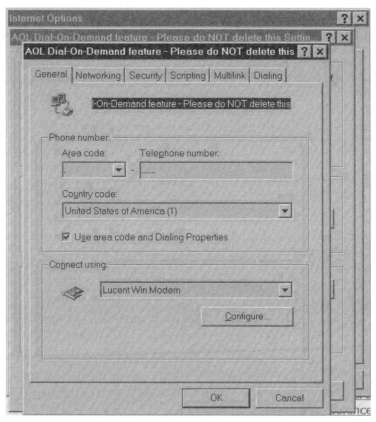

Fig.1.29 Checking the dialling properties

After making any necessary changes, operate the OK button to close the window, and then left-click the OK button on the next window to return to the Internet Properties window. If you use more than one Internet service provider this process should be repeated for each of the others.

Reinstallation

Reinstallation of the offending software is the only cure if there is a recurring problem with the connection not being terminated. It is advisable to remove the existing software first and then reinstall it from scratch. With a service provider such as AOL, which installs its own

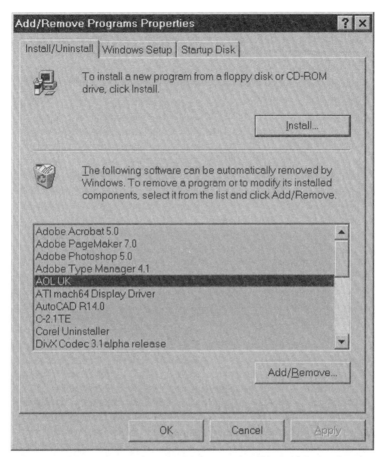

Fig.1.30 Windows has built-in facilities for removing installed software, which includes the software supplied by some ISPs

software during the sign-up process, it is clearly this software that must be removed. Select Settings from the Start menu to launch the Control Panel and then double-click on the Add/Remove programs icon. This will produce a window like the one of Figure 1.30, which includes a list of all the software that has been installed in Windows. Scroll down the list to find the entry for your Internet service provider's software and then operate the Add/Remove button.

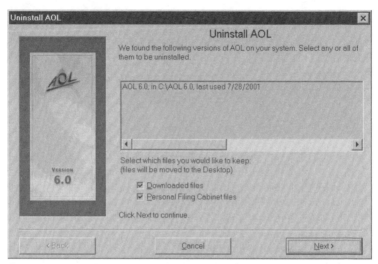

Fig.1.31 Uninstalling software is largely automatic, but you may be presented with some options

The process from thereon varies from one piece of software to another. The process is largely automatic, and you may have to do nothing more than confirm that you wish to completely remove the program. In other cases you may have a few options available, as in the example of Figure 1.31, which is the initial screen when uninstalling version 6 of AOL's software. Where the option is available you will presumably wish to keep downloaded files, etc., so that they are available when the software is reinstalled. When uninstalling software it is quite likely that you will be asked if you wish to delete one or more shared files that are no longer required. As the software will be immediately reinstalled it probably does not matter what you answer, but the No button is always the safer option.

If you are using a service provider that utilises the standard Windows Internet facilities you can try removing and reinstalling Internet Explorer and the associated software. This should be included in the list of installed software as something like "Internet Explorer 5.5 and Internet Tools". Having removed and reinstalled Internet Explorer you will need to go through the sign up process again with you service provider, and you will need any screen names, passwords, etc., used for the initial signup. This type of information is also needed when reinstalling the service provider's own software, or you will find yourself setting up a new account.

Random reset

I have occasionally encountered problems with systems that randomly reset themselves when connected to the Internet. In some cases it only occurs very infrequently, but in others it can happen quite often. In one case it was impossible to set up a connection to one of the largest Internet service providers due to the system always resetting at a certain point in the sign-up process. This seems to be a problem with certain modems, or to be more precise, with the device drivers for certain software modems. Software modems, which also known by such names as "soft" modems and "Winmodems", use relatively simple hardware. The inadequacies of the hardware have to be compensated for by device drivers that are much more complex than normal modem drivers. The drivers do rather more than integrate the hardware into Windows, and carry out some of the encoding and decoding, error correction, etc.

Modems of this type are inexpensive but can work well provided they are used in a reasonably powerful PC and the drivers are well written. Unfortunately, some of the very low cost generic modems of this type seem to be supplied with drivers that are not as reliable as they should be. It might be possible to find a more recent version of the driver software that works more reliably. If not, the only solution might be to replace the modem with a more reliable unit. Finding and installing new drivers is covered in the next chapter, as is replacing a modem, so these subjects will not be pursued further here.

Call waiting

The modern telephone system provides all sorts of clever features, but they can give problems when using a modem. Call waiting can be troublesome as it can result in an incoming call producing signals on the line that result in the Internet connection being lost. Call waiting can be disabled by dialling the correct code, which is normally *43#. It can be enabled again by dialling the reactivation code, which is usually #43#.

There is a facility in Windows that enables the appropriate code to be dialled prior to the Internet service provider's number being dialled. Select Settings and then Control Panel from the Start menu to launch the Windows Control Panel and then double-click on the Modems icon. In the new window that appears left-click the Dialling Properties button, and another window should pop up on the screen (Figure 1.32). Tick the checkbox labelled "To disable call waiting, dial" and then add the appropriate code into the textbox. Operate the Apply and OK buttons to

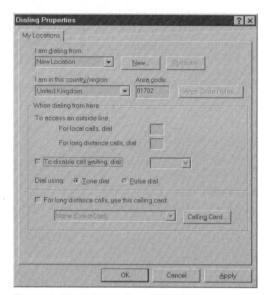

Fig.1.32 Disabling call waiting

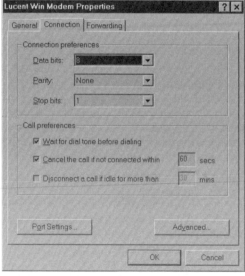

Fig.1.33 Avoiding the dialling tone check

make the changes take effect, and then left-click the OK button to close the Modems Properties window.

Some services, but particularly BT's Call Minder facility, can result in the dialling tone disappearing from time to time. The telephone system still works perfectly, but when someone has left a message the dialling tone becomes intermittent or simply disappears for a while. While this may not seem to be of any practical importance it can prevent the modem from dialling your Internet service provider. The modem fails to detect a dialling tone and assumes that there is a fault on the line or it is not connected to the telephone system.

The solution to this problem is to go into the Windows Control Panel, double-click the Modems icon, operate the Properties button in the new window that appears, and then operate the Connection tab. This should give a window like the one of Figure 1.33. Remove the tick in the checkbox labelled "Wait for dialling tone before dialling". The modem will then dial your Internet service provider whether or not a dialling tone is detected.

Reduced wait

It is also possible to cure another problem using this window. There can sometimes be a problem with the modem taking a long time to detect that its attempt at getting connected has failed. This is most likely to occur when a line is overloaded and a recorded message to this effect is received instead of a carrier signal. By default the modem will wait 60 seconds before it decides that there is a problem and it needs to redial. It is worthwhile reducing the 60-second timeout if this happens quite frequently. First make sure that there is a tick in the checkbox labelled "Cancel the call if not connected within" and then use a shorter time in the textbox to its right. A timeout of about 25 or 30 seconds should be more than adequate. Once the required changes have been made, operate the OK button to close the window and the Close button of the Modem Properties window.

Dual ISPs

One of the most common causes of connection problems is adding a second Internet service provider to a PC. In theory there should be no problem in having two or more service providers installed, but in practice things are not always done "by the book". The usual problem is that things work perfectly when using the last service provider to be installed on the system, but using previous installations fails to work. Some Internet service providers have information about curing this type of thing in the FAQ section of their web site. They presumably know better than anyone else does how to unravel the problem they have caused, so this should be the first port of call.

A common cause of problems is a proxy server being enabled. To check for this go to the Windows Control Panel and double-click on the Internet Options icon. Left-click the Connection tab followed by the Settings button. This should produce a window like the one in Figure 1.34. If there is a tick in the checkbox marked "Use a proxy server", try removing it.

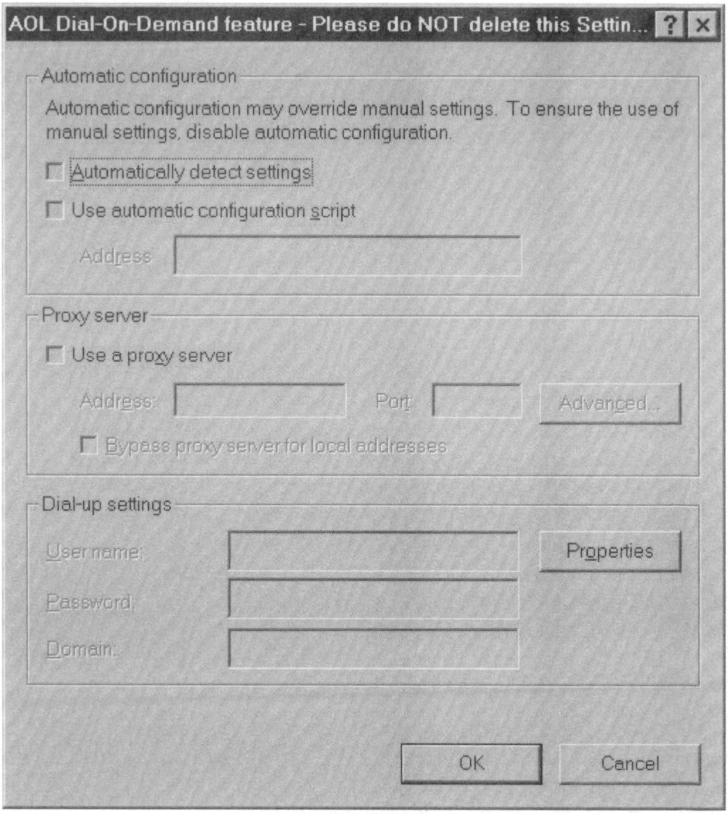

Fig.1.34 Make sure that the proxy server option is not enabled

Default ISP

When you add a new Internet service provider to your PC it not unreasonably sets itself as the default provider. When you activate Internet Explorer it will therefore start the dialling process for the new provider. This may be what you require, or you may have simply added the new provider as a standby in case there are connection difficulties with your main provider. Changing the default setting is very easy, and the process starts by going to the Windows Control Panel and selecting Internet Options and then operating the Connections tab in the new window that

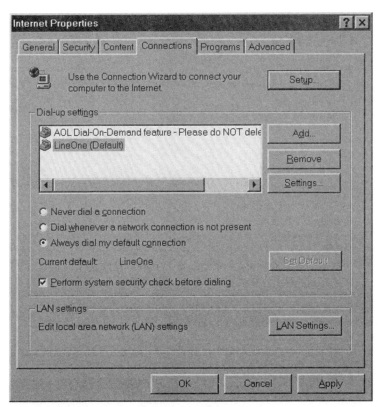

Fig.1.35 Getting a list of the installed ISPs

pops up. The installed Internet service providers are shown in the top section of the window (Figure 1.35). To set one as the default, first left-click on its entry to select it and then operate the Set Default button. Left-click the Apply and OK buttons to make the change take effect.

The home page will change to that of the new service provider, but it is easily changed back to its original setting, or any other page on the Internet come to that. Operate the General tab on the Internet Properties window and then type the full web address into the Address textbox (Figure 1.36). Left-click the Apply button to make the changes take effect and then operate the OK button to close the window.

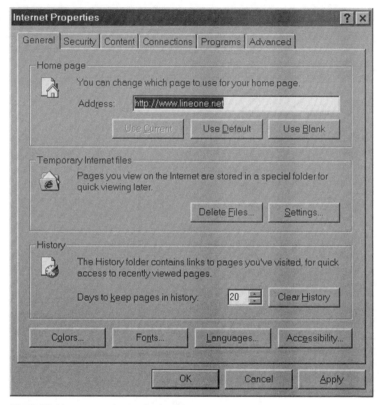

Fig.1.36 You can set any desired home page

Using a second ISP

With two or more service providers installed on the PC, how do you use one that is not set as the default provider? First double-click on the My computer icon on the Windows desktop and then double-click on the Dial-up Networking icon. With Windows ME you will have to operate the Dial-up Networking link in the left-hand section of the window. Either way you will obtain a list of the installed service providers. Simply double-click on one to activate it. A better way of handling things is to place a shortcut to the service provider on the Windows desktop. Right-click on the appropriate icon to produce a small popup menu (Figure 1.37), and then select the Create Shortcut option. Left-click the Yes button if you get an error message like the one in Figure 1.38.

The shortcut should appear on the desktop and double clicking it should get you connected to the Internet. A window like the one in Figure 1.39 will probably appear first. The password must be typed into the appropriate textbox if the Save password feature is not being used. Operate the Connect button to proceed with the connection process. A message like the one in Figure 1.40 will appear on the screen once the connection has been made, or there will be an error message if the connection process fails. Start whatever browser you normally use and it should use the Internet connection so that you can start browsing.

Note that the Internet connection will not be terminated when the browser program is closed. In order to

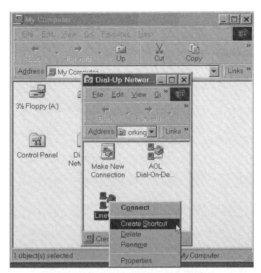

Fig.1.37 Creating a shortcut to an ISP

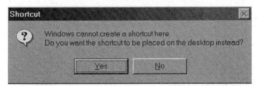

Fig.1.38 Answer Yes to create the shortcut

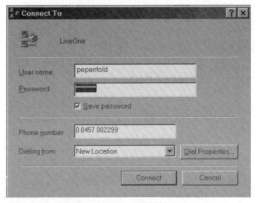

Fig.1.39 Starting the connection process

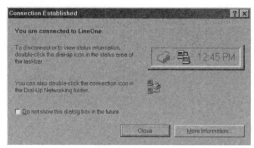

Fig.1.40   Confirmation that the connection has been made

switch off the connection, right-click on the connection icon near the bottom right-hand corner of the desktop (Figure 1.41). Select the Disconnect option and the connection should be terminated immediately.

Fig.1.41   Ending the connection

Removing an ISP

When you no longer wish to use an Internet service provider it is easy to remove them from your PC. The method varies depending on whether the provider has its own software or was added to Windows in the normal way. With a provider such as AOL that uses its own Internet software, it is removed from the system by uninstalling that software. The standard method is used, which means going to the Windows Control Panel and double-clicking the Add/Remove Programs icon. Select the service provider from the list of installed software and operate the Add/Remove button. It may be necessary to answer a few questions and do some button clicking, but uninstalling most software is largely automatic.

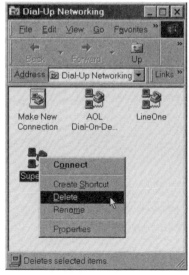

Fig.1.42   Deleting an ISP

Where a provider has been added in the normal way it can be removed from the system by

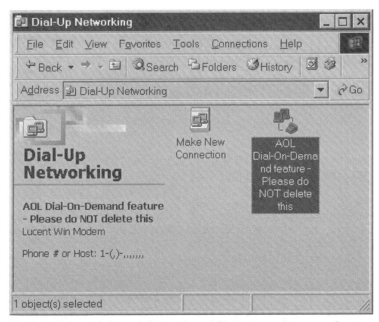

Fig.1.43 Do not delete an ISP such as AOL that uses its own software

going to the Windows desktop and double clicking on the My Computer icon. Then right-click on the icon for the provider you wish to remove, and select the Delete option from the small popup menu (Figure 1.42). Operate the Yes button when you are asked if you are sure that you wish to delete the item. Do not use this method with a provider that supplies their own software. Apart from the fact that it will leave the software on the hard disc, there is also a risk that it will get Windows rather confused. AOL includes a warning in the caption for the icon (Figure 1.43) and this should be heeded.

Points to remember

If there are warning messages along the lines "no modem" detected or the system does not get as far as dialling the Internet service provider, the problem is almost certainly due to a problem with the modem or its device drivers. Check Device Manager for indications of problems with the drivers, and check the cables, etc., for physical problems.

Try uninstalling and reinstalling the modem to see if this helps. If possible, get updated device drivers.

A USB modem stands no chance of working unless the USB ports are switched on and properly integrated with Windows. Users of Windows 95 will probably have to upgrade to Windows 98 or beyond in order to get the USB ports to function properly.

Hardware conflicts can be difficult or even impossible to resolve, but the Windows Troubleshooter will guide you through the process. Some simple port swapping will sometimes remedy faults.

If there are two or more entries in Device Manager, etc., for a single modem, delete all occurrences of the modem and then reinstall it from scratch.

If the modem is correctly installed it should produce sensible results when the Windows diagnostics facility is used. There is no point in checking the dialling settings, etc., until the modem is properly installing and responding properly.

Where there are major problems with Internet Explorer or another browser, the browser should be uninstalled and then reinstalled. In the vast majority of cases this will restore normal operation. If it does not, it is probably not the browser software that is causing the problem.

When a PC has a habit or resetting itself while you are online the problem is probably usually due to inadequate device drivers for a software modem. You either need updated and fully operational drivers or a new modem.

Clever services provided by telephone companies can lead to problems with the Internet connection being lost. Disable such services before going online. The right setting in Windows will permit the modem to dial the Internet service provider even if there is no dialling tone.

It is possible to use multiple service providers, but it will usually be necessary to do some "fine tuning" of the Windows settings in order to get things working as desired.

With an Internet service provider that does things "by the book" it is possible to remove the service from your PC by deleting its entry in Dial-Up Networking window. Where the service provider's own software is used, this software must be removed using the normal uninstall procedure. Simply deleting the relevant icon from the Dial-up Networking window will not work properly, and could get the Windows installation out of kilter.

1   Getting connected

Speeding up

Connection type

Unless you are lucky enough to have some form of broadband Internet connection it is likely that you are sometimes dissatisfied with the connection speed of your internet connection. If you are unlucky you may well be dissatisfied with the connection speed on a permanent basis. According to the popular joke, WWW stands for worldwide wait rather than worldwide web. The electronic superhighway title seems inappropriate when you are sitting in front of a PC waiting a couple of minutes for each page to download.

If you genuinely require a fast connection for some reason, there is no real alternative to using some kind of broadband connection such as ADSL. The fastest rate achievable using a telephone line and an ordinary modem is 56 kilobaud, but note that this means 56000 bits per second and not 56000 bytes per second. Taking into account the bits used for synchronisation purposes, the actual download rate is around 5600 bytes (5.6k) per second. Bear in mind that the rate at which data can be uploaded from the PC to a server is 33600 baud, or about 3360 bytes (3.36k) per second.

Both of these rates assume a theoretically perfect connection, which will rarely be achieved in practice. In fact the full upload and download rates may never be achieved using most "real world" telephone lines. Telephone modem technology seems to have progressed about as far as it is ever going to, so upload and download rates of 33 and 56 kilobaud respectively are close to the maximum that can be achieved using this method.

Slow progress

Bear in mind that having everything set up for rapid access at your end of the system does not guarantee that you will always achieve rapid download times. The slowest device in the signal chain largely governs the speed at which data is downloaded. If a traffic jam somewhere on the electronic superhighway is reducing the flow of data to one kilobyte per second, then one kilobyte per second is the highest download speed that can be achieved. Even if your Internet connection and equipment can handle a megabyte per second, the Internet traffic jam will still limit the download rate to just one kilobyte per second.

Although Internet traffic is currently much heavier than it was a few years ago, really slow results are actually less common. The rapid expansion of the Web meant that much of the infrastructure was not up to the task, and the Web was a victim of its own success. While I would certainly not claim that things are now perfect, they are definitely better than they were a few years ago. When trying to download new drivers from the sites of hardware manufacturers it was not uncommon to be faced with download speeds of less than one kilobyte per second. Using the site of one of the largest printer makers in the world I never managed to sustain a rate of more than about 165 bytes per second, and on one occasion gave up with the count at 85 bytes per second!

Perfect timing

This type of thing is now quite rare, but sites that simply can not cope with the amount of traffic they receive are not unknown. In fact most of the very popular sites noticeably slow down at times of high demand, and may even grind to a halt when there is exceptional demand. Many financial sites prove problematic when things "hot up" on the world's stock markets, and there can be similar problems with news and sports sites when a big story breaks. No doubt there are many other examples. Where possible it certainly pays to avoid the peak times and use the Internet at slack times as far as possible.

I originally did most of my surfing during the evenings in order to take advantage of cheap telephone rate, but I eventually moved to an unmetered service and accessed the Web mainly in the mornings. The difference between accessing the Web in the evenings and mornings was much greater than I had expected. With evening access it was often quite difficult and time consuming to get connected in the first place, and at times it was not possible at all. In the mornings it was a whole new world with rapid access and much faster results once connected.

The easier connection to the ISP was due to fewer UK users being online at that time. This partially accounts for the generally faster operation once connected, but the improved performance in the mornings probably has more to do with a lack of users on a worldwide basis at that time. A substantial percentage of Web users live and work in North America and the Far East. During the mornings in the UK it is the small hours in the Americas and the late evening in the Far East. Many potential Web users are asleep or offline.

From the congestion point of view, probably the best time to go online in the UK is in the middle of the night. At this time there are few users in the UK and the rest of Europe, and things should be slack in America where it will be quite late at night. Unfortunately, unless you suffer from chronic insomnia this approach is unlikely to be a practical proposition. However, some users start large downloads last thing at night and then leave their computer to get on with it into the small hours. There is actually software that can handle this type of download for you.

If you are interested in looking for times of low Internet activity there are plenty of statistics available on the Internet. However, with something like this the only sure way to find the good, bad, and indifferent times is to try the "suck it and see" approach. Obviously it might not be practical for you to surf at other than peak times, but where a choice is available it is certainly worth finding the best times to surf. This is true whether you use a standard telephone line or some form of broadband connection.

If at first...

You may sometimes find that on connection to the Internet you are actually connected to a subset of the Internet. To put it another way, you find that some sites are available but others simply produce error messages such as "site not found" and can not be contacted. Do not jump to conclusions if the odd site here and there can not be contacted. Sites do go offline from time to time, and some sites seem to make a habit of it. If a substantial percentage of sites are unavailable it is a different matter. While it is not totally inconceivable that the problem could be due to the sites having gone down, it is unlikely.

It is more likely that there is a problem with your Internet connection. This type of problem often seems to occur when there is a lot of upgrading going on, and there may be no option other than to put up with random bits of the Internet going "absent without leave" for a while. However, closing the connection and re-establishing it sometimes gives full coverage.

Hanging up the connection and starting again is usually the best course of action when things start to slow down to an unacceptable degree.

You may occasionally find that things do not work well right from the start. Pages that should load in a second or two take half a minute or more, or simply timeout before they load properly. More usually things work fine at first, but at some point in the proceedings the download rate drops to a very low level. In other cases there is a gradual slow down until things virtually grind to a halt. If you are lucky, it will be possible to restore normality by closing the browser and launching it again. Switching to a different browser program might help.

In most cases though, the only way of restoring a fast connection is to hang-up the connection and start again. This is clearly time consuming and inconvenient, but pressing on with an Internet connection that is operating at less than 10 percent of the normal speed is not the right approach. What should be a few minutes work could take an hour or two and might never be completed. Establishing a new connection is likely to be very much quicker. Also, a very slow connection is useless when undertaking things like ordering products online. Due to the slowness and lack of reliability you are likely to find that the order has not gone through properly or you have repeated the order. Never settle for anything less than a reasonably fast connection when undertaking anything that requires good reliability. Battling on regardless can cause no end of problems.

Modem problems

Any modern modem should give quite good results provided it is properly installed, but some modems still work better than others. Modern modems certainly work better than those of a few years ago, which had maximum download speeds of 2800 or 3360 bps (bits per second), or even less with the older designs. Such is the cost of modern 56k modems that it is usually well worthwhile upgrading slower types with a modern 56k type. Download times will be substantially reduced and there are plenty of good low cost modems to choose from. If the PC you use for accessing the Internet is "not as young as it used to be", it pays to choose a new modem carefully.

Modems fall into two main categories, which are the "soft" and "hardware" varieties. The soft type, which are also known as "Winmodems" and similar names, are not modems in the conventional sense. With this type of modem the hardware is actually a form of soundcard. A hardware modem is a true modem with hardware to do the encoding and decoding, and it is perhaps best to consider this type first. A normal modem connects to a port of the computer such as a serial or USB port. In order to send data from the modem the computer merely has to send the bytes of data to the appropriate port and the modem does the rest.

In the early days the modems represented the 1s and 0s in bytes of data as two different audio tones, giving the warbling sounds associated with early modems. Modern modems still support some of the early communication standards and a low speed is usually utilized when initiating a connection. More sophisticated methods are used for high-speed connections, giving what usually sounds like nothing more than high-pitched noise. The basic system is still the same though, with the computer communicating with the modem via a port, and the hardware in the modem producing the appropriate signals that are then sent down the telephone line. The modem decodes the received sounds into bytes of data that can then be read by the computer via the serial or USB port.

The important point here is that the modem is doing the encoding and decoding with no help from the computer. It will also undertake things like error correction. The computer still has to process the data to produce the right text and graphics on the screen, but the basic encoding and decoding process is handled entirely by the modem's hardware. With this type of modem the device can be an internal or external device. If it is an internal type in the form of a PC expansion card, the card will include the port hardware in addition to the electronics for the modem. It will therefore appear in the Windows Device Manager utility as both a port and a modem. The port is invariably a serial (COM) type.

Soft modem

With soft modems the PC is responsible for the encoding and decoding process. The driver software for a soft modem is much more complicated than the driver for a hardware modem. The soundcard can make the right "noises" for a modem and send them down the telephone line, but the PC has to directly control the sound generating hardware. Sending bytes of data to a hardware modem requires a minimal amount of processing power, but directly controlling the sound generation hardware is much more demanding.

The same is true when data is received by the modem. Reading bytes of data from a hardware type requires a minimal amount of processing power. With a software modem the received signals are digitised, and the PC must then decode the streams of numbers into the bytes of data that they represent. This requires much more processing.

The advantage of a soft modem is that it uses relatively simple hardware, and this gives cost savings. The savings were quite large when these devices were first introduced, and they were often less than half the price of a hardware equivalent. There is still some difference in cost, but it is now relatively small. The drawback of a soft modem is that it places more demands on the host PC, and the PC needs to be reasonably powerful in order to produce acceptable results. Minimum requirements are usually quite modest by current standards, with something like a 100MHz or 200MHz Pentium processor being required. Minimum memory requirements usually depend on the operating system in use, but would normally be around 16 to 32 megabytes.

Hard or soft

It is important to realise that the minimum requirements indicate the lowest hardware specification that will provide workable results. Using a PC having the bare minimum hardware specification is unlikely to give anything approaching optimum results for a 56k modem. This is one reason that hardware modems are generally considered superior to the software variety. A hardware modem will always download data at full speed even if the PC has a poor specification. It takes a fair amount of processing to turn the received data into completed pages, particularly when graphics are involved. This could slow things down, but the modem itself will always operate at full speed.

With a soft modem it takes a significant amount of computing power to decode the received signal, and then still more processing to convert the data into the finished pages. With a PC of modest specification the processing requirements could be so great that things grind along quite slowly at times. Even with a PC having a relatively high specification the amount of processing required to produce each page could be sufficient to slow things down slightly.

Rightly or wrongly, hardware modems are generally considered to be more reliable at decoding received signals. Due to the error checking used in modern digital communications this does not mean that a hardware modem with produce fewer errors in the data stream. It means that a hardware modem is likely to be faster as it will require fewer packets of data to be sent again. The validity of this argument is debatable, and in theory a software modem could probably produce equal or superior results. In practice, if you wish to be certain of the highest possible performance a hardware modem is a safer bet than a software type.

Drivers

Where a soft modem seems to be performing below par it is worth checking the manufacturer's web site to see if updated drivers are available. The drivers for most pieces of computer hardware seem to get at least one or two upgrades after the initial launch of the product, and soft modems are certainly no exception. Searching for improved drivers should present no difficulty if the modem is from one of the well-known manufacturers. Their site should have a section devoted to driver software, and there is usually helpful advice to make sure that you accurately identify the modem you have. Due care must be exercised, because computer hardware manufacturers often produce several pieces of hardware with very similar names or type numbers.

Matters are more difficult if your modem is one of the generic devices that come from a no-name manufacturer. The instruction leaflet supplied with the modem might have a Web address where any updated drivers can be found, but there will often be no assistance of this type. This is not to say that there is no hope of finding newer drivers, but it does mean that finding them will be more difficult. Computer chip manufacturers often produce generic driver software for their products. If you know that your modem is based on (say) a Motorola chipset, the obvious starting point is the Motorola web site. Any search engine should soon locate the manufacturer's web site. This will not necessarily produce a source of suitable drivers. Quite reasonably, the manufacturer of the chips might consider that it is the job of the equipment producer to supply support for their products. However, in practice the sites of chip makers often prove helpful.

Learner drivers

If a search of the chip manufacturer's site proves to be fruitless there are other avenues that can be pursued. There are plenty of sites that offer help with device drivers, and using "device drivers" as the search string in the Yahoo search engine will produce a useful list of driver sites. These sites mostly offer a great deal of general information about software drivers, plus advice for beginners on installing them. In most cases there are also search facilities and advice on finding suitable driver programs.

One example of such a site is DriverGuide.com (Figure 2.1). You have to register in order to utilize this site, but registration is free. Amongst other things it includes search facilities that enable the user to search for a certain manufacturer, drivers for a certain type of hardware, and so on

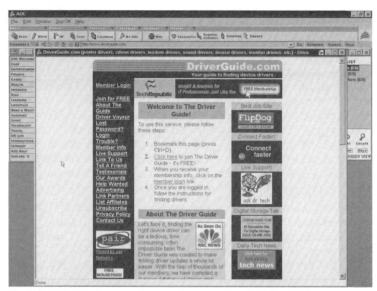

*Fig.2.1 DriverGuide.com is one of many sites that deal with
device drivers*

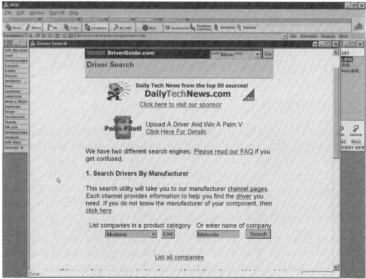

Fig.2.2 DriverGuide.com includes a search facility

Fig.2.3 WinDrivers.com is one of the best known device driver sites

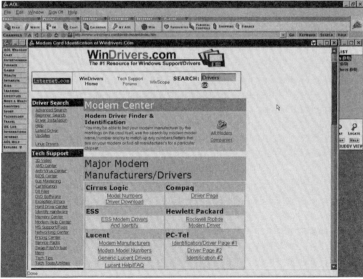

Fig.2.4 WinDrivers.com also includes a search facility

(Figure 2.2). Probably the best know site for device drivers is WinDrivers.com (Figure 2.3). This site provides a lot of general advice together with useful search facilities (Figure 2.4). I have found HelpDrivers.com to be very useful when tracking down drivers. On one occasion I managed to find the drivers I needed even though I had nothing more to go on than the markings on the main chip of the modem's circuit board.

Installation

Methods of installing updated drivers vary somewhat. The downloaded driver file is often a ZIP file, which is used as a compact and convenient way of storing several files. One of these will often be a Read.me file or a text file having a "txt" extension. Either way the file will be a simple text file that gives installation instructions for the driver files. Some driver files are a bit confusing in that they are downloaded in the form of an EXE (executable) file, giving the impression that you merely have to run the file in order to install the new drivers.

In most cases it is a so-called self-extraction file. In other words it is a form of compressed file, and on running it the file or files it contains are automatically unpacked. The uncompressed files are normally placed in the same directory as the source file. When unpacking any form of compressed file it is a good idea to place the source file in a temporary directory, and then use the same directory for the files that are extracted. By viewing the contents of the folder using a file browser such as Windows Explorer you can then see what files have been produced.

Sometimes the driver file is an executable file, usually called something like Install.exe. This type is the easiest to use, since it is merely necessary to run the file in order to install the updated drivers. You invariably have to reboot the computer in order to make the new drivers take effect, but this is a standard requirement whichever method of installation is used. It is unlikely that there will be any problems if the installation program is run by double clicking on its entry in Windows Explorer, but this is not the approved way of doing things.

Any form of installation program normally requires that no other programs are running during the installation program. This minimises the risk of the installation program being blocked from altering a file because the file is in use. It is not normally necessary to bother about shutting down the background tasks that seem to be a feature of every Windows PC these days, but normal applications such as word processors, DTP programs, and file browsers should be shut down.

The approved way of running the installation program is to use the Run option in the Windows Start menu. This brings up a small window like the one in Figure 2.5.

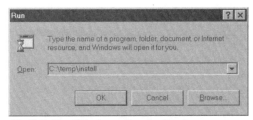

The name of the installation file is entered into the textbox, and the full path must be included. In other words, if the installation file is in a folder called "temp" which is off the root directory of drive C:,

Fig.2.5 The Windows Run facility is an option in the Start menu

the name would be entered as "C:\temp\Install", and not simply as "Install". The ".exe" extension is not required, but the program should

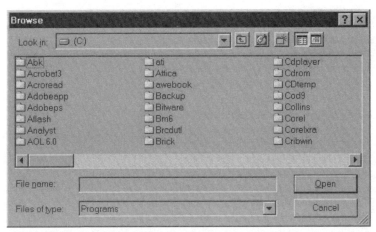

Fig.2.6 The filename and full path can be entered in the textbox or the usual Windows file browser can be used instead

still run properly if the extension is included. The easier way of selecting the file is to operate the Browse button and then use the standard Windows browser (Figure 2.6) to locate and select the file.

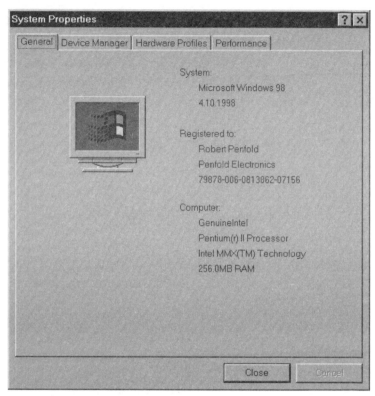

Fig.2.7 The System Properties window

Setup program

Another method of installation is for one of the files to be a Setup program, and the file will normally be called Setup.exe. The Run option in the Start menu is used to run the Setup program, which then goes through a standard Windows style installation process. You merely have to operate the right buttons when prompted in order to complete the installation process.

In some cases you may simply be provided with the driver files and nothing more. This seems to be unusual these days, but installing device drivers without any automated help is not usually difficult. This is actually the Windows "approved" way of handling things. The first step is to go

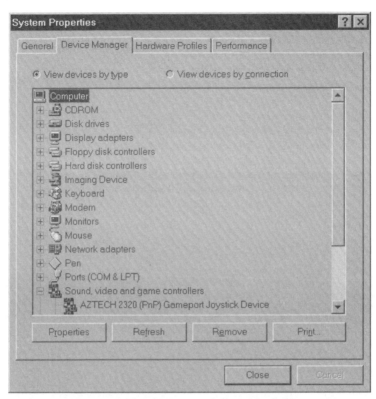

Fig.2.8 The list of installed hardware in Device Manager

to the Windows control panel. One route is via the Start menu, with Settings being selected followed by Control Panel. Double clicking on the My Computer icon and then the Control Panel icon is another way of launching the control panel. The options available from the Control Panel depend on the configuration of your PC, but there should always be a System option. Doubling clicking on this produces a window like the one in Figure 2.7.

Next left-click on the Device Manager tab at the top of the window to change the window to something like Figure 2.8. Again, the appearance of this window will depend on the configuration of your PC. The list shows all the hardware devices and ports of the PC, including the modem. Double-click on the modem entry and it will expand to show a list of the

Fig.2.9 There will usually be a single modem listed

Fig.2.10 The General page of the Modem Properties window

modems fitted to your PC, but in most cases there will only be one modem fitted (Figure 2.9). Next double-click on the modem's entry in the list in order to bring up its Properties window (Figure 2.10). By default the general section will be displayed, but it is the Driver section that is required in this case. Left clicking on the Driver tab at the top of the window selects this section, giving something like Figure 2.11.

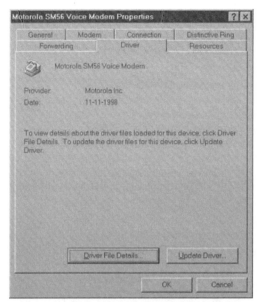

Fig.2.11 The Modem Properties Driver page

Fig.2.12 The initial window when updating device drivers

*Fig.2.13 The list of device drivers is of no interest, but use the radio
buttons to select the bottom option anyway*

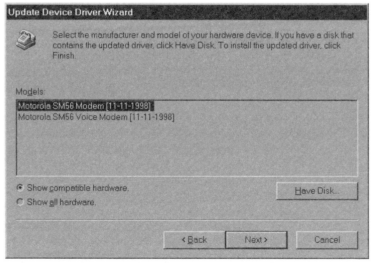

*Fig.2.14 Operate the Have Disk button so that you can point Windows
to the location of the new device drivers*

Left click on the Update Driver button, which will first bring up the information window of Figure 2.12. Operate the Next button to move on to the next window (Figure 2.13) where radio buttons are used to select the desired option. Select the bottom option and operate the Next button. A new window (Figure 2.14) shows the compatible device drivers that Windows detects on the system, which will normally be the

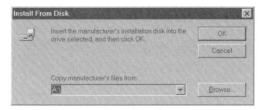

Fig.2.15 You can type the location into the textbox or use the Browse button

current driver and any additional device drivers provided by the hardware manufacturer. We need to point the system to the location of the new driver, and this is done by operating the Have Disk button. This produces the small window of Figure 2.15 where the location of the new device driver can be typed into the textbox. Alternatively, operate the Browse button and use the file browser (Figure 2.16) to select the correct location.

Once the location has been selected, left-click the OK button to return to the previous window, which should now look something like Figure 2.17. If the system will not accept the location you give it is likely that you have not pointed it to the precise location of the driver files. Alternatively, the files might not be valid device driver files. Perhaps the downloaded file

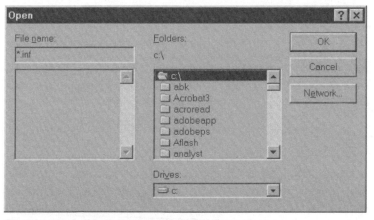

Fig.2.16 Using the file browser to locate the drivers

or files need to be unzipped before they can be used. There should be a file with an "inf" extension, not an "exe", "zip", etc.

To go ahead with the update operate the OK button, and then follow any onscreen instructions that appear. If all is not well you will get an error message. Probably the most common problem is a warning that you

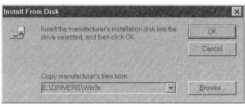

are about to replace a file with one that is older than the existing version. In other words, your new device driver is older than the one already in use. When given the option, never allow an older file to overwrite a

Fig.2.17 The drivers have been located and installation can proceed

newer version. The only possible exception to this is where new device driver has failed to work properly and you wish to go back to the previous version. If you have obtained an incompatible driver for your modem it is likely that this will be detected and that the update will be aborted. You will then need to search again for the correct driver software.

From the top

Updating device drivers does not always run smoothly. If you are unlucky there may be a major problem somewhere that prevents the new drivers from being installed properly. When things get into a muddle the best option is to remove the hardware and drivers from the system and start "from scratch". If necessary, remove the modem's entry in Device Manager, close down Windows and switch off the PC, and then remove the modem. Boot the system again and check that the modem's entry is still absent in Device Manager. Close down Windows, switch off the PC, and then reinstall the modem. Boot up the PC again and install the new drivers for the modem.

Hardware change

Particularly with an early example of a software modem, updating the device driver stands a reasonable chance of giving a worthwhile improvement in speed. However, with an older PC or a modem that simply does not work very well due to design inadequacies, changing to a hardware modem is a better bet, and is almost certain to bring a worthwhile improvement in results. With an old 28.8k or 33.3k modem the problem is simply the relatively low speed of the modem, and a change to a 56k modem should always bring a very significant improvement in performance. If you are not sure which type of modem is fitted to your PC, how do you find out?

Things should be straightforward provided you still have the documentation that was supplied with the PC or with the modem if it was bought separately. The documentation should give some basic details about the modem, including its speed and type. Some delving will be necessary if the documentation has been lost or if the PC was not supplied with adequate documentation. Many second-hand PCs fall into this second category, with little or none of the original documentation being passed on to the second owner.

You may be able to glean some information from Windows by going to the Control Panel and double clicking on the Modems icon. This will produce a window like the one of Figure 2.18, which will probably not be very informative. It will give the name of the modem, and this will often indicate its maximum speed. In this example the SM56 name indicates that it is a 56k modem.

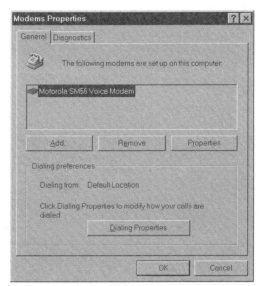

Try operating the Diagnostics tab to produce a window like Figure 2.19, select the modem from the list of ports and devices, and then operate the More Info... button. After a short delay

Fig.2.18 The Modem Proprties window may indicate the type of modem installed

while the modem is accessed a window like the one in Figure 2.20 will appear. This does indicate that the modem is a software type. Note that

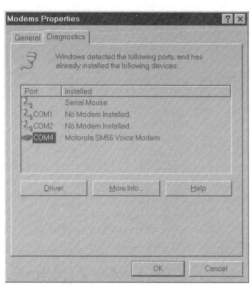

Fig.2.19 Operate the More Info button to run the diagnostics

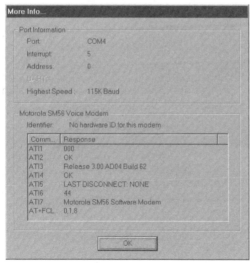

Fig.2.20 The dianostic tests confirm that this is a software modem

the indicated speed is the maximum rate for the port that the modem is connected to, and not the maximum speed of the modem.

You may find that the list of hardware in Device Manager includes two modem entries. One of these will be the usual "Modem" entry, while the other will be called something like "HSFMODEM". This indicates that the modem is a software type, and the additional entry is for some of the extra driver software that this type of modem requires.

It is unlikely that anything worthwhile can be deduced by looking at the modem card itself. If it is an old ISA type expansion card (Figure 2.21) it is probably a hardware modem, but its speed will probably be 33k or less. However, a few 56k modems were produced in ISA versions. There is

Fig.2.21 An old 33.6k modem for an ISA expansion slot

little difference between software and hardware versions of PCI modem cards (Figures 2.22 and 2.23 respectively). Unless you are an expert on modem chipsets the board is unlikely to reveal anything worthwhile. If you do not know the make and model of the modem it may be included somewhere on the card, and the manufacturer's web site should then provide at least some basic details for the unit.

AMR and external

Some modems fit into a special expansion slot on the motherboard, which is usually an AMR (audio modem riser) type. A modem of this type uses software plus the facilities of the motherboard to do most of the work, and an AMR modem is therefore a software type. External modems, whether of the serial port or USB variety, invariably seem to be hardware types. I suppose it might be possible to produce a USB software modem, but "real world" USB modems seem to be of the standard hardware variety. USB modems are reputed to be slightly faster than serial port units due to the faster transfer speeds available using a USB

Fig.2.22 A 56k (V90) software modem

Fig.2.23 This hardware V90 modem looks much the same as the
V90 software modem

port. However, the maximum rate for most serial ports is 115 kilobaud, which is substantially higher than the 56/33 kilobaud rate of a V90 modem. Do not expect a large difference in performance between a USB and serial port modems.

All change

Due to the falling cost of computer hardware in recent years the cost of some internal hardware modems is not much different to that of budget internal software models. If you feel that your current modem is not up to the task, switching to a new hardware modem will no longer cost a proverbial "arm and a leg". At the time of writing this piece it is certainly possible to obtain a 56k hardware modem from a well known

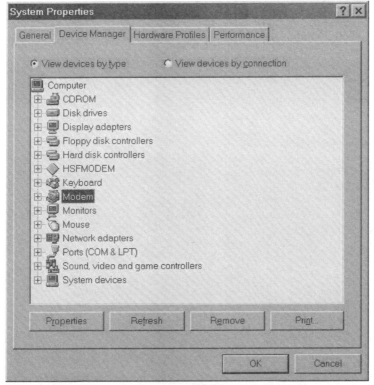

Fig.2.24 Here there are two modem entries in Device Manager

manufacturer for less than 20 pounds. Should you decide to go "all the
way" and obtain an external USB type it is likely to cost more than twice
as much. With an external USB modem it should be possible to leave
the existing modem in place, but my preference would be to remove the
internal modem. It might be possible to have two internal modems
installed, but I would definitely not recommend trying to do this. It is
better to keep things straightforward by having only one or the other
installed.

Software uninstall

The first task is to uninstall the driver software for the old modem. As
pointed out previously, software modems tend to have more than one
entry in Device Manager, so you need to carefully check the list of devices

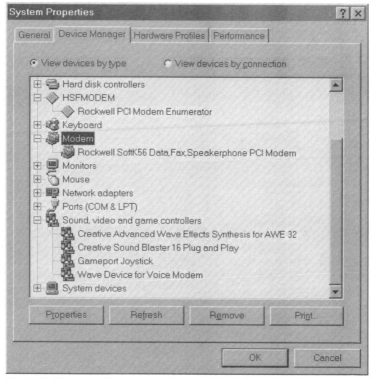

Fig.2.25 There are three entries for a single software modem

to find the ones that
relate to the modem.
In the example of
Figure 2.24 the usual
modem entry is
present, but there is
also an entry called
"HSFMODEM". In
many cases there will
be an entry in the
"Sound, video and
game controllers"

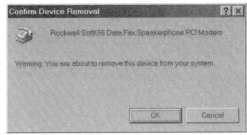

*Fig.2.26 Operate the OK button to uninstall
the modem*

section. Figure 2.25 shows the relevant sections of the list expanded to
show all the entries for the example modem. In order to remove an entry

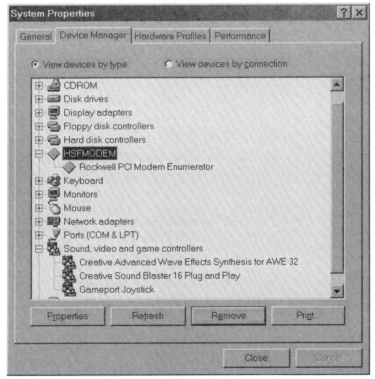

Fig.2.27 The Modem entry has been completely removed

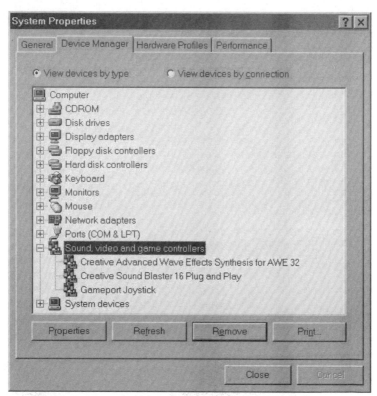

Fig.2.28 All the entries for the modem have been removed

simply left-click on the entry to select it, and then operate the Remove button. This will bring up a warning message like the one in Figure 2.26. Operate the OK button to remove the driver and its entry in Device Manager.

Note that you can not remove a category such as Modem, and can only delete individual entries within the categories. If you try to remove a category you will simply get a message explaining that this is not possible. When all the entries within a category have been removed, the category itself will be automatically removed from the list. Figure 2.27 for example, shows the list after the entry for the Rockwell soft modem has been deleted. This has resulted in the Modem entry being removed as well. Figure 2.28 shows the list in Device Manager once all the entries for the modem have been removed. Next Windows should be shut down and it then time to remove the modem itself.

Hardware swapping

The PC must be switched off before you start work on it, and it should preferably be switched off at the mains socket. In order to remove the old modem the outer casing of the case must be removed. There are various types of case currently in use, and if your PC uses one of the more unusual case styles it may take some time to "crack" it. Most AT style cases (the narrower type) have an outer casing that consists of the top and two sides in a single piece. Removing four or six screws at the rear of the case enables the outer casing to be slid backwards and free of the main chassis.

Note that there are often additional screws on the rear panel to hold the power supply and various odds and ends in place. Look carefully before removing any screws. It is usually pretty obvious which ones hold the outer casing in place. The wider ATX cases mostly have the outer casing in three separate sections. Two screws at the rear of the case hold each section in place. Removing the two screws enables the relevant section

Fig.2.29 There are four expansion cards in this PC

*Fig.2.30 The old card should pull free once the mounting bolt
has been removed, but some wiggling will probably
be required*

to be pulled away to the rear and free of the chassis. In order to remove
expansion cards it is only necessary to remove the left-hand panel (as
viwed from the front).

The expansion cards, including the modem, fit into expansion slots at
the rear of the PC and are held in place by a metal bracket. The number
of expansion cards varies from one PC to another, but there are usually
two or three including the modem. In the example of Figure 2.29 the
case is an AT mini tower and there are four expansion cards. Since a
socket on the back of the modem connects to the telephone socket
there should be no difficulty in determining which card is the modem.

Disconnect the cable that connects the modem to the telephone outlet
and also disconnect any internal cables that connect to the modem card.
There will not necessarily be any internal cables of this type, but some
modems have facilities that require a connection to the motherboard.
For example, some modems can automatically switch the PC from
standby mode to normal operation when a telephone call is received. If

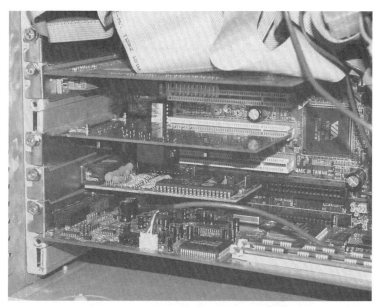

Fig.2.31 The new modem card installed in the computer

you wish to use a feature of this type it is clearly imperative to obtain a modem that supports the facility.

A largish cross-head screwdriver is needed to remove the screw that holds the card in place, and the card can then be pulled free (Figure 2.30). If the card is reluctant to pull free, which is more than likely, a rocking motion should gradually work it loose. It is then a matter of replacing the old card with the new one. Make sure that the card's connector is fully pushed down into the expansion slot at both ends. If it is not fully inserted into the expansion slot it is virtually certain that the modem will not work.

If the card is fully inserted at one end of the expansion slot but not at the other there is no chance of it working. In fact there is little chance of the PC working, and it could be damaged. With the card inserted at an angle it tends to short-circuit the terminals of the expansion slot. When the card is properly bedded down in the expansion slot the fixing screw is added. This should leave the computer looking much as it did before the changeover (Figure 2.31). To complete the physical installation the cables are reconnected.

Non-PCI modems

It has been assumed here that the old modem uses a PCI expansion slot and that the new modem will occupy the same expansion slot as the old one. If the old modem occupies an AMR or ISA expansion slot it is removed in much the same way as a PCI card. It will only be possible to install the new modem if there is a spare PCI expansion slot, which there almost certainly will be. Modern motherboards tend to have facilities such as the ports, sound generator, and even the video system built-in. This leaves most of the expansion slots free.

A few motherboards even have a built-in software modem. It would presumably be possible to have the new modem installed with the built-in modem still active, but to avoid possible conflicts it is advisable to disable the built-in modem where this is possible. The instruction manual supplied with the PC should indicate whether or not it is possible to switch off the integral modem, and if so how this can be achieved. In most cases there will be a switch or jumper on the motherboard that has to be adjusted. The modem might be controlled via the BIOS Setup program. Either way, the computer's instruction manual should give clear instructions showing how to disable the modem.

Any free PCI slot will do for the new modem. There will almost certainly be a blanking plate at the rear of the slot, and with luck it will be held in place by a fixing screw. With this screw removed the blanking plate can be removed and the modem card can then be pushed into place. With modern cases the blanking plates are usually held in place by metal lugs. Repeatedly twisting the plate from side to side breaks the lugs so that the plate can be removed. This sometimes leaves some sharp edges so dispose of the plate carefully. The modem card can then be slotted and bolted into place.

Static problems

These days any information about upgrading a PC has to be accompanied by warnings that computer equipment is vulnerable to damage by static electricity. If you buy practically any piece of computer hardware it is likely to come complete with dire warnings about the consequences of not taking the appropriate precautions to avoid damage by static charges. Probably most readers are not familiar with these precautions, and I will therefore outline the basic steps necessary to ensure that no components, including modem cards, are accidentally "zapped".

I think it is worth making the point that it does not take a large static charge complete with sparks and "cracking" sounds to damage sensitive electronic components. Large static discharges of that type are sufficient to damage most semiconductor components, and not just the more sensitive ones. Many of the components used in computing are so sensitive to static charges that they can be damaged by relatively small voltages. In this context "small" still means a potential of a hundred volts or so, but by static standards this is not particularly large. Charges of this order will not generate noticeable sparks or make your hair stand on end, but they are nevertheless harmful to many electronic components. Hence you can "zap" these components simply by touching them, and in most cases would not be aware that anything had happened.

I think it is also worth making the point that although it is the processor and memory modules that are the most vulnerable and require the greatest care, completed circuit boards such as modems and soundcards are also vulnerable to static damage. They are mostly more hardy, but most modern expansion cards and all motherboards are vulnerable to damage from static charges. Even components such as the hard disc drive and CD-ROM drive can be damaged by static charges. It is really only the power supply assembly plus purely mechanical components that you can assume to be zap-proof. Everything else should be regarded as potentially at risk and handled accordingly.

When handling any vulnerable computer components you should always keep well away from any known or likely sources of static electricity. These include such things as computer monitors, television sets, any carpets or furnishings that are known to be prone to static generation, and even any pets that are known to get charged-up fur coats. Also avoid wearing any clothes that are known to give problems with static charges. This seems to be less of a problem than it once was, because few clothes these days are made from a cloth that consists entirely of man-made fibres. There is normally a significant content of natural fibres, and this seems to be sufficient to prevent any significant build-up of static charges. However, if you should have any garments that might give problems, make sure that you do not wear them when handling any computer equipment or components.

Anti-static equipment

Electronics and computing professionals often use quite expensive equipment to ensure that static charges are kept at bay. Most of these are not practical propositions for amateur computer enthusiasts or those

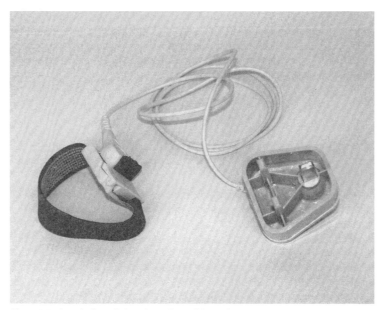

Fig.2.32 A wristband, lead, and earthing plug

who only deal with computers professionally on a very part-time basis. If you will only be working on computers from time to time, some very simple anti-static equipment is all that you need in order to ensure that there are no expensive accidents. In fact it is not essential to have any anti-static equipment if you will only be dealing with the odd expansion card here and there.

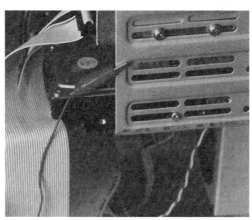

Fig.2.33 A crocodile earthing clip

If you wish to make quite sure that your body remains static-free you can earth yourself to the computer by way of a proper earthing wristband. This is basically just a wristband made from electrically conductive material that connects to earth via a lead and a high value resistor. The resistor does not prevent any static build-up in your body from leaking away to earth, but it will protect you from a significant shock if a fault should result in the earthing point becoming "live".

Most of the larger computer component suppliers now sell inexpensive anti-static wristbands. Some have a sort of dummy mains plug that is largely made from plastic. The wristband connects to the earth pin of the plug, which is the only pin that is made of metal (Figure 2.32). The alternative is to have a crocodile clip instead of the mains plug. This clip connects to the chassis of the computer (Figure 2.33). The PC should be plugged into the mains supply, but switched off. The mains should also be switched off at the mains socket. This still leaves the chassis connected to the mains earth.

Simple precautions

If you do not want to go to the expense of buying a wristband, a simple but effective alternative is to touch the metal chassis of the computer from time to time, and always prior to picking up a computer component. This will leak away any gradual build-up of static electricity in your body before it has time to reach dangerous proportions, and ensure that you are charge-free before handling any components. Again the computer must be connected to the mains supply, but it should be switched off and the mains supply should be switched off at the mains outlet. This avoids the risk of the computer being switched on accidentally while you are working on it, but the chassis will still be earthed.

That is really all there is to it. Simply having a large chunk of earthed metal (in the form of the computer case) near the work area helps to discourage the build-up of any static charges in the first place. The few simple precautions outlined previously are then sufficient to ensure that there is no significant risk to the modem card. Do not be tempted to simply ignore the dangers of static electricity when handling computer components. When building electronic gadgets I often ignore static precautions, but I am dealing with components that cost a matter of pence each. If one or two of the components should be zapped by a static charge, no great harm is done. The same is not true when dealing with computer components, some of which could cost in excess of a hundred pounds.

Anti-static packing

One final point is that any static sensitive components will be supplied in some form of anti-static packaging. This is usually nothing more than a plastic bag that is made from a special plastic that is slightly conductive. Expansion cards such as modems are invariably supplied in one of these bags, which are usually black or have a pattern of black lines.

Although it is tempting to remove the components from the packing to have a good look at them, try to keep this type of thing to a minimum. When you do remove the components from the bags make sure that you and the bags are earthed first. Simply touching the earthed chassis of a computer while holding the component in its bag should ensure that everything is charge-free. Make sure that you always handle the components in an environment that is free from any likely sources of static charges. There will then be a minimal risk of any damage occurring.

Plug and play

Having physically installed the modem card in the case it is time to move on to the software side of installation. Soft modems can give problems with plug and play installation due to the fact much of the hardware is of what I suppose could be termed the virtual variety. This can tend to confuse the operating system, and some manufacturers opt for their own installation software. This type of thing is rarer with hardware modems, which should go through the standard plug and play installation process with a minimum of fuss.

However, as always when installing computer hardware, read the instruction manual to see if a non-standard installation process is involved. Where the manufacturer supplies an installer program, always use this and do not try the plug and play approach. If the new hardware is detected by the operating system during the boot process, use the Cancel button to abort the automatic installation process. Then run the manufacturer's installer program once into Windows.

Assuming that the plug and play method is to be utilized, during the boot process a message like the one in Figure 2.34 will appear on the screen. Operate the Next button to proceed with the installation process, and a window like the one in Figure 2.35 will appear. Select the lower option using the radio buttons, and then operate the Next button. The next window offers various hardware categories, and in this case it is clearly the Modem entry that should be chosen (Figure 2.36). You will

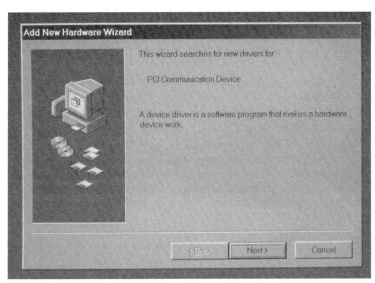

Fig.2.34 The installation process starts with this message

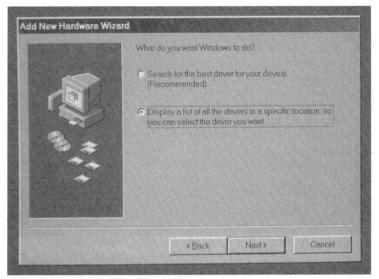

Fig.2.35 Opt to display a list of drivers

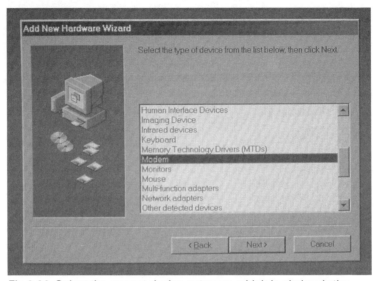

Fig.2.36 Select the correct device category, which is obviously the
Modem category in this case

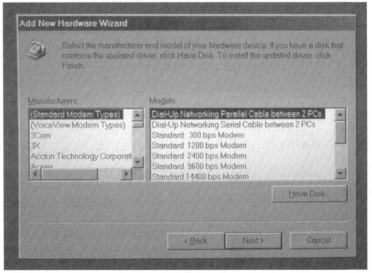

Fig.2.37 Next operate the Have Disk button

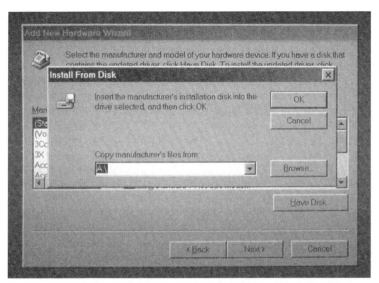

Fig.2.38 The location of the drivers can be entered into the textbox

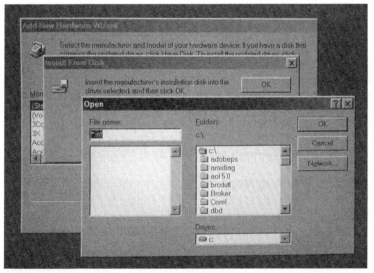

Fig.2.39 Alternatively, use the browser to locate the correct folder

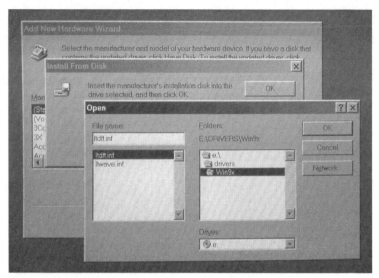

Fig.2.40 In this example two INF files have been located

then be shown lists of standard modems and modem manufacturers (Figure 2.37), but it is unlikely that the particular model you are using will be one that is covered by a standard Windows driver. Instead, place the drivers disc supplied with the modem in the appropriate drive and operate the Have Disk button.

A small window then pops up (Figure 2.38), and the path to the device drivers can then be typed into the textbox. The instruction leaflet or on-disc manual for the modem should give the location of the drivers. Rather than typing the path you may prefer to use the Browse facility to locate the right directory, which is generally the easier and more reliable method. A conventional Windows file browser will appear (Figure 2.39), and you can then select the appropriate disc drive and locate the directory containing the drivers. When the right directory has been found there should be one or two files having "inf" extensions shown in the left-hand section of the browser's window (Figure 2.40). Select the top entry if there is more than one, and then operate the OK button.

Having pointed Windows to the correct location for the drivers you should then have a window that looks something like Figure 2.41, with the new modem now listed. Operate the Next button to continue, and then again on the following information window (Figure 2.42). After some hard disc

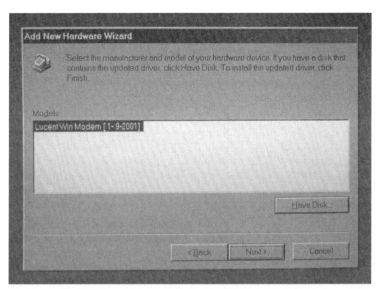

Fig.2.41 Back at the main window and ready to proceed

Fig.2.42 Operate the Next button when this window appears

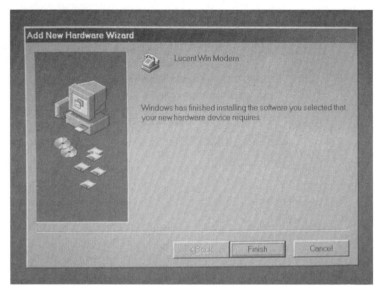

Fig.2.43 The installation has been completed successfully

activity a window like the one in Figure 2.43 should be produced, indicating that the device drivers have been installed correctly. Operate the finish button, and the boot process will then continue. However, it may be necessary to install further drivers, and this whole process will then be repeated. The only difference is that on the second time around you must choose the lower "inf" file when pointing Windows to the correct drivers. With the second device driver installed the boot process should continue normally.

Checking installation

Once Windows has booted you can check that the modem has been successfully integrated with Windows. Go to the Control Panel and double-click on the modem entry. The new modem should be shown in the list of installed modems, where it will presumably be the only entry (Figure 2.44). Left-click on its entry to select it and then operate the Properties button to bring up a window like the one in Figure 2.45. The Maximum Speed section at the bottom of the window includes a menu where the connection speed to the modem can be selected. This does not affect the speed at which the modem operates. It controls the speed of the serial port to which the modem is connected. It will probably default to the maximum rate, but it is as well to check this point and manually adjusted it to the highest setting if necessary. Some advocate always setting the connection speed at the highest possible setting. Others recommend using the lowest rate that is higher than the speed of the modem in order to avoid the possibility of packet errors. With a 56k modem this is likely to work out at the maximum 115.2k setting whichever of these methods is used.

In the case of an internal hardware or software modem the serial port is included on the modem card. Most PCs have two built-in serial ports, so the new modem will usually connect to serial port 3 or 4 (COM3 or COM4). It seems to be the convention that software modems

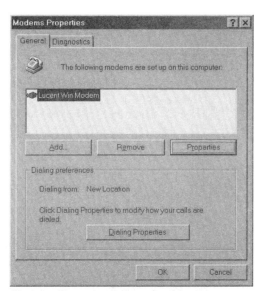

Fig.2.44 The new modem should appear in the list of installed modems

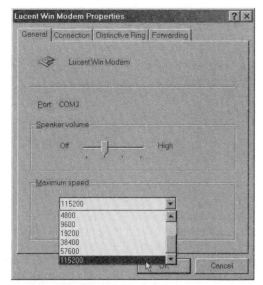

Fig.2.45 The serial port speed settings

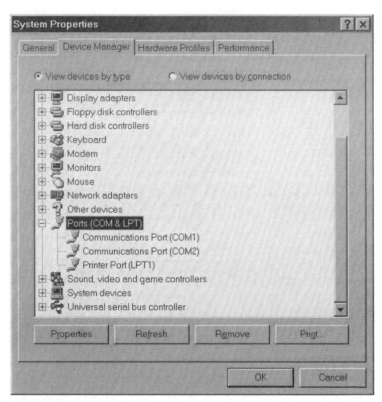

Fig.2.46 Do not worry if the modem's serial port is not listed

connect to port 4 and the hardware variety connects to port 3, but there may well be some exceptions to this. The port used for the modem will be shown in the main Modem Properties window.

There is no need for concern if the port used by the modem does not appear in the list of ports in Device Manager (Figure 2.46). How can the modem connect to COM3 or COM4 if it does not exist? In the days when modems used ISA expansion slots the modem's built-in serial port would normally appear in the list of ports, and the built-in port would be a standard PC serial type. It is not possible to have a conventional PC serial port on a PCI bus, which gives a slight problem with modern modem cards. The device driver plus some hardware on the card has to "bridge the gap" between Windows and the modem's main hardware using a sort of pseudo serial port. Due to the non-standard nature of this port it does not usually appear in the list of ports in Device Manager, but it should still work perfectly well.

Speed test

If the new modem is faster and more reliable than its predecessor was, this fact should be fairly obvious in use. You may prefer to conduct some speed tests to confirm this, in which case the old modem should be tested prior to its removal. The problem in speed testing is that it is the overall speed of the system that is being tested and not just the modem, so results have to be taken with the proverbial "pinch of salt". If results are bad it could simply be because you have chosen a bad time on the wrong day to conduct the tests.

You can try your own tests, downloading files and checking the times taken for example. Another method is to use one of the Internet speed testing sites. For example, you can try the site at:

http://msnhomepages.talkcity.com/windowsway/diagnostics/modem/modem1.html

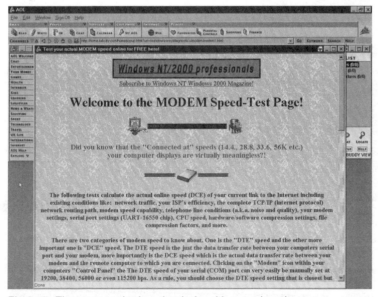

Fig.2.47 There are web sites that help with speed testing

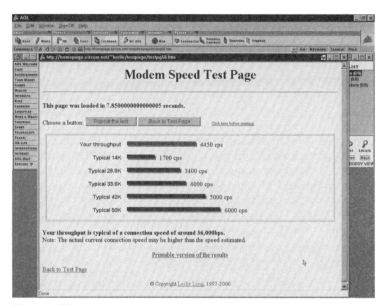

Fig.2.48 The best result obtained using the software modem

This provides some useful information about modem speeds and the terminology involved (Figure 2.47), plus some links to other sites. The second test takes you to a page where the speed can be tested by downloading either a small GIF image file or a much larger (470k) file. The test results are provided as soon as the file has downloaded. Figure 2.48 shows the best result obtained using a software modem, and the small file. Figure 2.49 shows the slowest result obtained using the hardware replacement and the small file.

Neither result is particularly close to the theoretical speed of the modems, but even on its worst showing the hardware modem does seem to be somewhat faster than this particular software modem's best performance. Do not worry if your modem fails to achieve something close to the theoretical maximum speed. In practice a connection rate of 46 to 49 kilobaud is about the maximum most users ever achieve.

Home page

The speed at which your modem accesses the Internet is not the only factor that governs how fast (or otherwise) you surf the Web. There are some useful tricks that can be used to streamline things. One of these is

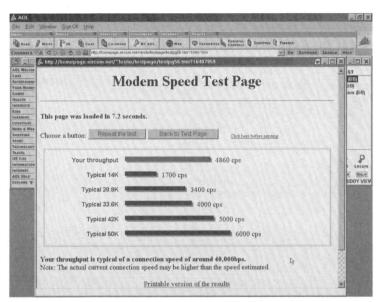

Fig.2.49 The worst result produced by the hardware modem

to set your home page to something more useful than the default page. The home page is the page that loads automatically each time you connect to the Internet. Understandably, this page is usually set to the index page of your ISP's Internet site by the installation software supplied by the ISP. If you are happy to start at this page each time there is no problem, but it is likely that you would prefer a different start-up page.

You do not have wait for the home page to finish loading before moving on to another page, but things are even quicker and more convenient if you simply change the home page to one that you view regularly. For example, if you are interested in sport you may like to go to your favourite sports news site each time you logon to the Internet. In order to change the home page setting go to the Windows Control Panel and double click on the Internet Options icon. This will produce a window like the one of Figure 2.50. Edit the Home page textbox to remove the existing address and add the full address of the selected web page. Left-click the Apply button and then the OK button and the browser should then go to the selected page each time you logon to the Internet.

Note that you do not have to go to the main page of a site, and can go direct to any page within the site provided you know its exact address.

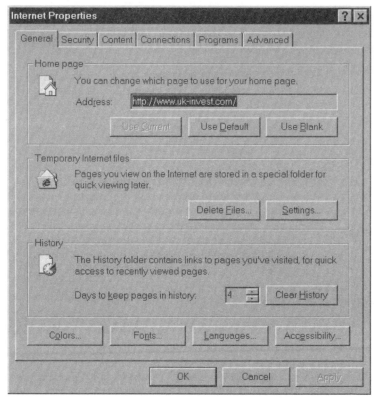

Fig.2.50 The home page can be set as any accessible web page

The obvious exceptions are any pages that have restricted access with some form of password protection for example. If you do not know the address of a page, simply go to that page and look at the address field of the browser. Web addresses for anything other than main pages are often quite long, but you can double-click on the address to highlight it, and then press the Control and C keys to copy it to the Windows Clipboard. It can then be pasted into the textbox in the Internet Options window by first clearing the existing address and then pressing the Control and V keys.

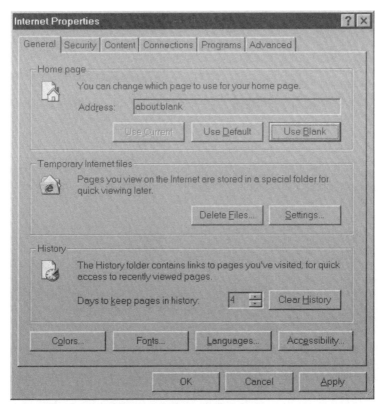

Fig.2.51 It is not mandatory to have a home page

Blank page

It is not essential to have a home page at all, and it may be better to opt for a blank page at start-up if there is no site that you wish to visit each time you logon. In order to do this go to the Internet Options window, and then operate the Use Blank button. The address in the text box will change to "about blank" (Figure 2.51). Next operate the Apply button, and then the OK button to exit and close the window. Next time you logon to the Internet the browser should initially display a blank page (Figure 2.52), avoiding any unnecessary download time.

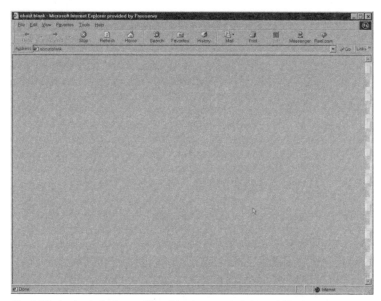

Fig.2.52 Instant start-up with a blank page in Internet Explorer

To select a home page using Netscape Communicator or Navigator, first select Preferences from the Edit menu. This produces a window like the one of Figure 2.53. The three radio buttons near the top of the page enable navigation to start using either a blank page, the selected page, or the last page visited. If you wish to specify the address for the home page, it is added into the large textbox. Note that it is the home page settings of Netscape Communicator or Navigator that will be used by these programs, and not those set in Windows. However, the Netscape settings will not affect another browser such as Internet Explorer, which does use the Windows settings. The Windows and Internet Explorer home page settings are actually one and the same.

It is only fair to point out that the software of some ISPs tends to take over your computer and do its own thing. With AOL for example, the choice of home page is largely irrelevant. When you logon you always get the AOL browser with an array of AOL pages on display. However, if you minimise the AOL browser and activate an alternative such as Internet Explorer, this browser should use the selected home page or blank initial page.

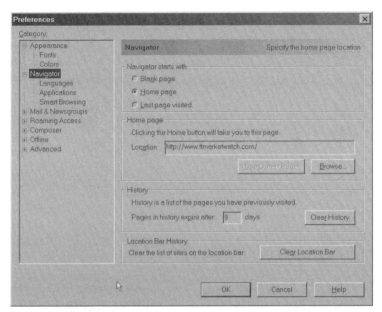

Fig.2.53 Setting a blank home page with a Netscape browser

Long and short of it

Some advocate having the PC as close the telephone socket as possible,
and preferably as close as possible to the main socket (the one that
connects directly to the outside wiring). The logic of this is sound in that
the longer the total cable length, the more the signal will be degraded.
However, it seems unlikely that an extra few metres of wire will significantly
reduce the signal quality. I tried speed tests with and without a 10-metre
extension cable in use, and there was no significant difference in the
results. It makes sense not to use cabling that is much longer than it
really needs to be, but relocating a computer in the hope of increased
speed is unlikely to be successful.

New browser

Some advocate a change of browser in order to obtain nippier Internet
performance. This is not in order to obtain a faster transfer of data, but is
instead aimed at getting a browser program that is more rapid in
operation. Browsers like Internet Explorer and Netscape Navigator

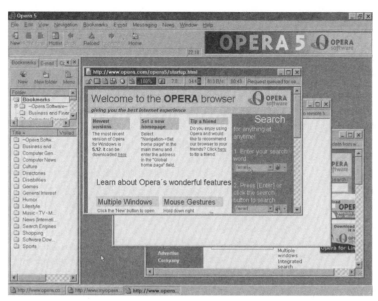

Fig.2.54 Opera 5.12 in action

require a fair amount of resources in order to run well. Using a modern version of either in conjunction with an older PC of modest specification can give sluggish results, especially if the modem is of the software variety. With a hardware modem fitted in a "dream machine" PC, any increase in the speed obtained using a less demanding browser program is likely to be less noticeable.

One option is to use an old version of Internet Explorer or a Netscape browser. In this context the word "old" means a version that would have been current when the PC was new, or something approximating to this. The obvious drawback of this approach is that the browser will be a bit out of date and might not work well with all web sites. In fact it might not work at all with some sites. In particular, secure sites and those that utilise the latest clever programming tricks are likely to give problems. Even sites that use frames might be problematic in some cases.

Many Web users overlook the fact that there are other browsers, and it is not mandatory to use the Microsoft and Netscape offerings. Probably the most popular alternative browser is one called Opera, which is produced by Opera Software. The latest version should be available from any of the major software download sites, and it is often included on the cover-mount discs supplied with computer magazines. Version 5.12 is the latest one at the time this was written, and it offers multiple windows (Figure 2.54) and built-in Flash support. It is a compact program, and the download is just 2.2 megabytes. It certainly seems to work well with old or new hardware, and it is well worth giving this browser a try. It is free if you are prepared to put up with the banner advertising.

Bare minimum

An alternative approach is to settle for Internet Explorer, but to disable some of the more advanced features that are not really needed. These can be switched off by going to the Windows Control Panel, double-clicking on the Internet Options icon, and then operating the Advanced tab. Scroll down the list of settings until the Multimedia section is reached (Figure 2.55). Here things such as sounds, animations, and even pictures can be switched off. A facility is switched on if its checkbox is ticked, or off if the tick is removed.

The greatest gain in download time can be obtained by switching off pictures, which prevents practically any type of graphic content from being downloaded. On the face of it, pictures are unnecessary most of the time, since it is the text content that is usually required. Unfortunately, it is now less practical to switch off pictures than it was in the past. Many sites now feature menus that utilise fancy control buttons (Flash buttons), and these buttons are graphics objects. If you switch off pictures, menus that use Flash buttons will disappear along with photographs, etc.

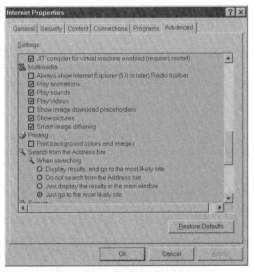

Fig.2.55 Switching off some features can give speedier Internet access

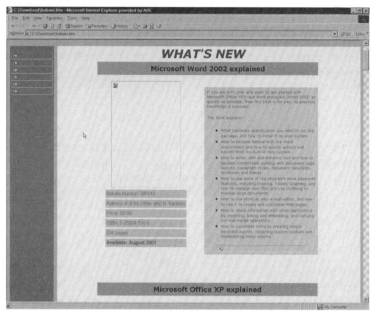

Fig.2.56 All graphics, including the menu buttons on the left, have been removed

This can be seen in the example of Figure 2.56 where the menu near the top right-hand corner of the page has failed to materialise. Pages will load much more quickly, but this is of little use if it is not possible to navigate sites properly. Although there are just blank spaces instead of buttons, left-clicking the blank space does actually operate the non-existent button! Obviously this problem does not afflict all web pages, and much surfing can be undertaken with pictures deactivated. The reduction in download times is quite surprising.

Wait reduction

A common mistake made by newcomers to the Internet is to wait unnecessarily for each page to download. If a menu has downloaded and appeared on the screen there is no need to wait for the rest of the page to load before selecting a menu item. Downloading of the current page should cease almost immediately when a menu entry is activated, and the next page will then start to download. With the penchant for large web pages this can save a huge amount of time.

REN

With the relaxation of the telephone regulations many houses suddenly gained a telephone in practically every room. When adding new telephones many people ignore the fact that there is a limit to the number that can be used per telephone line. Telephones have a REN (ring equivalence number) rating, which for most modern telephones is 1.0. This rating is usually show on the underside of the base unit, as part of the BABT approval sticker (Figure 2.57). The total REN value

Fig.2.57 Most equipment has a REN of 1.0

on one telephone line should not exceed 4.0. Note that this includes the REN ratings of any modems connected to the line, and not just telephones. The REN rating may be shown on a sticker on the modem itself, or it may appear on the box. It should also be included in the instruction manual.

If your telephones operate erratically, sometimes fail to ring, and reliable operation at a reasonable speed is not possible with your modem, check that the total REN rating of the units on the telephone line is no more than 4.0. It may be necessary to unplug some units in order to obtain good results with a modem where the total rating is being exceeded.

Points to remember

If you really must have a very fast connection there is no alternative to using some form of broadband Internet service. Tweaking settings and using clever software will help you to get the most from a V90 modem, but it will not get it to go faster than 56.6k.

The Internet works best when the fewest people are using it. Where possible, do your surfing at these times of low activity, which mainly means the small hours and early morning.

If you are still using a 33.6k or a slower modem such as a 28.8k type it is definitely worthwhile upgrading to a V90 (56.6k) modem.

Some early software modems do not work particularly well, especially when used in an older PC. Upgrading to a 56k hardware modem will usually give significantly better performance. In general, hardware modems work somewhat better than the software variety even in a modern super-fast PC.

When dealing with any PC hardware bear in mind that most of it is vulnerable to damage from static charges. Take at least a few basic precautions to guard against accidentally zapping things.

If you would prefer not to replace a software modem that seems to be performing below par, see if you can find improved device drivers for the old one.

Where only a subset of the Internet can be accessed and (or) pages are loading in slow motion, try logging off and signing on again. Things are unlikely to improve if you stay online and press on regardless.

There are web sites and software than can help you to test the connection speed of your modem. It is advisable to repeat these tests, preferably at different times of day. A single bad result might just be down to the test being made at a time of high congestion.

You are not obliged to have the home page set by your service provider. In fact your home page can be any page on the Internet to which there is free access. If you visit a page very frequently, save time by setting this page as your home page.

A less demanding browser may speed things up slightly when using an older PC. With any PC, things can be speeded up considerably by switching off sounds, animations, etc., although this will result in some web sites being at least partially unusable.

Your modem, and your other telephone equipment come to that, may not work well if the total REN value of the various units on the line exceeds 4.0. Remember that the modem itself has a REN value that must be included in the total.

2   Speeding up

Download
managers

Accelerator strategies

If you have an Internet connection via a standard telephone line and you regularly achieve something close to the theoretical maximum data transfer figures, there is no point in trying to obtain faster connection speeds other than changing to a faster method of connection such as ADSL. Even if you were to achieve theoretically perfect results the improvement in performance would be minimal. This is not to say that it is not possible to streamline things and reduce the time it requires online to carry out a certain set of tasks.

One popular strategy is to avoid downloading things that are unnecessary. For example, practically every web page seems to come complete with at least one banner advertisement, and it is increasingly common for pages to be accompanied by so-called pop-ups. In other words, an advertisement that pops up in a new window when a page is loaded. Using a program that filters out banner advertisements and pop-ups can significantly boost the rate at which you surf the Internet.

This sort of thing does not help when downloading large music files, videos, etc. It is possible to streamline things when dealing with large files such as these, and the normal approach is to use a program called a download manager. A program of this type tries to make sure that the rate at which data is downloaded is as close as possible to the maximum rate that your modem supports. There are two main approaches, and one of these is to test the various sources of the file so that the fastest server or servers can be used.

The other is to use settings that are likely to give optimum results when downloading large files. A program that only adjusts settings is usually called an optimiser or accelerator rather than a download manager. However, the terminology of these programs is rather loosely applied,

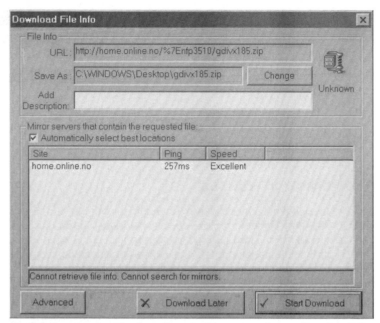

Fig.3.1 Accelerator Plus in action. In this case only one download site has been found

so you need to read the "fine print" in order to determine the exact facilities provided by any programs of this genre.

A download manager can also be used to carry on where you left off if the connection to the server is lost. Normally there is no way of continuing with a download if the connection is lost. Establishing the connection again and continuing with the download will almost invariably result in the process starting "from scratch", and the part of the file downloaded previously will be lost. Even if there were only a few bytes of a 100-megabyte file left to go when the connection went down, the part of the file that was downloaded will be lost!

With large files and unreliable servers it may only be possible to download large files with the aid of a download manager. Without one you might never get more than half the file downloaded. In less severe instances it can still save a lot of wasted time, since you will not keep downloading the same data over and over again until the complete file is eventually downloaded in one lump.

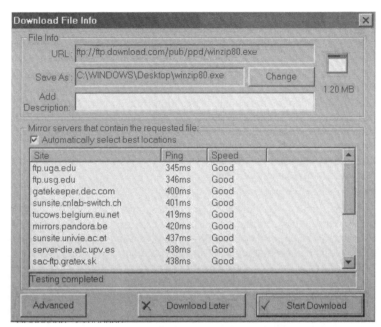

Fig.3.2 *In this example Accelerator Plus has found about 20 sources for the file*

The right connections

A download manager that searches for the best download sites and (or) can resume where it left off, is normally set to popup automatically when a download is about to commence. Figure 3.1 shows Accelerator Plus in operation, and in this case it has not been able to find any information about alternative download sites, or "mirror" sites as they are termed. This gives no option but to download the file from the original site.

The chances of finding mirror sites depend on the popularity of the file you are trying to download. With a very popular download there could be dozens of alternative sites available. Figure 3.2 shows the result when trying to download the popular Winzip program. In this case there are so many mirror sites that the list has gained a scrollbar.

Pinging

The list includes a ping time for each site and a rating of that ping time. Pinging is sending a small packet of data to a server and back again. The shorter the time this takes the faster the download is likely to be. It tends to be assumed that the rate at which data can be downloaded is purely dependent on the quality of the connection to the Internet service provider and the speed at which the server can send data. However, data is not downloaded from the server in the form of one continuous stream of data. It is sent in smaller chunks called "packets", and a dialogue is needed between your PC and the server in order to ensure that everything works smoothly.

Time is lost each time your PC and the server try to establish contact. Pinging is used to measure how quickly (or otherwise) your PC and the server can establish contact, rather than just measuring the rate at which data can be transferred between the two. With a short ping time there is relatively little time wasted trying to establish contact so that messages or packets of data can be exchanged efficiently. Of course, if the rate of data flow is very low, this will also produce a long ping time.

The obvious approach is to use whichever site gives the shortest response time, but many download managers take things a step further. The fastest site is used initially, but if this site fails to live up to expectations another fast site will be tried instead. There may be an option to manually select the sites to use, but automatic selection is easier and likely to yield the best results. Operating the Start Download button gets things underway, and a small window then appears. This shows how things are progressing (Figure

Fig.3.3 The program has selected and is using four download sites

3.3) and also indicates if it is possible to resume a broken download, which it normally is. Where appropriate, the bottom section gives details of how the data is being downloaded using simultaneous connection to several sites.

Registry

Most Internet accelerator programs operate by altering parameters in the Windows Registry. Probably most Windows users have heard of the Registry, but it seems to be a little understood aspect of this operating system. I suppose that this is reasonable, since it is an aspect of Windows that most users do not have to deal with directly. Indeed, you are definitely discouraged from tampering with the Registry in case a mistake results in the PC refusing to boot properly, or malfunctioning in some other way.

You are almost certain to make changes to the Registry unless you leave your PC with its factory settings and add no new software or hardware. However, you will probably be unaware that you have made these changes. You make changes to the Registry each time you change the screen resolution, add a new piece of hardware, alter the Windows colour scheme, or make practically any change to the system. The changes are made via indirect means though, hiding the Windows Registry from the user

There are numerous settings in the registry that can not be altered via the Control Panel and the other standard methods of control. It is this factor that makes the Registry so popular with hackers and tweakers, who can access various features that are otherwise "out of bounds". Accessing the Registry is easy enough, and Windows includes a simple utility program called Regedit specifically for this purpose. Although the name suggests that the Registry is one file, it is actually two hidden files in the Windows folder that are called System.dat and User.dat. However, Regedit hides this fact from users.

Regedit

One way to run Regedit is to go to the Start menu, choose Run, type "regedit" in the text box, and then operate the OK button (Figure 3.4). There is no need to include the path to the Regedit.exe file; Windows will know where to find it. Alternatively, use the Run function but use the Browse facility to locate the Regedit.exe file and then operate the OK button. This will bring up the rather blank looking initial screen of Figure

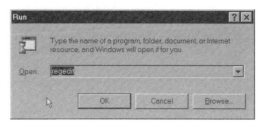

3.5. There is no harm in looking at the contents of the Registry, but never alter a Registry setting unless you are sure you know what you are doing.

Fig.3.4 Running the Regedit program

In operation Regedit is designed to be much like Windows Explorer. There are what appear to be files and folders, and there is no hint that it is actually two files that are being edited. You need to bear in mind the program is showing the contents of a database, and that it can not be used in exactly the same way as Windows Explorer. For example, the drag and drop approach does not work when using Regedit. Double clicking on one of the entries in the left-hand section of the screen expands it, as in Figure 3.6, to show what appear to be subfolders.

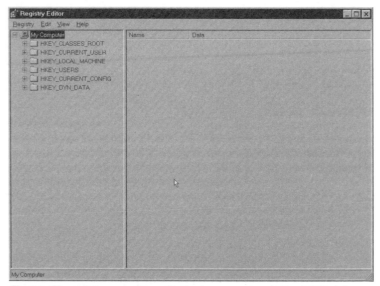

Fig.3.5 Regedit in operation with the keys on view in the left-hand section of the window

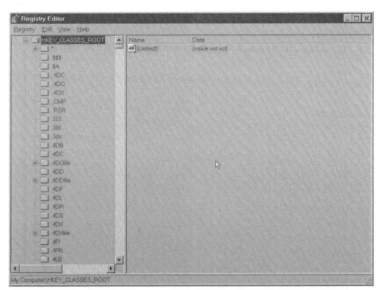

Fig.3.6 The keys can be expanded to show the sub-keys, which in most cases can also be expanded to show further sub-keys

In Windows Registry terminology the left-hand section of the screen shows keys, and double clicking on one of these expands its entry to show the sub-keys. With subfolders double clicking on an entry will sometimes reveal further subfolders. Likewise, double clicking on sub-keys will sometimes reveal a further layer of the key structure. A mark beside a key icon indicates that a further layer of sub-keys is available.

Once the lowest level in the key structure has been reached, double clicking on an entry produces something like the window of Figure 3.7. Including the icons on the left, the right-hand section of the screen breaks down into three sections. The icon indicates the type of data stored in the key. An icon containing "ab" indicates that the key holds a string, which means that it contains letters and (or) numbers. The string is always contained within double quotation marks (").

An icon containing "011110" indicates that the key holds a numerical code, which is often in the form of a binary number and not an ordinary decimal type. The hexadecimal numbering system is also used, and numbers of this type are preceded by "0x" to show that they are in this numbering system. No quotation marks are used for numeric values.

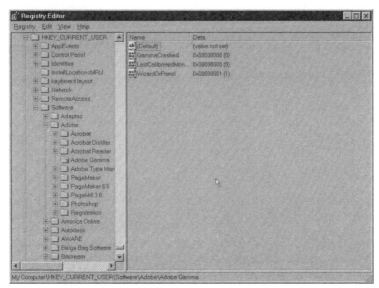

*Fig.3.7   The right-hand section of the window shows the Value
and Data fields*

Next to the icons in the Name column are the values, but this term is
perhaps a bit misleading. The Name heading at the top of this column is
more accurate, since the values are names that tell you which piece of
data is stored for each entry in the database. Fortunately, the names
used here usually give a good idea as to the purpose of each piece of
data, although the names have to be kept reasonably short and therefore
tend to be a bit cryptic. The third column is the actual data stored in
each value.

Navigation

You do not have to move around the Registry for long in order to realise
that the number of values stored there is vast. I do not know how many
values are to be found in an average Windows Registry, but it must be
many thousands. There are six main Registry keys in the "root directory",
which are known as "hive" keys incidentally. It is obviously much easier
to find the required value if you understand the significance of the hive
keys, and know which one to search. These are the six hive keys and
the types of value that each one contains:

HKEY_CLASSES_ROOT

All the file associations are stored within this key. This includes OLE information, shortcut data, and file associations for the recognised file types.

INKEY_CURRENT_USER

The desktop preferences are stored in this key. This mainly means parameters that are set via the Control Panel, but other data is stored here. Under the Software sub-key there is a further sub-key for each item of installed software, so there can be a vast number or entries here as well.

HKEY_LOCAL_MACHINE

Machine in a Windows context means the PC that it is running on. This hive key therefore contains data that is specific to the particular PC concerned. As one would expect, there is a Hardware sub-key here, but there are others such as a Network sub-key and a security type. There is a Software sub-key here as well, but it is different to the one found under the HKEY_CURRENT_USER hive key. The information stored in this Software sub-key seems to be largely associated with hardware configuration and uninstalling the software, rather than things like screen colours.

HKEY_USERS

If the PC has more than one user, this hive key is used to store the preferences for each user. In most cases the users feature of Windows is not utilised, so the information here will simply duplicate that stored in the HKEY_CURRENT_USER hive key. Perhaps more accurately, HKEY_CURRENT USERS will duplicate the data stored in HKEY_USERS.

HKEY_CURRENT_CONFIG

This key contains the current software and hardware configuration data. In the likely event that you are only using one configuration, it will contain the same data as HKEY_LOCAL_MACHINE.

HKEY_DYN_DATA

The dynamic data is stored in this hive key. Dynamic in this context means that it is data that must always be stored in memory so that it can be accessed quickly. As one would expect, the data stored here is highly technical in nature.

Even if you know what you are looking for and roughly where to find it, searching through the numerous entries in the Registry can still be very

Fig.3.8 Using Regedit's Find facility

time consuming. Fortunately, the Registry Checker has a Find facility that is similar to the Find Files and Folders facility of Windows Explorer. Selecting Find from the Edit menu brings up a Window like the one of Figure 3.8. Use the textbox to enter the text you wish to search for, and select the fields of the Registry you wish to search.

You can also opt for a whole string search. In other words, a match will only be produced if the full string in the Registry matches the one you have entered. If this option is not selected, a match will be produced if the string you entered matches part of an entry in the Registry. The whole string option can help to keep the number of matches to more manageable proportions, but you have to know precisely what you are looking for. Press the Find Next button to search for the string. If a match is found, it will be shown highlighted in the main window of the Registry Editor. If this one is not the entry you are looking for, call up the Find facility again and operate the Find Next button. Keep doing this until the required entry is located or the whole of the Registry has been searched.

In order to edit a Registry entry, double-click on it to bring up the editing window, as in Figure 3.9. Both the value name and data can then be edited in the normal way. Left-click the OK button when you have finished, or the Cancel button if you change your mind. It is also possible to left-click on an entry and then use the Edit menu to either delete or rename it. Clearly it is necessary to know exactly what you are doing before altering any registry entries. Unless you have the necessary expertise it is better to alter the Registry only via indirect routes, such as using the Control Panel or utility programs that are designed to make a specific set of changes to the Registry safe and easy.

Registry backup

Although Windows makes its own backup copies of the Registry, some users prefer to have an additional backup copy. If you are going to alter a Registry setting using Regedit or a utility program it is not a bad idea to make a backup copy first. Since the file sizes involved are quite small it

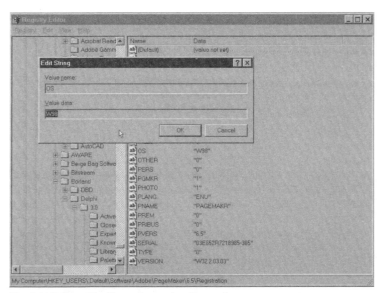

Fig.3.9 Editing Registry data using Regedit

makes sense to keep the backup copies on floppy discs, a Zip disc, etc., rather than on the hard disc where they are vulnerable to disc failures. The Windows Registry sounds as though it should be a single file, but as explained previously it is actually system data contained in two files called User.dat and System.dat. In order to backup these files it is merely necessary to locate them on the hard disc using Windows Explorer and then drag them to a floppy drive, Zip drive, or whatever.

Bear in mind that these are system files, and that using the default settings of Windows Explorer they are hidden from view. However, it only requires one easy change in order to make the files visible using Windows Explorer. Activate the View menu and then select Folder Options. Operate the View tab of the new window that appears, which will produce a number of check boxes and radio buttons that can be used to select the desired options (Figure 3.10). Under the Hidden files section make sure that the Show all files radio button is selected. Left-click the Apply button and then the OK button to apply the new setting and close the window.

The User.dat file is usually quite small and will fit onto a 1.44-megabyte floppy disc quite comfortably. The System.dat file tends to vary in size quite substantially from one PC to another, but in general it seems to be

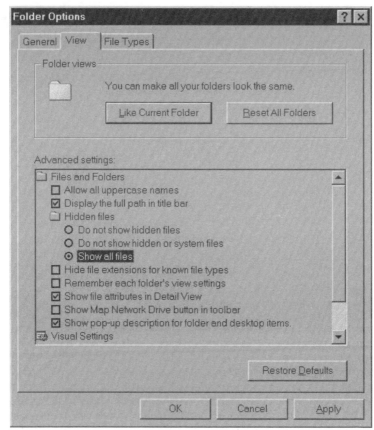

Fig.3.10 Making hidden files visible using Windows Explorer

much larger and can be several megabytes in size. Even using compression it is unlikely that this file will fit on a single floppy disc, but there are programs that can spread large files across several floppy discs and reconstitute then again. For instance, later versions of the popular Winzip program can accomplish this. Using this program to produce a compressed file on a hard disc is covered in chapter 5. The process is much the same using floppy discs, but you have to change discs when prompted. Alternatively, copy this file to a higher capacity disc such as a CD-RW or Zip type.

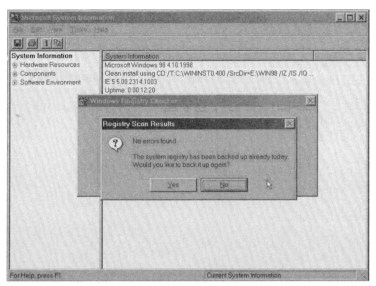

Fig.3.11 Operate the Yes button to backup the Registry

Windows does actually have a facility to backup and restore the Registry, and you may prefer to use this to ensure that there is a fully working copy stored on the hard disc drive. Apart from when you make alterations to the Registry using Regedit or another special utility, it is not a bad idea to have backed-up the Registry before installing any software of unknown quality that has been downloaded from the Web. In order to backup the registry select Programs from the Start menu, followed by Accessories, System tools, and Registry Checker. The Registry Checker will look for errors in the Registry, but it will presumably fail to find any. It will then display the message of Figure 3.11. The last backup copy made by the system automatically is probably sufficient, but operate the Yes button to ensure that there is a fully up to date backup copy of the Registry.

Restore

The Registry Checker runs automatically each time the computer is booted, and it will ask for confirmation that you wish to resort to a backup copy if the Registry is found to be damaged. It makes sense to restore an earlier version of the Registry when major corruption has been detected, since there is little chance of the computer booting and running

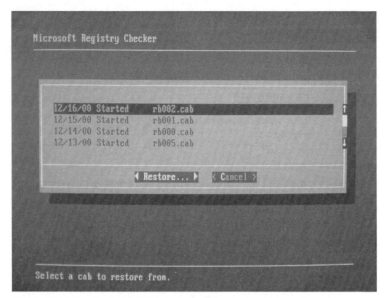

Fig.3.12 Using Scanreg's Restore facility

properly using the corrupted Registry. The Registry Checker program will not always detect a problem in the Registry, and it is mainly designed to find something fairly major such as part of the file being obliterated. Consequently, the Registry Checker may fail to find any problems but a Registry fault could still result in the computer failing to boot properly or other problems.

Restoring your own copies of the Registry files is just a matter of copying them to the Windows folder on the hard disc. It is advisable to rename the old files first rather than simply overwriting them. That way you can change back again if the need should arise. Reverting to one of the backup copies produced automatically by Windows is slightly more complicated. The first step is to boot into MS/DOS. Booting from drive A: using a Windows Startup disc or from C: using MS/DOS mode are both acceptable in this case. Next type this command and press Return, which will produce a screen like the one in Figure 3.12:

C:\windows\command\scanreg /restore

This command includes the full path to the Scanreg program, so the system does not have to be in a particular drive or directory when it is issued. By default, Windows keeps five copies of the Registry, but this includes the one that is currently in use. This screen enables any of the four backup copies to be restored. Thus, if the most recent backup is faulty, you can revert to an earlier version and try again. Use the up and down cursor keys to select the backup copy you require and then press enter. If you change your mind and do not wish to reinstate a backup copy of the registry, press the right cursor key to highlight the Cancel option and then press Return.

The backup copies of the Registry files can also be restored from within Windows. The backup copies are stored in cabinet files in the \Windows\sysbckup folder, but this is a hidden folder so it will only be visible to Windows Explorer if it is set to show hidden files and folders. There are several cabinet files in this folder (the ones having a "cab" extension), and the dates of the files indicate the ages of the backup copies that they contain. To restore a pair of backup files they are extracted from the cabinet file and copied to the main Windows directory. The existing Registry files will have to be overwritten so answer "yes" if you are asked if you wish to overwrite them. Alternatively, rename the existing Registry files first, and then copy the backup files into the Windows directory.

MTU and MSS

The two Registry tweaks that are normally used to improve results with modems are the MTU and MSS settings. MTU stands for Maximum Transmission Unit, and it sets the maximum size for a packet of data. It is normally set at 1500 bytes, which is fine for a local area network (LAN). It can be too high for use with a dial-up modem, giving reduced performance. Although the packet size may seem to be of no great consequence, you have to bear in mind that with this type of link it is not unusual for errors to occur. The system includes error checking, and this does not give problems with corrupted data.

If a packet contains errors that can not be corrected, the whole packet is sent again. Taking an extreme example, with a packet size of one million bytes, an error free packet might never be received. At the other extreme, taking things on a byte by byte basis would waste a lot of time regulating the flow of data. What is needed is a good compromise between these two extremes.

Another train of thought about MTU is that setting it too large results in packets of data to or from your PC being larger than the packet size used by your Internet service provider. This results in the packets being broken down into smaller packets and then reassembled at the

Fig.3.13 Expanding the HKEY_LOCAL_MACHINE folder

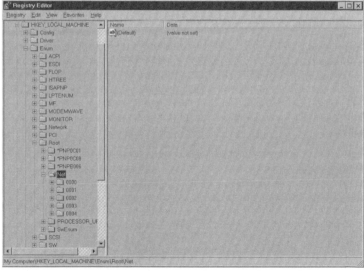

Fig.3.14 Next the Enum, Root, and Net folders are expanded

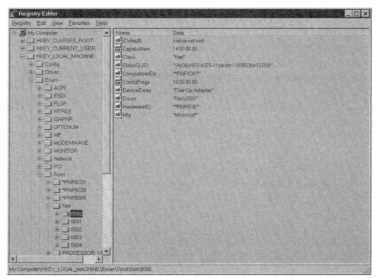

Fig.3.15 Find the subfolder with "DeviceDesc" in the Name field

destination, which reduces efficiency. Whichever way you look at it, a smaller packet size can be beneficial.

The MSS (Maximum Segment Size) value controls the maximum amount of data that can be sent in a packet. At first sight it may seem that this is the same as the MTU value, but you have to bear in mind that each packet actually contains more than the data. For example, it contains addresses that enable it to find its way from the server to your PC. Consequently, the MSS value is slightly smaller than the one for the MTU setting.

Tweaking

You can tweak Registry values using either Regedit or a special utility program. Both methods will be described here, starting with the Regedit method. Any alterations to the Registry are made at your own risk, and this is something that should not be tried unless you have at least a basic understanding of what you are doing. Remember to make backup copies of the existing registry files before making any changes.

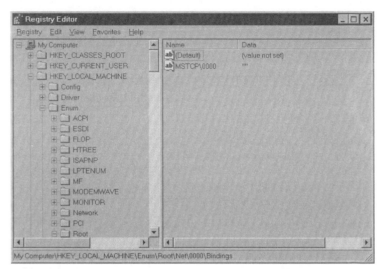

Fig.3.16 Here there should be an entry that starts "MSTCP"

The first task is to find the section of the registry that deals with the dialup adapter. Start the Registry Editor program and left-click on the HKEY_LOCAL_MACHINE folder. This should result in something like Figure 3.13. Next expand the Enum, Root, and Net folders so that you have something like Figure 3.14. Every PC is different, so the exact Registry entries may be different on your PC, but there should be several subfolders of the Net folder with names like 000, 0001, 0002, etc.

Now left-click on each of these folders in turn, and look at the data that appears in the right-hand section of the window. You are looking for the entry that has "DeviceDesc" in the Name field and "Dial-Up Adapter" in the Data field. This will probably be found in the first of the folders (Figure 3.15). The folder that contains this entry should have a subfolder called Bindings, which should now be expanded. This subfolder should contain an Entry in the name field that starts "MSTCP/", followed by a four-digit number. Make a note of this number, which will probably just be 0000 (Figure 3.16). Next go to:

HKEY_LOCAL_MACHINE\Enum\Network\MSTCP\xxxx

Here xxxx is the four-digit number noted previously. In this folder there should be a Value entry called Driver, and its Data entry will be something like "NetTrans0000" (Figure 3.17). It is the four-digit number in the Data entry that is required.

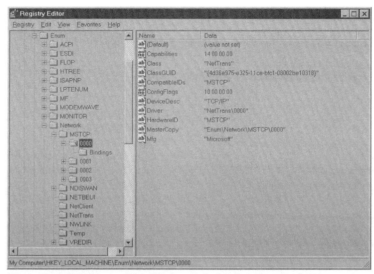

Fig.3.17 At this page of the Registry it is the Driver entry that is of interest

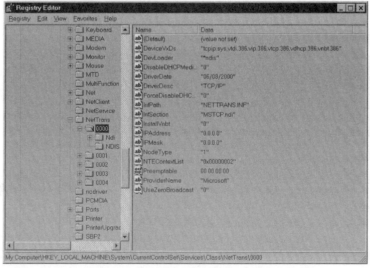

Fig.3.18 At last, this page is where the changes are made

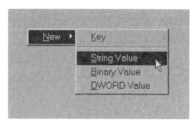

Fig.3.19 Use this menu to create a new string value

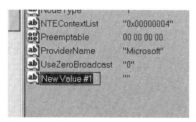

Fig.3.20 The newly created entry

Close the subfolders to remove the clutter in the left-hand side of the screen and return to the basic keys. To make the changes to the Registry go to HKEY_LOCAL_MACHINE again and go down the directory structure through System, CurrentControlSet, Services, Class, NetTrans, and 000x. Here 000x is the number of the dialup adapter that you determined previously, or 0000 in this example. This should give you something like Figure 3.18. Right-click in the right-hand section of the screen to produce a small popup menu (Figure 3.19) and select the String Value option. A new Value entry then appears in the list (Figure 3.20), and this is edited to read "MaxMTU". Then double-click on the new entry to produce the window of Figure 3.21 where a value of 576 should be entered.

Repeat this process, but the second time use "MaxMSS" for the Value field and 536 as the Data value. Next choose Exit from the File menu to close Regedit and then reboot the computer so that the changes can take effect. Run Regedit again and check that the changes are present and correct (Figure 3.22). Close Regedit and go online to see if the new settings have the desired effect.

There are no entries for MTU and MSS already present in the Registry because the default values are built into the Windows program code

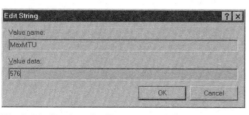

Fig.3.21 Setting the Data part of the new entry

and are not normally controlled by way of the Registry. Thus the entries first have to be generated and then given data values. If you find entries for MTU and MSS already present, either

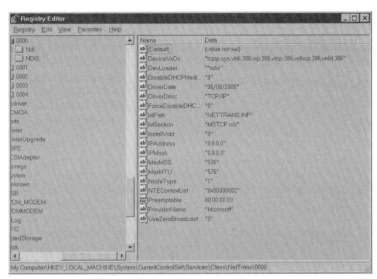

Fig.3.22 The two new entries in position on the correct page

someone has already added them manually or an accelerator program has put them there. Note that tweaking MTU and MSS must be repeated for each dialup adapter if there is more than one installed. There will almost certainly be more than one if you are using two or more Internet service provider. Additional adapters will be found in the keys called 0001, 0002, etc., when initially searching the Registry for the main dialup adapter's entry.

Easy tweaking

If you do not wish to delve into the Windows Registry directly, and I would certainly not recommend it, the easy alternative is to use one of the many programs that make it easy to change the default values. Here the popular TweakDUN program will be used as an example of this type of acceleration program. This should be available from any of the large software download sites or the manufacture's site at:

www.pattersondesigns.com.

Unregistered versions of the program are only partially operational, but do enable the MTU and MSS settings to be changed. When first run there is a splash screen followed by a menu that permits the desired

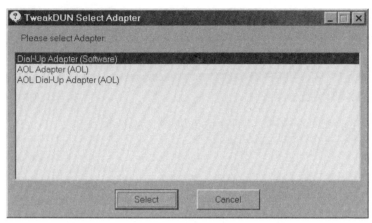

Fig.3.23 Selecting the dialup adapter for Tweak DUN to change

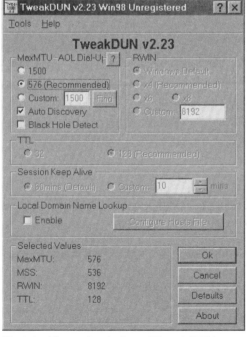

Fig.3.24 The main window of Tweak DUN

adapter to be selected (Figure 3.23). The adapters listed here will obviously depend on the set-up of your PC. Left-click on the entry for the adapter you wish to modify and then operate the Select button.

The program then moves to the main screen (Figure 3.24) where the MTU value of 576 can be selected using the appropriate radio button. Operate the OK button to implement the changes and then the Yes button when asked if you wish to restart the computer. Once the computer has rebooted the changes will have taken effect and it is ready for testing online. This method is certainly a lot easier than manually delving around in the Windows Registry, and it should be equally effective.

Other software

There are plenty of programs that will help to speed up your Internet access if it is below par. Some have the option of fully automating the process, with the program running tests to determine the best settings. There is another type of software that tries to speed things up by filtering out items that you do not require, which usually means banner advertisements and pop-ups. An advantage of this approach is that it should always speed things up, even if you system is already working very efficiently. However, it only works when downloading web pages, and this approach will not usually bring any benefit when downloading large files. It might bring a marginal improvement if the download site makes heavy use of banner advertising.

A potential problem with programs that remove banner advertising is that other material might also be filtered out. Figure 3.25 shows a web page that has been filtered using a program that removes banner advertisements, and Figure 3.26 shows the same page on a PC that does not use any filtering. The missing items from Figure 3.25 are not actually banner advertisements, but are not essential parts of the page either. However, be warned, programs of this type can sometimes remove menu buttons, making a page unusable.

Efficient PC

One final point is that you should make sure that your PC is running efficiently. If it runs slowly with frequent crashes when running offline, it is not reasonable to expect it to work well online. There are web sites that can provide help to diagnose problems with PCs and correct them, and there is also plenty of PC diagnostics software available. However, where a PC has become seriously "gummed up" the best course of action is probably to backup important data to onto CD-RWs or some other removable storage medium, reformat the hard disc, and then reinstall everything from scratch.

Fig.3.25 A web page with banner advertisements filtered out

Fig.3.26 The same page without any filtering applied

Points to remember

Some download managers try to obtain fast downloads by using mirror sites. Data is downloaded from whichever site provides the fastest download rate at the time.

Probably the most useful facility of a download manager is its ability to continue where it left off in the event that the connection is lost. This is especially important if your Internet service provider has an automatic cut-off after an hour or two. Large downloads are then impossible without a download manager.

Internet access speeds can sometimes be improved by tweaking the Registry settings, either manually or indirectly using a suitable acceleration program. The MTU and MSS settings are the ones that are normally modified. You really need to learn a bit about the Registry and the Regedit program before trying to make changes manually.

Before modifying Registry settings, either directly or indirectly, it is a good idea to back up both of the Registry files. Restoring the backup files should cure the problem if things go badly wrong.

Even if the Registry is not backed up prior to making changes, it should be possible to rectify matters if things go wrong. Boot-up using a Windows recovery disc and then use the Scanreg program to restore one of the automatic backup copies from a previous day.

Programs that filter out banner advertisements and the like can produce speedier surfing, but can sometimes remove important page content.

3   Download managers

Browser problems

The big two

There are a number of browser programs currently in use, but the vast majority of Internet users rely on Microsoft's Internet Explorer or a Netscape browser such as Navigator. Consequently it is primarily Microsoft and Netscape browsers that will be discussed here. In fact we will be largely concerned with Internet Explorer, as this is now the most popular browser.

Text size

The size of computer screens has gradually increased over the years, as have screen resolutions. A resolution of 640 by 480 pixels on a 14-inch monitor was once the height of luxury, but these days many "budget" PCs are supplied complete with 15-inch or even 17-inch monitors. Even 19-inch monitors are not exactly a rarity these days. Screen resolutions of around 1024 by 768 to 1600 by 1200 pixels have become the norm. Web pages tend to be designed so that they are usable by visitors using relatively small monitors and low screen resolutions. The lowest common denominator approach is understandable, but it can produce problems when browsing using a high-resolution screen. The problem is worst when using high resolution relative to the size of the monitor's screen. A resolution of 1024 by 768 on a 14-inch screen for example.

The usual problem is that much of the lettering is so small that it is difficult to read. There can also be problems with the layout of some pages looking rather rough. This occurs because the lettering is either too big to fit its allotted space, or occupies only a fraction of the available space. An HTML web page can have various text sizes, but the actual displayed

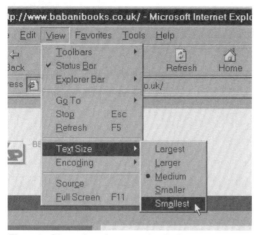

Fig.4.1 Changing the text size in Internet Explorer

size is dependent on the way in which the browser program interprets the HTML code. The same web page viewed using two different browsers can have noticeable differences. The obvious way of overcoming the small text problem is to maximise the page so that it completely fills the screen. In practice this is often unsuccessful, with the page staying the same size. The screen is padded out with empty space, usually down the right-hand side of the screen.

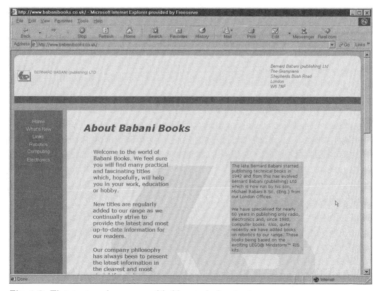

Fig.4.2 The example page with Normal size text

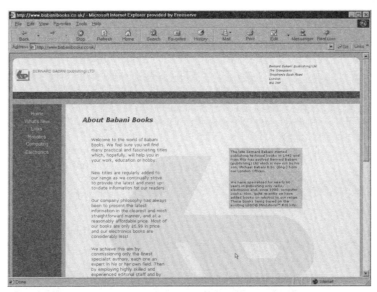

Fig.4.3 The example page using the smallest text setting

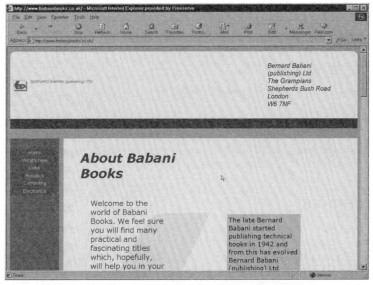

Fig.4.4 The same page, but this time using the largest text

In Internet Explorer it is possible to adjust the text size by going to the View menu and selecting the Text Size option. This produces the submenu of Figure 4.1, offering five text sizes. These are the normal size, plus two smaller and two larger sizes. Figure 4.2 shows an example web with text at the normal size, while Figures 4.3 and 4.4 respectively show the same page using the smallest and largest text sizes.

Most browser programs have a similar facility. In Netscape Communicator for example, there are Increase Font and Decrease Font commands available from the View menu (Figure 4.5). As one would expect, these respectively give larger and smaller text sizes. If you have problems with uncomfortably small text it is worthwhile trying the larger sizes to see if they provide more usable results. A smaller text size can be beneficial if page layouts sometimes seem to go awry, perhaps with text that is inaccessible.

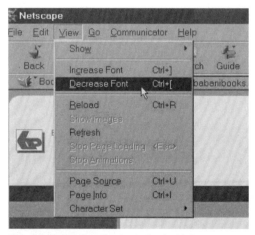

Fig.4.5 Adjusting the text size in Netscape

It is only fair to point out that some web pages use coding that specifies absolute text sizes, and prevents the browser from interpreting things as it sees fit. This ensures that page layouts are reproduced accurately with no problems such as text extending beyond its allotted space. Unfortunately, it also means that setting larger or smaller text sizes has no effect on these pages.

Hard copy

Hard copy from a browser can live up to its name, with printouts often lacking some of the bits you need, or including masses of material that you do not require. In fairness to browser programs, web pages vary enormously in size and content, making it impossible for a simple print facility to produce exactly what you require every time. The basic process

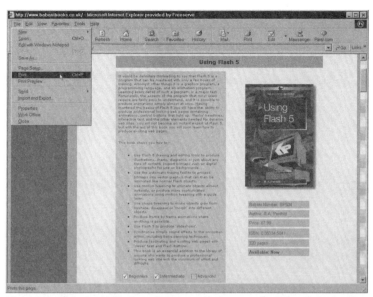

Fig.4.6 In standard Windows fashion, the Internet Explorer Print facility is available from the File menu

of printing a page is very straightforward. Start by selecting Print from the File menu. Figure 4.6 shows the File menu of Internet Explorer 5.5, but the same route is used in the Netscape browsers, and practically every Windows program come to that.

The Print window (Figure 4.7) will then appear, and here you can select the correct printer, the number of

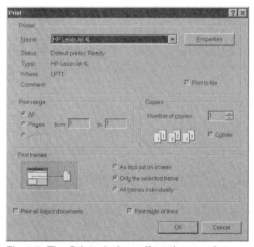

Fig.4.7 The Print window offers the usual facilities

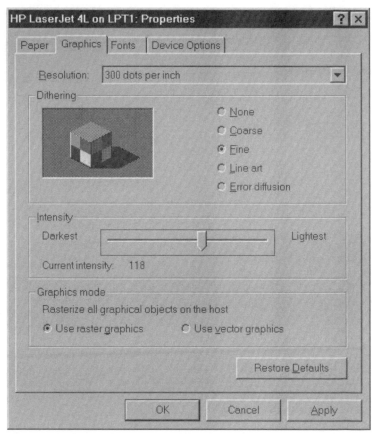

Fig.4.8 The Properties window for the printer. This is different for each printer

copies required, and so on. Operating the Properties button brings up a control window for the selected printer (Figure 4.8). The exact facilities vary from one printer to another, but there are typically controls for such things as the print quality, paper size, orientation (landscape or portrait), and media type. Operate the Apply and OK buttons to implement any changes and return to the Print window. Then operate the OK button to print the page.

Internet Explorer 5.5 introduced a useful Print Preview facility that is available from the file menu. This shows exactly what will be printed,

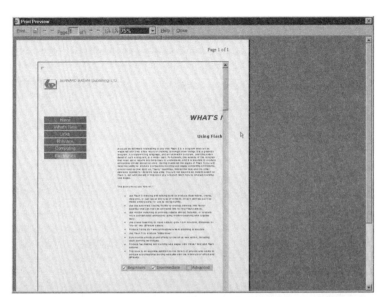

Fig.4.9 The Print Preview facility of Internet Explorer

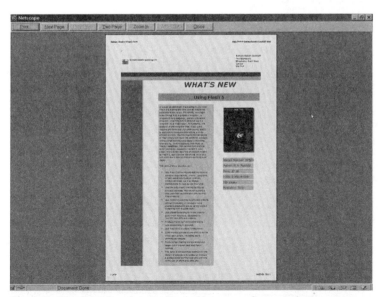

Fig.4.10 The Print Preview facility in Netscape Communicator

and avoids wasting paper and ink or toner on pages that will not be printed to your satisfaction. Figure 4.9 shows the Print Preview facility of Internet Explorer 5.5 in action. There is a similar facility in Netscape Communicator (Figure 4.10). Both programs have a page setup facility that gives control over things such as margin widths. Figure 4.11 shows the Page Setup window of Netscape Communicator.

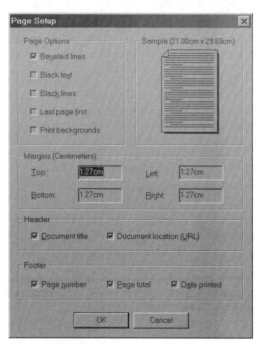

You may sometimes go to print a page only to find that the Print entry in the File menu is greyed out and unusable. This usually occurs because the page has not finished downloading. Either wait until it has finished downloading, or operate the refresh button to try again if things seem to have ground to a halt before the loading process was completed.

Fig.4.11   The Page Setup window of Netscape Communicator

Over the edge

Some web pages have a strip down the right-hand side missing when they are printed out. This occurs simply because the page is too wide to fit the printed page. If a page is too wide to fit the screen a horizontal scrollbar comes to the rescue, but there is no equivalent when printing. However, the printer setup page should offer the choice of portrait or landscape printing. This is normally set to portrait printing, and by switching to landscape mode the effective page width is increased by

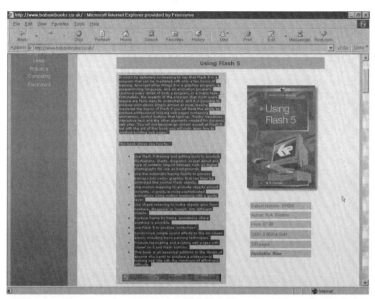

*Fig.4.12 Dragging can be used to select the required text on a
web page*

around 50 percent. This will usually be sufficient to get everything onto
the page. Of course, the available page height is reduced, and the web
page will be printed over more paper pages.

Being selective

A common problem in producing hard copy is that you get all sorts of
extraneous material in addition to part or parts that you actually require.
With some programs it is possible to select part of a document and then
print out only the selected section. This method is unusual with Windows
programs though, and it does not work with a browser such as Internet
Explorer. Text can be selected in standard Windows fashion by dragging
the pointer over the required block of text, and the selected text will be
highlighted (Figure 4.12). The easiest way to print the selected text is to
first use the Copy facility of the browser to place the text on the Windows
Clipboard. Either select Copy from the Edit window or press the Control
and C keys.

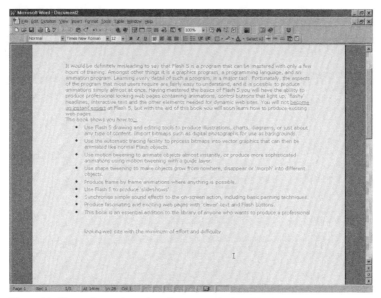

Fig.4.13 The selected text has been copied to Word 97

With the text selected and copied it can be pasted into another program such as a word processor. Open a fresh document in the other program and then either select Paste from its Edit menu or press the Control and V keys. The text should then be loaded into the new document. Figure 4.13 shows some text that has been copied from Internet Explorer 5.5 and then pasted into Microsoft Word 97. Even the Wordpad program that is supplied as part of Windows is sufficient to extract and print the required text.

Once in a word processor the text can be edited, and the font, text size, colour, etc., can be altered if desired. A text colour that is fine for a web site is often inappropriate for hard copy, so a change of text colour will often be needed. Where necessary, several blocks of text can be copied to the word processor using separate cut and paste operations. The facilities of the word processor can be used to format the text in the required fashion, or it can even be copied to a desktop publishing program if a complex layout is required.

Fig.4.14 To copy an image, right-click on it and select Copy from the popup menu

Printing frames

Pages that use frames can sometimes be awkward when printing. The way in which frames are handled seems to be to some extent dependent on the printer driver. Sometimes the entire page with all frames is printed, while in others only one frame makes it to the printed page. If only one frame at a time is printed, make sure that the text cursor is on the frame that you wish to print. Check the print options of your printer, as these sometimes give a few options when printing frames. For example, my Brother printer enables all the frames to be printed together or on separate sheets.

Graphics

A common complaint is that graphics can not be copied and pasted in the same way as text. Also, if the Save facility is used to save a web page to disc, when the page is loaded into an HTML editor or a browser any graphic elements are absent. There is a simple solution to copying and pasting graphics, and Windows does include means for doing this.

Fig.4.15 The image pasted into Word 97

Fig.4.16 Once in another program the image can be processed

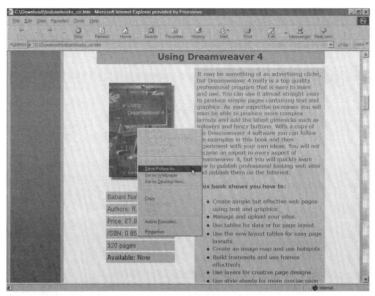

Fig.4.17 A web image can be saved to disc

The process is not quite the same as for text though. In order to copy a graphic element you must first right-click the mouse on the appropriate part of the screen. This produces a pop-up menu like the one of Figure 4.14. Select the Copy option and the graphic will be copied to the clipboard.

It can then be pasted into any application that can handle the type of graphic element involved. This does not just mean graphics programs, and any desktop publishing program should be able to take web graphics. In fact most modern word processors will accept graphics, including those from web pages. Figure 4.15 shows a photograph pasted into Word 97. The basic editing facilities of the program should be available, enabling the graphic to be resized and reshaped for instance (Figure 4.16). In fact the full range of editing facilities should be available if it is loaded into a good quality graphics package.

There is an alternative way of extracting an image from a web page and importing it into another program. In Internet Explorer, right-click on the image as before but this time select the Save Picture As option (Figure 4.17). The same procedure is used in Netscape Communicator, but the

Fig.4.18 Use the Save Image As option when using a Netscape browser

Save Image As option is selected (Figure 4.18). Either way, the standard Windows file browser should appear (Figure 4.19).

File formats

You are not usually "spoilt for choice" when it comes to the available file formats that can be used when saving the file. With Internet Explorer the usual choice is between the Jpeg and BMP formats, and the required format is selected via the Save As Type menu near the bottom of the window. Netscape Communicator mostly offers a Ford choice of any format you

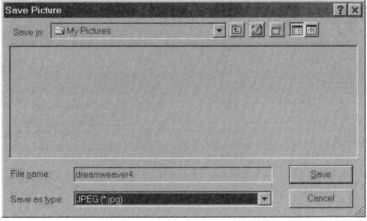

Fig.4.19 The usual Windows file browser is used when saving images

like provided it is Jpeg. Jpeg is the most common form of web graphic, and it is a bitmap format. In other words, it saves the image in the form of screen pixels, as does the Windows BMP format.

The difference is that Jpeg normally uses compression in order to keep file sizes and download times as small as possible. The BMP format does not use compression, which ensures no loss of quality but also gives what are usually much larger file sizes. In fact the BMP file size is likely to be three to 10 times larger, depending on the level of compression used in the Jpeg version, and how easily it compresses. The BMP option is the safer one, since practically any graphics program can handle this format, and optimum quality is guaranteed. Due to its more compact file sizes, Jpeg is still the preferred format for most, and it is now usable with practically any graphics software.

Jpeg problems

However, there can be problems with Jpeg due to the use of more than one type of compression. Figure 4.20 shows a window that appears when saving files in Jpeg format using PhotoShop 5.0. There are three types of compression available, and most programs use the standard version. There are two alternative types available, and these seem to be used by a small but significant minority of web sites. Browsers should have no problem with any form of Jpeg file, but having saved a file in this format it might not be compatible with your graphics software, even if it has basic Jpeg support. Note

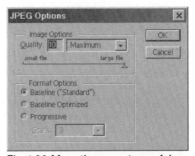

Fig.4.20 More than one type of Jpeg compression is in use

that the amount of compression used should not affect compatibility. Images that use large amounts of compression to achieve small file sizes are likely to be lacking in technical quality but will be equally compatible or incompatible with graphics programs.

If your graphics program is not very accommodating with non-standard Jpeg files, the easiest solution is to save images in BMP format. You can then save the file in Jpeg format from the graphics program and delete the original BMP file. This ensures that you always obtain compatible Jpeg files and avoids the relatively large file sizes associated with BMP files. Alternatively, just work with BMP files and put up with the larger file sizes. Modern computers have huge disc drive capacities and large file sizes are not of great importance for files that are not destined for use on the Web.

Other formats

There are other formats in use with web pages, including the PNG (pronounced "ping") format. This format is increasingly used for web graphics, and it was designed to be the eventual standard format for all web graphics. Current browsers load PNG images without any problems, but only offer Jpeg or BMP as options when saving images to disc. Using Internet Explorer it is actually possible to obtain images in their native format by saving the entire page to disc, as explained later in this chapter.

Some web images are in the GIF format, which is primarily used for vector graphics, or line art as it is also known. In other words it is used for things like charts, diagrams, and cartoons rather than photographic images. However, the GIF format is sometimes used for monochrome photographs, and pseudo photographic images. It is also used for simple animations. If you try to save an image of this type, the GIF format will probably be offered as one of the file type options, possibly with BMP as an alternative. BMP is the safer option because it is more widely supported than GIF. Most paint programs for example, can only handle bitmaps and can not import a vector graphic format such as GIF. As discussed later in this chapter, GIF offers higher quality if you wish to produce large printouts. Consequently, it is better to stay with the GIF format where this is possible.

Fig.4.21 The ART format is available when using AOL's browser

AOL ART

AOL users are offered a choice of ART and BMP formats when saving bitmaps (Figure 4.21). The ART format seems to be one that has been devised by AOL, and it is little used other than by AOL browsers. Some graphics software can import this format, but this facility is something of a rarity. One option is to simply use the BMP format. Another is to minimise the AOL browser and launch another browser program such as Internet Explorer or Netscape Communicator. The non-AOL browser should offer the usual Jpeg option provided the image in question has not already been loaded into the AOL browser. Presumably the image file is stored in cache of temporary Internet files in ART form, and it is this file that is loaded into the new browser instead of the original file.

Anyway, if you will need to save bitmaps in Jpeg form, switch to the non-AOL browser before going in search of the images. Once an image has been loaded into the AOL it is still possible to save it in Jpeg format by switching to another browser, but the temporary Internet files must be deleted first. In order to do this from within Internet Explorer select Internet Options from the Tools menu (Figure 4.22). This produces the Internet Options window of Figure 4.23. Another way of launching this window is to go to the Windows Control Panel and double-click on the Internet Options icon.

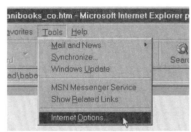

Fig.4.22 Internet Options is available from the Tools menu

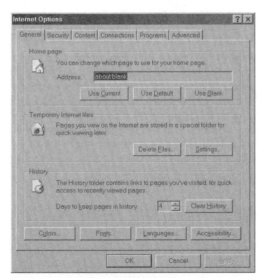

Fig.4.23 The General section of the Internet Options window

In the middle section of the window that is headed "Temporary Internet files", operate the Delete Files button. This produces a warning message, and the

OK button is operated if you wish to go ahead and delete the files. Then operate the OK button in the Internet Options window in order to close it. Note that deleting the temporary Internet files will slow access if you return to pages that you have visited recently. The files for those pages will have to be downloaded again since they will no longer be available in the store of temporary Internet files.

Resolution problems

Once an image file has been loaded into a word processor, desktop publishing program, or whatever, the graphic can be printed using the print command of the program. In most cases the printed images are either of reasonably quality but of postage stamp proportions, or a reasonable size but of very poor technical quality. The vector graphics of the GIF format generally fair much better than any form of bitmap when printing web images. Dealing with images is easier if you understand the way in which the two systems operate.

Photo-editing programs are primarily designed to operate with images in bitmap form. In other words, the image is formed from thousands or even millions of dots of different colours. The dots are called pixels, and this method is the one used to produce the picture on the screen of a monitor. Popular programs that are primarily designed for use with bitmaps include Adobe PhotoShop, and Corel Photo-Paint.

Programs such as Corel Draw! and Adobe Illustrator are line art programs where the image is comprised of so-called graphics primitives or just primitives. These are lines, circles, and other shapes, plus fill colours, patterns, etc. Objects are usually stored in the computer's memory using a co-ordinate system, and a straight line would be stored as a line from one co-ordinate to another, plus additional information such as its width, colour, and style (solid, dashed, etc.).

Line art, which is also know as vector graphics, does not lend itself well to all types of image. In particular, it is not well suited to colour photographic images, which in most cases do not readily boil down into primitive objects, colour fills, and so on. As explained previously, line art is well suited to charts, diagrams, cartoons, or anything of these general types. An advantage of line art in many applications is that the file sizes tend to be relatively small. With a really complex image the file size might actually go into the realm of megabytes, but in most cases files are measured in kilobytes rather than hundreds of kilobytes or megabytes. The file size is also largely independent of the final image size and resolution.

Fig.4.24 Vector graphics utilise the available resolution

Fig.4.25 The pixels are obvious when bitmaps are enlarged

Images are usually stored using a high resolution co-ordinate system, which is scaled down to produce something like a small image on the screen of a monitor. For high-resolution output to a printer the co-ordinate system would still have to be scaled to suit the printer, but it would probably be more than adequate to provide accurate placement of all the objects.

Line art makes the best of the available resolution, which is important when blowing up a small image to make it large, or when reproducing an image on a high resolution output device. Figure 4.24 shows some small text added to the drawing area in Macromedia Flash 5, with the Zoom tool used to enlarge this part of the drawing so that it virtually fills the relevant section of the screen. This program uses vector graphics. The outline of the text makes full use of the available resolution, giving letters that are free from any obvious stepping or any other roughness on the edges.

A similar procedure with a bitmap in Adobe PhotoShop has not faired so well (Figure 4.25). The individual pixels have been scaled up to produce giant size pixels, and a few compromises have been made in order to get the text the right size.

Low resolution

The problem with bitmaps downloaded from the Web is that the resolution tends to be quite low. Even using compression, large bitmaps produce huge files that could take a minute or five to download using a 56k modem. Consequently, most web images have a resolution of only about 250 by 200 pixels, and the larger images are generally only about 600 by 450 pixels. This gives acceptable results when viewed on the screen of a monitor, but not when printed out at a decent size. It is generally accepted that an absolute minimum of 150 pixels to the inch (60 pixels per centimetre) is required for good results on printouts. Ideally the resolution should be 200 pixels per inch (80 pixels per centimetre) or more.

Therefore, an image that is 250 pixels wide should be printed to a width of no more than 1.66 inches, or 4.16 centimetres. Ideally it would be printed to a width of no more than 1.25 inches or 3.12 centimetres. Even an image that is 600 pixels wide would ideally be printed to a maximum width of 4 inches (10 centimetres), and would preferably be limited to a width of 3 inches (7.5 centimetres). Clearly the average web bitmap is unsuitable for producing decent size prints without some additional processing.

Smoothing images

Vector graphics are clearly superior where a small image may need to be scaled up or printed at high resolution, but it is a fact of Web life that most of the images used on web pages are bitmaps. Most web images are colour photographs, and vector graphics are not well suited to

Fig.4.26 The original photograph

Fig.4.27 The enlarged section shows some rough edges

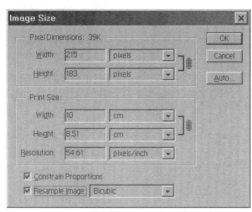

this type of image. Fortunately there are ways of enlarging bitmaps and smoothing out the rough edges so that better-looking results are obtained. It is important to emphasise that it is not possible to put in details that are not present on the original image. The idea is to get rid of pixels that are so large that they can be

Fig.4.28 Boosting the number of pixels using PhotoShop 5.0

Fig.4.29 The edges have been smoothed, but no detail has been added

clearly seen by the viewer. This also avoids the obvious stepping that occurs on anything other than vertical or horizontal lines.

Some printers have a built-in resolution enhancement facility or are supplied with software that adds this facility. Where applicable, this is likely to be the easiest way of enhancing web graphics and avoiding over-obvious pixels. The same effect can be obtained using most modern bitmap graphics programs. For this example the photograph of a bee on a flower in Figure 4.26 will be used. This is reproduced at about 180 pixels to the inch, which should give reasonable but not spectacular results. Figure 4.27 shows an enlargement of part of the photograph, and the quality is clearly very poor. Look at the jagged edge on some of the petals for instance. This lack of quality is not surprising since the picture is being reproduced at only about 50 or so pixels per inch.

The method of increasing the number of pixels varies from one graphics program to another, and the method here is the one used in PhotoShop. Selecting Image Size from the Image menu produces a window like the one in Figure 4.28. This shows that the fragment of the original image is some 215 pixels wide. With the Restrain Proportions and Resample Image boxes both ticked, the required width in pixels is typed into the Width textbox.

In this case we will increase the number of pixels by a factor of four in both directions, increasing the number of pixels by a factor of 16. This is rather more than would normally be used, but it will clearly show the effect of boosting the number of pixels. Click the OK button to exit the Image Size window and the newly enhanced picture (Figure 4.29) will appear. There is no more detail than on the original, but the jagged edges of the petals have clearly been smoothed quite significantly.

Sharpening

Most graphics software has filters that will try to give an apparent increase in sharpness. These generally work quite well provided you are prepared to settle for a modest amount of processing. Systems of this type mainly work by looking for small areas of the picture that contain a moderate amount of contrast. The contrast is those areas is then boosted slightly. A small overall increase in contrast might also be applied. Figure 4.30 shows the example picture with a small amount of sharpness filtering added. Try not to get carried away with this type of thing, as it can be counterproductive, undoing the smoothing applied previously (Figure 4.31).

Fig.4.30 Some sharpening added to the photograph

The boost in size that can be obtained depends on the nature and quality of the original image. Some web images are over-compressed, giving poor quality images that are covered in artefacts. This type of thing is unlikely to produce good results when printed small, and will certainly not give good results when processed and enlarged. A good clean image should produce good results if the number of pixels is double in each direction, giving an overall increase by a factor of four.

With enhanced images it is best to print at about 175 pixels to the inch or more. I have sometimes obtained good results by trebling the number of pixels in each direction and printing at about 200 pixels per inch. However, this requires a top quality original image. If the original scene is something fairly simple that lacks any fine detail it might be possible to use higher degrees of enlargement, but in the vast majority of cases this will not give worthwhile results.

Fig.4.31 Excessive sharpening can be counterproductive

Blank spaces

A common problem when saving pages to disc is that of blank spaces where there should be any form of graphic, including control buttons. Some browsers will in fact save an entire page to disc, but you may find that you are placing much more on the disc than you expected. To understand the cause of this problem it is necessary to look at the way that a web page is constructed. Web pages are written using what could be regarded as a form of programming language, known as HTML (hypertext mark-up language). As its name suggests, it is actually more like a mark-up language used in a desktop publishing program than a true programming language.

Those of us that can remember desktop publishing in the days before that term had been invented can also remember the relatively crude way in which pages were produced. There were no true WYSIWYG (what you see is what you get) desktop publishing programs for the early PCs

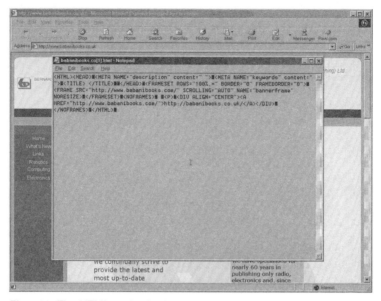

Fig.4.32 The HTML code displayed in Notepad

and other computers of that era. Instead, embedded codes were used to indicate that pieces of text should be in a certain font, style, and size. What appeared on the monitor was the text plus the embedded codes in the standard font of the text card. This was usually a pretty crude monospaced font. In order to see what a page looked like you had to print it out. If there were any problems or you simply did not like some aspect of the page design, the embedded codes had to be changed and then the page was printed out again. This sounds like slow and tough going, and it was.

Modern desktop publishing programs do not work on this basis, and the monitor does provide something close to a true WYSIWYG display. The resolution of even a good monitor is usually well below the final printed resolution, requiring some compromises to be made in the version displayed on the monitor, but you get a good idea of what the final printed version will look like before it is proof printed.

This is not to say that the embedded codes have disappeared, and they are still used by some programs. There is often a mode that enables the user to see the raw text plus these codes, and even make changes to the text and the embedded codes. However, with a modern WYSIWYG desktop publishing program there is no need to use or know anything about the method of coding. You can simply format pages using the palettes, pop-down menus, etc. The program displays a good facsimile of the final printed version, generates the embedded codes, and eventually converts the text and code into the finished product.

Originally it was necessary to understand HTML before you could produce web pages, because there was no WYSIWYG program that would do the job for you. The situation has changed over the years of course, and there are now plenty of programs that enable web pages to be produced by those having no understanding of HTML. In some cases the program may totally shield the user from the underlying HTML code, and the code is transparent to users of the page. However, even though you can not see it the code is still there. HTML is the language understood by web browsers, and it is what all web site and web page creation programs have to generate. If you select the Edit with Windows Notepad option from the file menu of Internet Explorer, the Windows Notepad text editor will appear, complete with the HTML code for the current page (Figure 4.32).

The whole picture

Items such as control buttons and images are added to the page by including codes to tell the browser where to find the relevant files, the size and position of the image, and so on. If the HTML code for a page is saved, items provided by additional files will not appear when the page is reloaded, because the computer will no longer have access to those files. The solution to the problem is to save the HTML code and any additional files needed to produce the complete page. This facility is not available from all browsers, but it is available in Internet Explorer from version 5.0 onwards. Select the

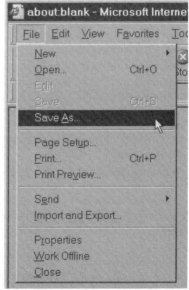

Fig.4.33 First select Save As

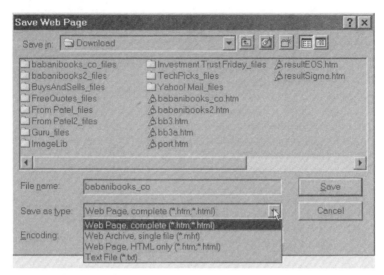

Fig.4.34 Selecting Save As brings up the usual file browser

Save As from the File menu (Figure 4.33) to produce the usual file browser window of Figure 4.34.

The "Save as type" menu offers four choices, two of which save the page in HTML form. The "Web page complete" option is the one to use if you wish to save the page complete with all the support files. If you save a page in this format and then locate the folder containing the HTML file using Windows Explorer, you will discover that there is a new folder with the same name that was used for the HTML file (Figure 4.35). This folder contains further folders that in turn contain the various source files, and there can be a substantial number even for a single page (Figure

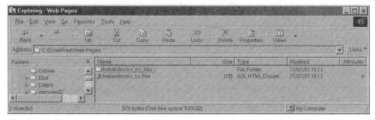

*Fig.4.35 By saving a complete page you save both the HTML
document and a folder containing the support files*

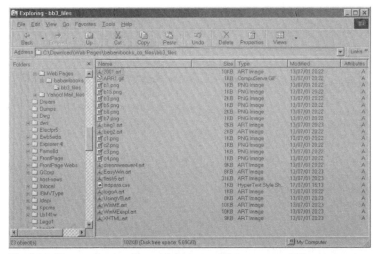

Fig.4.36 The contents of a subfolder containing some of the support files for a single web page.

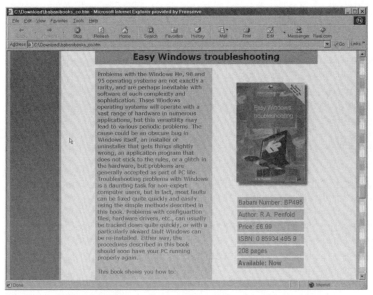

Fig.4.37 A page that has been saved to disc and reloaded into Internet Explorer

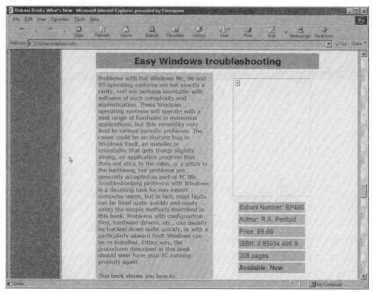

Fig.4.38 With only the HTML code saved, no graphics are included on the page

4.36). If you wish to delete the page it is necessary to remove both the HTML file and the associated folder structure. Note that the web page will be complete when it is viewed offline using the browser, and buttons, links, etc.. will all be active. However, the files to link to will not be available offline, so there is no point in operating buttons, menus, etc.

HTML only

In order to save the HTML page without the "extras", choose the "Web Page HTML only" option. How closely (or otherwise) a page saved in this form resembles the original depends on the amount of non-text content on the page. There is no certainty that anything will be lost, but these days most web pages contain a fair amount of graphics, and all this content will certainly be lost. Any sounds associated with the original page will also be absent. The general layout of the page will remain unaltered though. Figure 4.37 shows part of a page that has been saved in its entirety and reloaded into Internet Explorer. Figure 4.38 shows the same page with only the HTML code saved and reloaded. The text and background colours are the same in both cases, but the large image is not included in the HTML-only version. A blank area replaces it, together with a cross to indicate that an object has been omitted from the page.

Blank page

Unless you actually require the graphics it makes sense to save the HTML-only version. This avoids saving large numbers of files and directory structures that are not really needed. As pointed out previously, if you only require the text on a page it can be copied to another program using the Windows Cut and Paste commands. Once in a suitable program it can be viewed, edited, and printed out as required. Saving a web page as a plain text (txt) file offers an alternative method of transferring the text content of a page to another program such as a word processor. However, this method does not always have the desired effect, and the text file may lack some of the text on the original page when it is opened. In fact the screen may have a decidedly blank expression, with not a single text character in evidence!

With a simple web page there should be no problem. What the browser is actually doing is filtering out the HTML codes and saving the rest, which will normally be the raw text for the page. Things go wrong where the page is a complex type, particularly if it uses frames. The basic HTML code for the page points to the frames that contain the text, but the text does not actually appear in the HTML code for the page. Hence the saved text file contains little or no text. The copy and paste method is the more awkward method of extracting text from a page, but it is also the more reliable option. You know exactly what is being copied to the other program, and can see immediately if anything has gone slightly awry.

Web archive

Do not overlook the fourth option in the file type menu, which enables pages to be saved in web archive format. In other words, the file is saved in a non-standard form of HTML that puts everything into a single file. Pages can be loaded into Internet Explorer and viewed in the normal way, and should look exactly the same as the standard HTML version. The big advantage is that everything is compressed into a single file, thus avoiding the subfolders and numerous files that often result when pages are saved in standard HTML format. This option is the best one if you do not require access to the individual files from which the page is comprised, but you do require the page in its entirety.

PDF files

The Adobe PDF (portable document file) format is steadily gaining in popularity in the world of computing, and there are more and more PDF files appearing on the Web for downloading. The basic idea of PDF is that it should be a universal format that can be used by any computer, or any electronic gadget that can handle electronic documents. This book was supplied to the printer in the form of a huge PDF file for example. Universal formats designed to handle complex documents often suffer from problems with inaccuracies when the documents are viewed using some systems, or when they are printed out.

PDF is designed to handle text, vector graphics, and bitmaps without the common problems associated with universal formats. For example, you do not need the appropriate fonts installed on your PC for the text to be produced correctly. The font information, and all the other information needed to produce the page correctly is included in the file. If text should fit accurately into a box, with PDF the text will not spread outside the box, be offset to one side, or something of this general nature. It will always be the correct size and in the right place.

PDF can be used for low-resolution documents only designed for viewing on the screen of a monitor, but it is mainly used where high quality hard copy will be required. High-resolution documents can still be used on the screen though. Although PDF documents are stored in a highly compressed form, large documents in high-resolution form can still be quite large. A booklet in PDF format would typically be at least a few hundred kilobytes, and could well run to a few megabytes of data. A book the size of this one would typically be over 100 megabytes.

PDF problems

Problems with PDF files mainly occur due to users downloading a file and then trying to view it using a browser or a word processor. Although PDF is a common format there are relatively few programs that can read or write this format. Browsers can not handle the PDF format without some outside assistance. In order to view and print out these files it is necessary to have a suitable program installed on your PC, and the normal choice is Adobe's own Acrobat Reader program, which is free.

PC peripherals often have on-disc documentation in PDF format, and you may have a support disc that includes this program. It is often included on the "free" cover mounted discs included with computer magazines. Failing that, the latest version can be downloaded from the

Adobe web site at www.adobe.com. It is available for various computers and operating systems so make sure you download the right version.

Fig.4.39 A PDF file can be saved to disc in the usual way

One way of dealing with PDF files, and my preferred way of handling things, is to right click on the link to the file. In Internet Explorer this produces a small pop-up menu like the one in Figure 4.39. In order to save the file to disc choose the Save Target As option. With a Netscape browser right-click on the link and choose the Save Link As option (Figure 4.40). In either case the usual file browser should appear (Figure 4.41) so that the file can be renamed if desired, and then saved in the selected folder. Operate the OK button when you are ready to proceed, and a window like the one of Figure 4.42 should appear. This shows how far and how quickly the download is progressing. Once saved to disc the file can be viewed using the Acrobat Reader program.

Left clicking on the link rather than right clicking might produce the window of Figure 4.43. In order to save the file to disc, use the radio buttons to select the "Save

Fig.4.40 With a Netscape browser use Save Link As

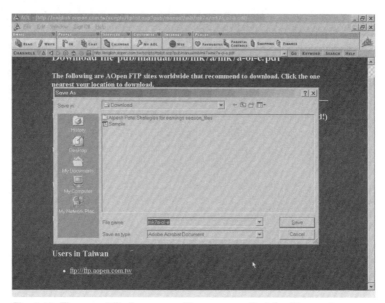

Fig.4.41 The usual file browser will appear so that the file can be saved to disc

this program to disk" option and then operate the OK button. The usual file browser, etc., are then used to save the file to the appropriate folder. With Adobe Acrobat Reader installed on your PC you may find that left clicking on the link results in some additional controls appearing on the browser's user interface. After a delay the PDF document will then be displayed, as in the example of Figure 4.44. In effect, Acrobat Reader is being run from within the browser, and the normal Acrobat Reader controls are

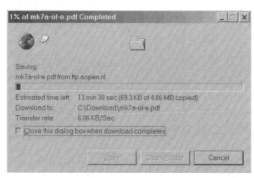

Fig.4.42 This window shows how the download is progressing

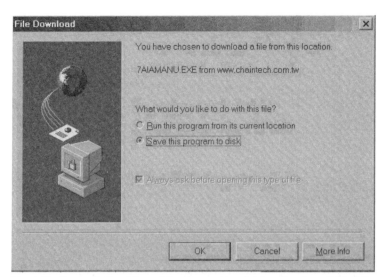

Fig.4.43 Normally the "Save this program to disk" option is selected if this window appears

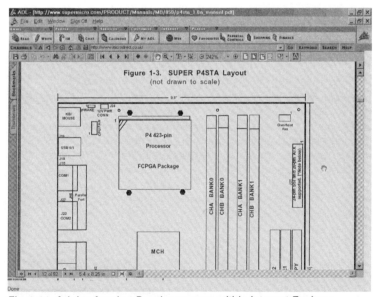

Fig.4.44 Adobe Acrobat Reader can run within Internet Explorer

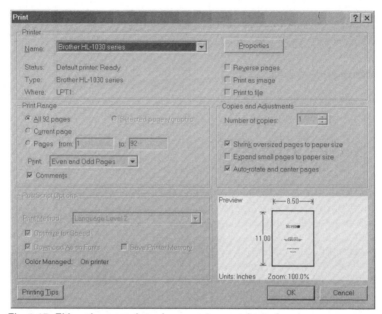

Fig.4.45 Either the complete document or a selected page range can be printed

available via the toolbar that is added near the top of the screen. There is a variation on this system that launches Acrobat Reader as a separate entity and then starts to load the document into the program.

The problem with either of these methods is that things can move along in a very hesitant fashion with the PC sometimes seeming to have hung-up. Its advantage is that it is possible to read the required pages of a document without having to download the entire document. If you decide to save the document to disc, operate the button on the extreme left-hand end of the Acrobat toolbar. This is the one having the icon that looks like a 3.5-inch floppy disc. This brings up the usual file browser window that enables the file to be renamed if required, and then saved in the appropriate folder. If the file has not fully downloaded there will be a delay while the download is completed. The document will then be saved to disc.

Operating the printer icon, which brings up a window like the one in Figure 4.45, enables the document to be printed. The complete document or selected pages can be printed. A common complaint about PDF documents is that they are difficult to edit. Acrobat Reader is only designed to permit documents to be read and printed, and it lacks any editing facilities. The full Adobe Acrobat program is needed in order to make changes to PDF documents. However, the text selection tool (the one with the "T" icon) enables text to be selected so that it can be copied and pasted to another program. The button immediately to the right of this one activates the graphics selection tool. This enables a rectangular section of the screen to be selected and copied to the Windows Clipboard.

File compression

When downloading files from the web you are likely to encounter ZIP files, particularly when downloading program files. ZIP files are files that have undergone compression in order to reduce the file size. Compressed files are very familiar to anyone involved with PCs in the early days when hard disc capacities were small and programs were distributed on floppy discs. Files were often compressed in order to save disc space, and practically any files swapped via a modem were compressed. File compression is used much less in these days of high capacity hard disc drives, CD-ROMs, and DVDs.

Even on the Internet ZIP files are less in evidence than was once the case. One reason for this is that many file formats now have a high degree of built-in compression, and any further processing is unlikely to produce a significant reduction in file size. Using data compression on a highly compressed Jpeg file for example, is unlikely to have much effect. Compression can still be used to good effect on some types of file though, and it is almost invariably used with program files that are downloaded via the Internet. It also works well with plain text files, some word processor file formats, and bitmap formats that do not utilize any form of built-in compression. The reduction in file size is usually around 45 to 65 percent. Compression is sometimes used for PDF files, although the reduction in file size is not usually very great.

Unzipping

Some ZIP files are in the form of a so-called self-extraction program. These sometimes cause confusion when downloading programs, because you appear to be downloading a non-compressed program file that is ready to be run. The file does indeed have an EXE extension, and it is a program of sorts, but it is not the program you downloaded in ready-to-run form. A file of this type it should be downloaded into an empty temporary folder and then run. The Run option in the Start menu can be used, or simply locate the file using Windows Explorer and then double-click on its entry. It is probably best to use Windows Explorer because it is then easy to see if the automatic file extraction has worked properly.

You may be given the option of specifying a destination folder for the decompressed file or files, in which case a window like the one in Figure 4.46 will appear. If you do not wish to use the default folder, edit the text in the textbox or use the Browse facility to locate the correct folder. Operate the Unzip button to decompress the contents of the file. In some cases the uncompressed data will simply be placed into the same folder as the source file. Having run the program, check with Windows Explorer to determine what new files have appeared. If the program is a fairly simple type it is possible that there will be a single file having an EXE extension, or a file of this type plus a text file containing documentation. These days it is far more likely that there will be a collection of files, including one called Setup.exe. Running this file should produce the usual Windows style installation process.

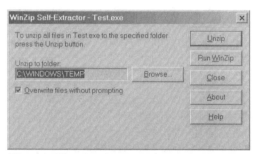

Fig.4.46   Files are decompressed into the specified folder

Winzip

Where the downloaded file has a ZIP extension it is necessary to decompress it using a suitable utility program. Numerous file compression/decompression programs have been produced over the years, but Winzip is now by far the most popular. This is included on many of the "free" discs given away with computer magazines, and the latest version can be downloaded from one of the software web sites such as www.download.com. It is also available from the web site of the manufacturer, Win-Zip Computing Inc., at www.winzip.com.

With Winzip installed on your PC it will be associated with files having a ZIP extension. Therefore, double-clicking on a ZIP file in Windows

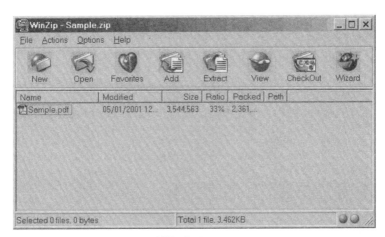

Fig.4.47 The main screen of Winzip 8

Explorer will result in Winzip being launched, and a window like the one of Figure 4.47 will appear. Actually, if you are using an unregistered copy of Winzip there will a screen prior to this one. This screen simply explains that you are using an evaluation copy of the program. Operate the I Agree button to move on to a screen like the one of Figure 4.47.

The bottom section of the window lists the files that are stored within the ZIP file, and in this example there is just a single PDF file. If you only wish to decompress some of the files, start by left clicking on one of the files that you wish to decompress. Then hold down the Control key and

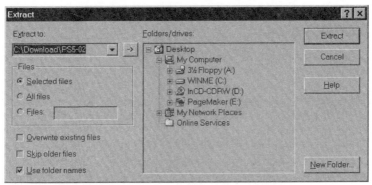

Fig.4.48 Selecting the destination folder using Winzip 8

left-click on the entries for the other files that you wish to process. In most cases all the files will have to be processed and they can all be selected by choosing Select All from the Actions menu. Having selected the appropriate files, operate the Extract button near the top of the screen.

This produces the window of Figure 4.48 where the destination folder for the files can be altered if the default is not suitable. Either type the name and path of the folder in the "Extract to" text box or select it using the file browser in the middle section of the window. The radio buttons and check boxes provide various options, but for most purposes the default settings will suffice. Operate the Extract button to decompress the files into the selected folder. Assuming there are no problems, the new window will then close and you will be returned to the main Winzip window. Use Windows Explorer to check that the new files have been created successfully.

Another way of doing things is to launch Winzip and then select the ZIP file to decompress. Select the Open Archive option from the File menu and then use the file browser to locate and select the file. Then operate the Open button, and the main Winzip window should then show the contents of the ZIP file. The files are then selected and decompressed in the usual way.

On installation you can opt to use a wizard rather than use the "classic" Winzip interface. The wizard can also be launched by operating the Wizard button near the top of the main Winzip window. Either way a window like the one of Figure 4.49 will be obtained. In standard wizard fashion, a series of windows are then used to tell the program what you wish to do. You may prefer to use this method, but extracting files is quicker using the "classic" interface.

Instant access

Using a recent version of Winzip it is not always necessary to unzip the files prior to using them. For example, with a PDF file it is possible to access it by double-clicking on its entry in the main Winzip window. Adobe Acrobat Reader will then be run and the PDF file will be loaded into it. Although the file appears to be running normally, it is being read via the Winzip program. Simple text files, word processor documents, graphics files, etc., can all be read in this way.

Bear in mind though, that additional processing is required in order to access the file and that this will inevitably slow down access to the file. With something like a movie or audio file it is safer to decompress it first

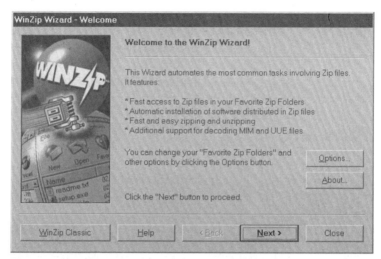

Fig.4.49 If preferred, Winzip 8 can be used with a wizard

and then use it in the normal way. In theory anyway, it is possible to run a Setup program via Winzip, and install a program without decompressing the files first. Setup programs do not like anything other than Windows itself running while they are in operation, but this method usually seems to be successful.

The rest

There are numerous types of compressed file and not just those that have a "zip" extension. Some of these file types are bordering on obsolescence, but they are still encountered from time to time on the Internet. Others are primarily used with Unix or Linux systems, but Windows users may still need to extract files from them. TAR, ARJ, GZ, ARC, and TAZ are just some of the file types that you might encounter. Winzip can handle most of these, but Winrar files are an exception. These have a "rar" extension, and can be decompressed using the Winrar program. This can be downloaded from one of the large software download sites.

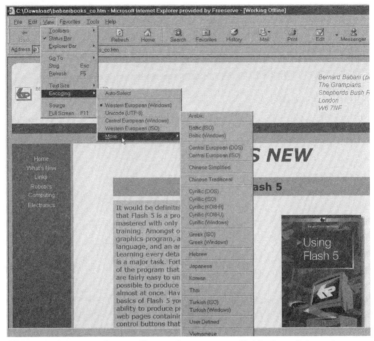

Fig.4.50 A range of encoding options are available from Internet
Explorer

Odd characters

I can not say that I have ever had this one happen to me, but it is
apparently possible to end up with your browser producing all sorts of
odd characters on the screen instead of normal text. The way a browser
interprets a page depends on the part of the world you live in, and the
character sets used by the sites you normally visit. Problems can arise if
you visit sites in other parts of the world that are intended for local
consumption. With sites of this type the browser program will tell you
that it is downloading the appropriate character set for the page you are
trying to view. There will be a Cancel button, and it is advisable to operate
this. There is no point in spending 10 or 20 minutes downloading a
character set if the right characters will be meaningless to you! For most
of us the page will be no more or less readable with the wrong characters.

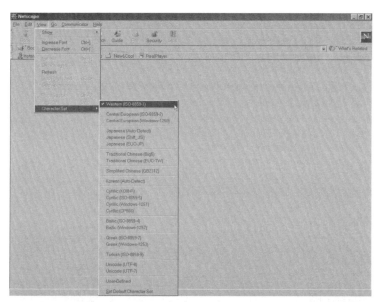

Fig.4.51 Netscape browsers also offer a number of encoding options

The pages of the web site should be displayed properly if you go ahead with the download, but there is a risk that things will not go back to normal when you return to English language sites. If a problem with strange looking pages should occur when using Internet Explorer, go to the View menu and select the Encoding option. Various types of encoding are offered here, with many others available under the More submenu (Figure 4.50). Assuming you are in the UK and using a Windows PC, the Western Europe (Windows) option is the right one. There is a similar facility available in Netscape Communicator. From the View menu select the Character Set option (Figure 4.51).

Reinstallation

In my experience it is not likely to be problems with the character set that produces problems with pages failing to load properly. In most cases it seems to be due to a major problem with the installation of the browser program. Often the easiest solution is to remove the browser and reinstall it from scratch. Note though, that any customisation of the program, including any bookmarks you have added, will be lost when the browser

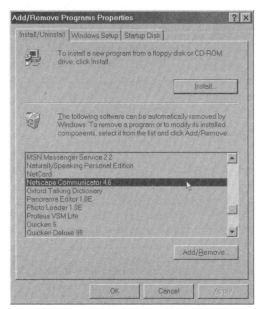

*Fig.4.52 The list shows all the installed
programs*

is uninstalled. Some customisation can be saved to disc and then restored after the browser has been reinstalled (refer to the final section of this chapter).

Even if you do not have an uninstaller program it should be easy to remove the browser. Go to the Windows Control Panel and double-click on the Add/Remove Programs icon. This will produce a list of the installed programs (Figure 4.52) where you should be able to find the browser program that you wish to remove. Left-click on the program to select it and then operate the Add/Remove button. This starts the routine that removes the program, and the exact routine varies from program to program. The process will be largely or totally automatic though. You may be asked if you wish to delete a shared file that is no longer used by other programs. The safe course of action is to operate the No button, just in case the file is still needed by other programs.

Size change

A mild annoyance with Internet Explorer is the size changes that sometimes afflict the default window size. These seem to occur at random. Normally the window is automatically maximised when it is opened, but for no apparent reason it opens in a tiny window going off the edge of the screen. Fortunately, altering the default window size is very simple. Open Internet Explorer, set its window at the required size and position on the screen, and then close it again. With older versions it may be necessary to hold down the Shift key while closing the program.

The next time the program is launched it should run in a window of the correct size and position on the screen.

Long search

Many web sites organise their content into relatively few pages in order to make navigation easier. On the other hand, it can sometimes take a while to search each page for the snippet of information that you require. The Find facility of Internet Explorer makes things easier, and this operates in much the same way as the equivalent feature of most word processors. You provide a search string and the program searches the page for any occurrence of that text. The find facility is accessed via the Edit menu (Figure 4.53). A small window like the one in Figure 4.54 appears, and the search string is entered into the textbox.

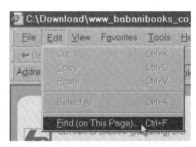

Fig.4.53 Selecting the Find facility

The radio buttons are used to search up or down from the current position in the document. Assuming that you start at the top, the default Down setting is clearly the one to use. Normally the search is not case sensitive, and the search string "jack jones" would match with "Jack Jones" in the document (or vice versa). The search can be made case sensitive by ticking the appropriate checkbox. If the "Match whole word only" checkbox is ticked the search will only find a match if a word in the document matches the search string. For example, "trouble" would

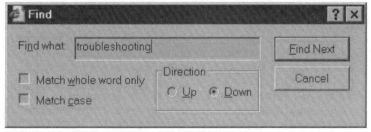

Fig.4.54 The search string is entered in the textbox

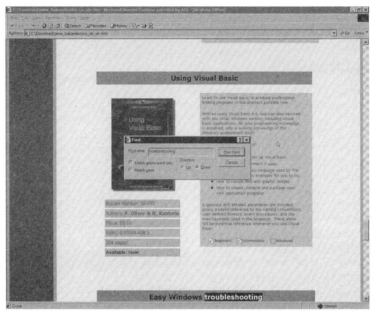

Fig.4.55 A match has been found and the word has been highlighted

normally match with "troubleshooting", but no match would be produced if the "Match whole word only" checkbox was ticked.

If a match is found, the matched text string is highlighted on the page (Figure 4.55).   Operate the Find Next button to search for a further occurrence, or the Cancel button to close the Find window.

Translation

You may occasionally encounter a web page that looks as though it might contain some useful information, but there is a slight problem in that it is in Spanish and you only speak English and a bit of French. There are programs that can attempt to translate text from one language to another, and it might be possible to cut and paste the text from the web page and into one of these programs. Another approach is to use the Translate function of Netscape Navigator 6. With the page for translation loaded into the browser, select the Translate option from the View menu. The translation seems to be provided by a web site rather

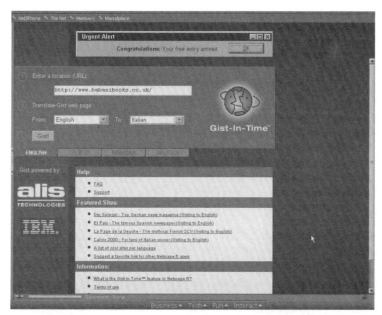

Fig.4.56 Various "From" and "To" languages are available

than the program itself, so there might be a delay before something like Figure 4.56 is displayed.

The two menus are used to select the language used in the web page and the language you wish to translate the text into. The URL of the web page will be automatically entered into the appropriate textbox. Operate the Gist! button to go ahead with the translation. In due course the translated version of the page will appear. Figure 4.57 shows the babanibooks.com homepage translated into Italian. Do not expect the text to be translated in "purple prose". It will probably read like the manual for a cheap piece of electronics from the Far East, but it should give you the gist of a page's content. Also, do not expect things like text on buttons or text in graphics to be translated. It is only the main block or blocks that are processed.

It is worth noting that some search engines now have a translation facility. For example, the Google and Alta Vista search engines have a facility of this type, and both of them can be very useful. Again, do not expect word perfect results, but you should be able to extract the required information from pages.

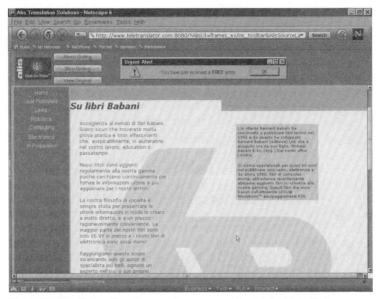

Fig.4.57 The Babanibooks.com home page translated into Italian

Auto connection

If you launch a browser with a view to working online you will almost certainly find that it starts to dialup your Internet service provider. There should be an opportunity to quickly dive for a Cancel button and prevent it from doing so, but life is easier if the browser can be persuaded not to start dialling in the first place. Probably the easiest solution to the problem is to set a blank home page. The reason the browser starts dialling is that it is trying to load the specified home page. This is a web address, so it goes online and then loads the page. If a blank page is specified as the home page there is nothing to load at start up, and the program does not try to connect to the Internet.

Setting a blank page as the home page was covered in chapter 2, so this process will not be described in detail again here. In Internet Explorer it is just a matter of going to the Windows Control Panel, double clicking on the Internet Options icon, and then operating the Use Blank button (Figure 4.58). Note that a blank page will be displayed when the Internet connection is activated, and not just when the browser is used offline. The home page can be an HTML file on the hard disc if you prefer not to

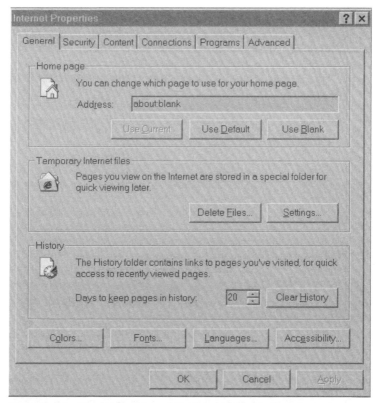

Fig.4.58 The General section of the Internet Properties window

start with a totally blank screen. Just type the name of the file, including the full path, into the Address textbox. Again, this will be used as the starting page when working offline or online.

De-branding

When a new Internet service provider is installed on your PC it is not uncommon for Internet Explorer to suddenly have a title bar that reads something like "Internet Explorer Provided by TheBestISP". This is not exactly true, since you almost certainly had Internet Explorer on your PC before the new service provider was installed. The new service provider's installation software has simply added its name to the title bar of the

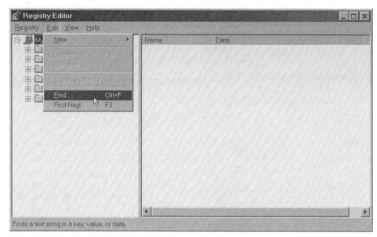

Fig.4.59 Accessing the Find feature of Regedit

existing installation of Internet Explorer. In any event, most people prefer not to have this branding on their browser program, and it can be especially annoying if you are stuck with the branding added by a company that you only used for two weeks in 1997!

Removing the title bar branding is not difficult, but whether it is removed directly or indirectly it requires changes to be made to the Registry. Take heed of the warnings about altering the Registry that were given in the previous chapter. Backup the Registry files before making any changes so that the original version can be restored if the need should arise. The branding can be removed by creating and running a small file or by directly editing the Registry. The second method is the one that will be used in this example.

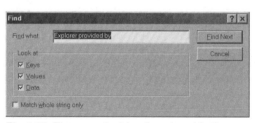

Fig.4.60 The search string is entered in the textbox

Select the Run option from the Start menu and type "regedit" into the textbox. And then operate the OK button to run the Regedit program. Probably the easiest way to find the entry that needs to be edited is to use the Find facility, which is available under the Edit menu (Figure 4.59).

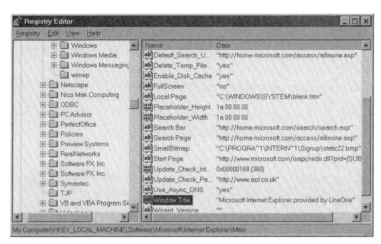

Fig.4.61 The search has been successful, and the right entry has
been found

This produces the window of Figure 4.60 where the search string is added
into the textbox. The search string is all or a substantial part of the text
that appears in the Internet Explorer title bar. If you use less than the full
title bar text, try to choose something that should only appear once in
the Registry. For example, "Explorer provided by" is a fairly safe bet,
whereas "Internet Explorer" is likely to appear time and time again in the
Registry.

With the search text added, operate the Find button and wait while the
program conducts its search. In due course it should locate the entry
you are looking for (Figure 4.61). You can search for the right entry
yourself, and it should be in:

HKEY_LOCAL_MACHINE\Software\Microsoft\Internet Explorer\Main

Either way, having
found the right entry
you can not simply
edit the text in the
Data field. Instead,
double-click on the
"Title Window" entry
in the Value field, and
then edit the text in
the window that pops

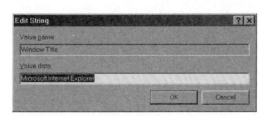

Fig.4.62 Editing the data for the new entry

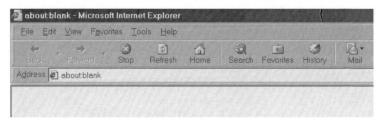

Fig.4.63 The Internet Explorer title bar minus the branding

up (Figure 4.62). Whatever text you have in this textbox will appear in the Internet Explorer title bar. Operate the OK button when you have finished, and then select Exit from the File menu to close the program. Note that you must reboot the PC for the changes to the Registry to take effect. The title bar should then be restored to normality (Figure 4.63).

Toolbar troubles

In a similar vein, installing some software results in a button added to Internet Explorers toolbar. In the Example of Figure 4.64, installing the popular RealPlayer program has resulted in the toolbar suddenly sprouting a "Real.com" button. The toolbar is customisable, so removing an unwanted button is very easy. Right-click on the toolbar and then choose Customise from the popup menu. This produces a window like the one shown in Figure 4.65.

Locate the button you wish to remove, which should be in the list in the right-hand section of the window. Left-click on its entry to select it and then operate the Remove button. The button's entry in the list on the

Fig.4.64 The toolbar, complete with the Real.com button

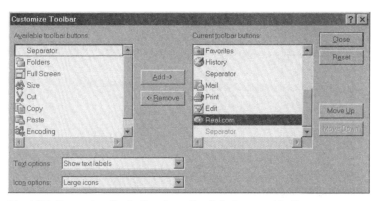

Fig.4.65 Removing the button from the list of current buttons

right will disappear, and it will reappear in the list on the left. Left-click the Close button and the toolbar should immediately reflect the change you made (Figure 4.66). If you change your mind later on, the button can be reinstated by returning to the Customise window. Select the button's entry in the list on the left and then operate the Add button. If the tool bar disappears altogether, it can be restored by going to the View menu and selecting first Toolbars and then Standard Buttons from the submenu.

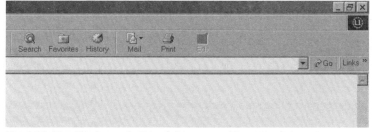

Fig.4.66 The Real.com button duly removed from the Internet Explorer toolbar

Reinstallation

Serious problems with a browser are not that uncommon, with it frequently causing the computer to hang-up perhaps, or maybe the browser simply vanishes "into thin air" without warning. Whatever browser you are using,

Fig.4.67 A wizard makes importing and exporting easy

the best approach is to uninstall it in the usual way and then reinstall it from scratch. You can use the Import and Export facility under the File menu to save cookies and favourites to disc. This feature is really intended as a means of transferring settings from one computer to another, but it can also be used to save certain settings so that they can be restored after the program has been reinstalled. This feature uses a wizard (Figure 4.67), so it is very straightforward to use.

Now you see it...

Something we all do from time to time is visit a useful site but then fail to add it to Favorites or make a note of its address. It can probably be found again with the aid of a search engine but there is an easier way provided it was days rather than months since you visited the site. Operating the History button in Internet Explorer's toolbar splits the main screen vertically, and there are four folders in the left-hand section (Figure 4.68). By default a record is kept for the last 22 days of Internet activity.

The four folders contain the names of the sites visited on the current day, one week ago, two weeks ago, and three weeks ago. Left-click on a folder in order to view its contents (Figure 4.69). Obviously there may be

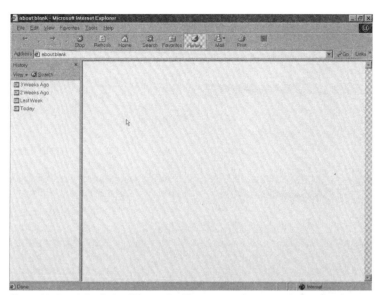

Fig.4.68 by default the History facility covers three weeks and a day

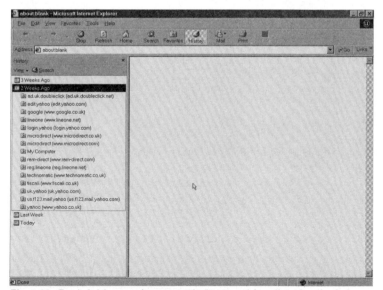

Fig.4.69 Each folder can be expanded to provide a list of web sites

Fig.4.70   The entry for each site can be expanded

a large number of sites listed, but it should not be too difficult to find the forgotten site. If you are not sure whether or not a listed site is the one your are after, try left clicking on its entry. This will provide a list of pages within the site that you visited (Figure 4.70), and may help to jog your memory. If you end up with three or four "possibles", it will not take long to visit them one by one until you find the right site.

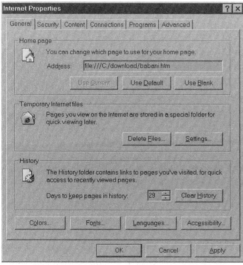

Fig.4.71   It is possible to set the number of days covered by the History facility

Note that the span covered by the History facility can be altered. Go to the Windows Control Panel and double-click on the Internet Options icon. This produces a window like Figure 4.71, and in the History section you can set the number of days that are stored in the history folders. Months or even years of Internet visits can be stored if desired, but years of data might use up significant amounts of hard disc space.

Points to remember

With both Internet Explorer and Netscape browsers it is possible to alter the displayed size of the text on most web pages. Unfortunately, it does not affect all web pages.

When printing a web page results in a loss of material down the right-hand side of the page, change the printer from portrait to landscape printing. This will usually ensure that the missing material is printed, but it might takes several sheets of paper per web page.

Text and graphics can be transferred from a web page to a program such as a word processor using the Windows Copy and Paste facilities. You can then format the material in the desired fashion prior to printing it.

Most small web graphics do not look good when printed large. The number of pixels in the image can be boosted using a suitable graphics program, and this will keep the pixels small when the image is printed large. However, it will not put in detail that is not present on the original.

A web page is usually comprised of some HTML code and a number of support files. This can make it difficult to save complete web pages, including any graphic content. However, complete pages can be saved to disc using a recent version of Internet Explorer.

Current web browsers can not handle files in Adobe PDF format. Internet Explorer can be used to this format provided a modern version of Adobe Acrobat Reader is installed on your PC. This program is free and should be considered an essential piece of software.

A web browser can not handle documents that are in some form of compressed file or an archive file. The file must be decompressed using a program such as Winzip, and then the file or files it contains must be read using the appropriate program.

Programs supplied in an archive file must also be decompressed before they can be installed. Where a program is downloaded as an EXE file, this file is unlikely to be the program in ready to run form. It is more likely to be a self extracting file which contains the program and any support files.

When your browser keeps trying to go online when you wish to work offline, try setting a blank home page.

Branding on Internet Explorer can be removed, but it requires alterations to the Registry. Unwanted buttons on the toolbar are more easily removed.

If you need to reinstall you Internet browser software, cookies and favourites can be saved to disc prior to removing the existing installation, and then imported into the newly installed browser.

A "lost" web site can be found using the History facility provided the site was visited within the last 22 days. The number of days stored by the History facility can be altered via the Internet Options in the Windows Control Panel.

Email problems

Large attachments

Email attachments are a great way of sending files that you need to get to someone in a hurry. However, there are some limitations on the size and number of files that can be attached to a single Email. The limits vary from one Email server to another, but the maximum size is often as small as one megabyte, and is not often more than two megabytes. If multiple attachments are permitted there may well be a limit of just two or three per Email. This is not to say that it is impossible to send larger amounts of data or a great number of attachments. It is possible to send the data with several Emails, effectively stretching both limits. It is also possible to merge several files into one attachment, which is then split back into its constituent parts by the recipient.

It is only fair to point out that even by using a few tricks, sending large amounts of data via Emails may not be a practical proposition. Using a V90 (56k) modem the download speed is theoretically 56000 bytes per second, but in practice is like to be more like 44000 to 48000 bytes per second. This equates to about 4.5 kilobytes of data per second, or almost four minutes to download a megabyte. The upload speed is 33.6k, which in practice is likely to mean data transfer at about 3 kilobytes per second. This equates to around 5.5 minutes per megabyte. Uploading and downloading many megabytes of data could take a long time. Also bear in mind that the recipient's Email server will almost certainly have a restriction on the maximum amount of data that can be stored in their inbox. Some files would have to be retrieved and deleted before others could be sent.

Sending

Sending an attachment is usually pretty straightforward. In Outlook Express the first step is to compose the Email in the normal way (Figure 5.1). Next operate the Attach button near the top of the window in which the Email has been composed. This produces a standard Windows file

5 Email problems

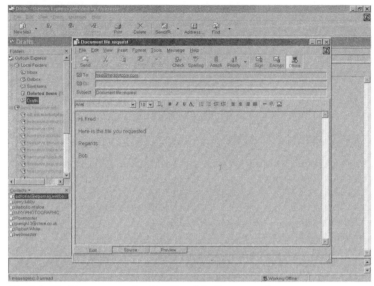

Fig.5.1 Start by composing the Email in the normal way

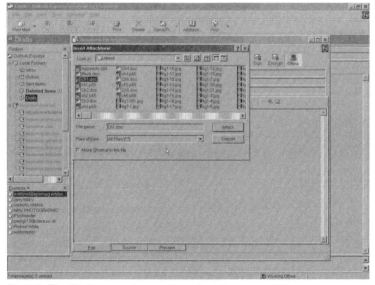

Fig.5.2 The file browser is used to select the correct file

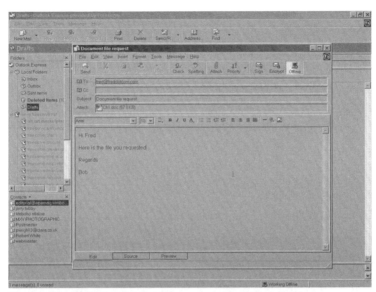

Fig.5.3 The file's details should appear in the Attach field

browser (Figure 5.2) where you can select the file for attachment to the Email. Operate the Attach button when the correct file has been located and selected. This takes the program back to the document window where the Attach field near the top should show the name of the attached file and its size (Figure 5.3). To attach more files to the Email just repeat this process as many times as necessary. The Attach field in the

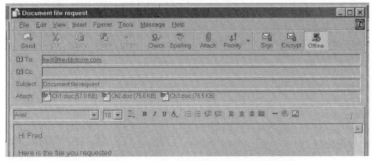

Fig.5.4 A number of files can be attached to each Email

document window will show the names and sizes of all the attached files (Figure 5.4).

Too many attachments

With a large number of attachments of small size it is generally more practical to merge them into a single file prior to transmission. The single file is split into its constituent parts once the recipient has downloaded it. There are a number of programs that can provide this merging and splitting action, but Winzip is the most popular choice for this type of thing. The evaluation version is available from numerous web sites and this program is also included on many of the "free" discs supplied with computer magazines.

Winzip is primarily a file compression program, and a useful byproduct of merging files is that the size of the archive file will usually be much less than the total size of the source files. With files that have already been compressed, such as Jpeg image files, the degree of compression obtained will only be very small. With non-compressed files the reduction in size is generally much greater at around 50 to 80 percent. Simple text files and bitmaps generally provide the best compression rates.

Using Winzip is very straightforward. When using an unregistered version you must first agree to the licensing conditions by operating the appropriate button, and then the main window will appear (Figure 5.5). It is assumed here that the "classic" interface was specified during the installation process. You can opt for the wizard approach if preferred. However, as the standard Winzip "classic" interface is not difficult to use

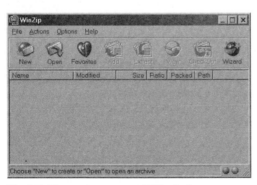

Fig.5.5 The main screen of Winzip 8

and it is generally quicker than using the wizard, I would recommend using the standard interface.

The first task is to tell Winzip where you wish to deposit the archive file, and to provide a name for the file. Select the New Archive option from the file menu

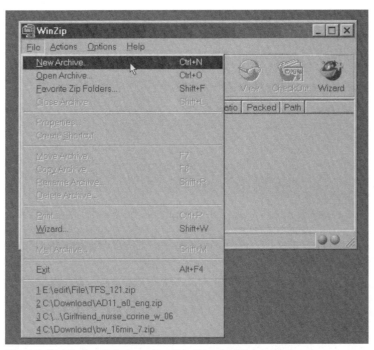

Fig.5.6 The first step is to select the New Archive option

(Figure 5.6) to bring up the usual file browser (figure 5.7). If necessary, use the menu at the top of the window to alter the folder to be used for the archive file. A name for the file is entered in the File Name text box, and there is no need to add the Zip extension. This will be added automatically by the program.

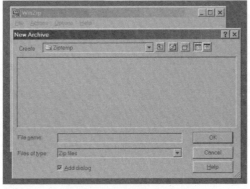

Fig.5.7 Selecting a filename and folder for the new archive file

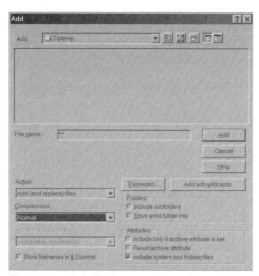

Fig.5.8 Another file browser is used to select the files that will go into the archive

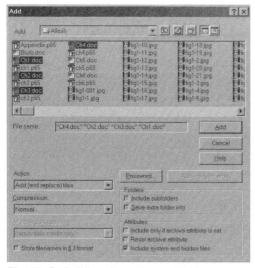

Fig.5.9 By holding down the control key a number of files can be selected

Operate the OK button to move on to the next window (Figure 5.8), where the files to be archived are selected. This is done using the top section of the window, which is a standard file browser. It is advisable to have all the files for the archive in a single folder as they can then be selected in one operation. Use the browser to locate the right folder and left-click on the first file to select it. Select the other files by holding down the Control key and left clicking on their entries in the file browser. There are various options available in the bottom section of the window, but for most purposes the defaults will suffice. With all the required files selected (Figure 5.9), operate the Add button to create the archive file.

The main window then returns, and it displays the contents of the newly created

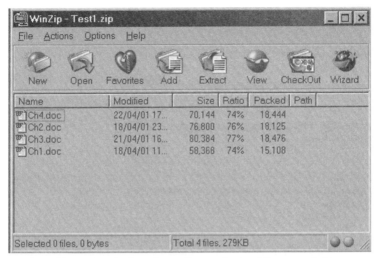

Fig.5.10 The main window shows the contents of the new archive

archive (Figure 5.10). It shows the original size of each file together with its compressed size and the degree of compression. In this case the Word DOC format files have been compressed by impressive ratios of around 74 to 77 percent. Some 279k of data have been compressed to a mere 69k. This shows the effectiveness of this method with the right types of file. A one-megabyte limit could effectively be increased to about four megabytes with suitable files.

Self-extracting

An ordinary ZIP file can be decompressed using Winzip, and the recipient must obviously have Winzip or an alternative compression/ decompression program for this system to work properly. Dealing with various types of file including the ZIP type was covered in chapter 4, so "unzipping" files will not be covered here. There is an alternative form of ZIP file called a self-extracting file. This is an executable program, and the file has the usual EXE extension. It is actually a basic decompression program and the compressed files merged into a single file.

In order to obtain the decompressed files it is basically just a matter of running the program. This avoids the need for the recipient to have a decompression program and the knowledge to use it. It is a simpler and more convenient way of doing things even if the recipient does have a suitable decompression program. The drawback is that the file size is increased by the need to include the decompression program with the compressed data.

In order to produce a self-extracting file using Winzip the steps for generating a standard ZIP file should be carried out first. Then select the Make EXE file from the Actions menu (Figure 5.11). This produces the new window of Figure 5.12. The file shown towards the top of the window should be the correct one, but if necessary it can be changed. By default a 32-bit program for use with Windows 95 and above will be produced, but there

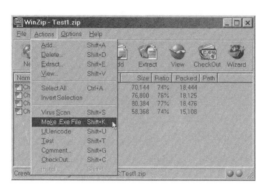

Fig.5.11 To produce a self-extracting file select the Make EXE option

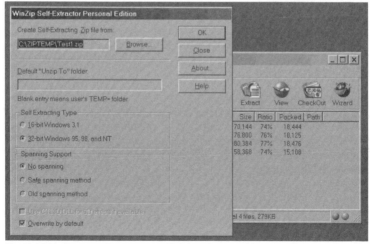

Fig.5.12 Various options are available when making a self-extraction file

is the option to produce a 16-bit file for use with Windows 3.1. Use the appropriate radio button in the Extraction Type section to select this option. Left-click the OK button to go ahead and create the self-extracting file.

If all goes well the window of Figure 5.13 will be produced. This gives the option of testing the newly created self-extracting file. It is advisable to test the file before it is sent, so the test may as well be carried out at this stage. Operating the Yes button produces the window of Figure 5.13, where the destination folder for the decompressed

*Fig.5.13 Always check that the new file
                    works properly*

files is selected. Operate the Unzip button to decompress the files into the selected folder. It is then a matter of checking the files to ensure that they are usable with the appropriate application program.

Overhead

The files used in this example were about 69k when compressed into a standard ZIP file, and about 99k when converted into a self-extracting file. In percentage perms this is a considerable increase in size, but the increase remains at about 30k if the process is used with much bigger files. Compared to one or two megabytes of compressed data an increase of 30k is not very great, and self-extracting files are a perfectly practical approach to file compression.

Attachment too large

Winzip is a possible solution where a file is only slightly too large for the Email service. As pointed out previously, some types of file compress very well while others remain virtually the same size after compression. The only way to tell how small or otherwise a file will be after compression is to try the "suck it and see" method. Where compression will make a file small enough to pass through the system, this almost certainly represents the best way of handling things.

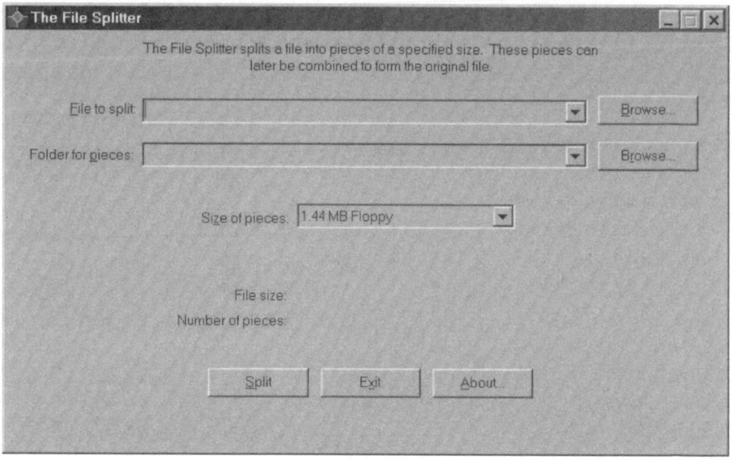

Fig.5.14 The initial screen of The File Splitter

With some types of file there is no major problem in breaking them into small pieces and reconstructing them again. With something like a large word processor file for example, there should be no difficulty in breaking the document into several chunks and then recombining them again using the word processor. This type of thing is clearly not applicable to all types of file, and it can not be used with a program file for instance. However, there are programs that can take any file, slice it into several pieces, and then combine the pieces again to produce the original file without a byte out of place. In fact the search engine of a major software download site will probably come up with about 50 or more programs of this general type.

A program by Marc Bjorklund called The File Splitter is one that I have found easy to use, and it is available from the big software download sites such as Download.com. It is freeware incidentally, so it offers a zero cost method of splitting and recombining files. Unlike many other file splitting utilities it does not require the recipient to have the program installed. The recombining of the file fragments is accomplished using a MS/DOS batch file and the standard MS/DOS facilities. Obviously the recipient must have a system that can provide these facilities, but there should be no problem using any PC running Windows 95, 98, or ME.

The window of Figure 5.14 appears when the program is run. By default the program breaks the source file into pieces that will fit onto standard

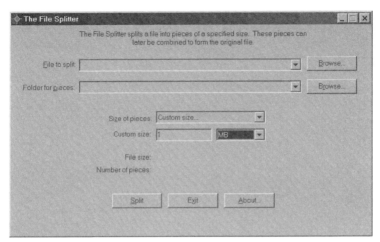

Fig.5.15 A maximum size can be set for the file fragments

3.5-inch 1.44-megabyte floppy discs. For use in an Email context it will normally be necessary to alter the size setting by selecting the Custom size option from the Size of pieces menu. The size is then entered into the Custom size textbox (Figure 5.15). The little drop-down menu to the right of this enables the size to be specified in bytes, kilobytes, or megabytes.

Size matters

It is advisable to be slightly conservative when selecting the file size. Bear in mind that the maximum size allowed by the Email service provider includes the Email itself, which will normally only be about one kilobyte. Another complication is that there are two definitions of a megabyte. Strictly speaking it is 1048576 bytes, but some consider a megabyte to be a straightforward one million bytes. File Splitter seems to work in terms of genuine megabytes. Consequently, it is advisable to make the file size slightly smaller than the stated maximum of your service provider.

The two browsers at the top of the window are used to select the file to be split and the folder for the files that are created. Note that File Splitter leaves the original file intact, so there is no need to make a copy for it to operate on. Having selected the source file and destination folder the window with display the size of the sources and the number of pieces

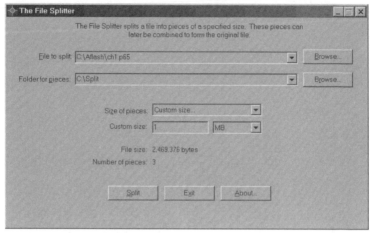

Fig.5.16 The program gives the size of the source and the number of
        pieces it will be broken into

that it will be broken into (Figure 5.16). In this example the source file is
just under 2.5 megabytes and it will be broken into three pieces.
Operating the Split button completes the process. A small window (Figure
5.17) shows the progress of the processing and indicates when it has
been completed.

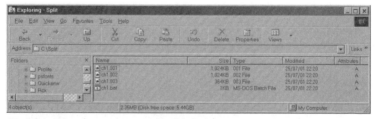

Fig.5.17 You can monitor progress of the splitting process, which
        generally takes a few seconds

Having completed the splitting process, Windows Explorer can be used
to check that the file fragments have been generated. This check will
show that an MS/DOS batch file has been created in addition to the
three file fragments. It is essential to send this file with the fragments,
because it is needed in order to reconstitute the original file from the
pieces.

Fig.5.18 Double-clicking the batch file opens a DOS window

Reconstruction

With most file splitting programs it is necessary to have the program in order to recombine the file fragments. As pointed out previously, this is not the case with The File Splitter. All the recipient has to do is place the pieces of the file and the batch file in any convenient folder, locate the batch file (the one with the "bat" extension) using Windows Explorer, and then double click on it. A MS/DOS window will appear, and should state that the new file has been created successfully (Figure 5.18). The new file will appear at the bottom of the list of files in Windows Explorer. The reconstructed file should be identical to the original. The PageMaker 6.5 file used in this example was certainly free of errors and loaded correctly into PageMaker (Figure 5.19).

Using Outlook

When using Outlook Express there is an option that results in Emails and attachments above a certain size being automatically split and recombined. In order to set up Outlook Express to automatically split

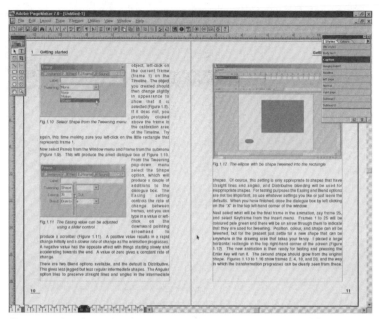

Fig.5.19 The reconstructed file should work perfectly, as in this case

Emails go to the Tools menu and select the Accounts option (Figure 5.20). This brings up a new window where the Mail tab is operated (Figure 5.21). Next left-click the Properties button to bring up another new window (Figure 5.22), and then operate the Advanced tab. This should give something like Figure 5.23, where the checkbox in the Sending section is ticked. A maximum size for Emails is then entered into the textbox. Operate the Apply button followed by the OK button to close the window. Finally, left-click on the Close button in the Internet Accounts window, and the program should then automatically apply the splitting.

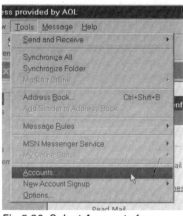

Fig.5.20 Select Accounts from
the menu

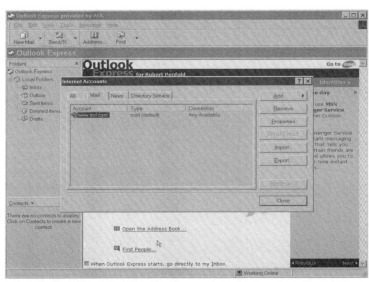

Fig.5.21 Operate the Mail tab in the new window

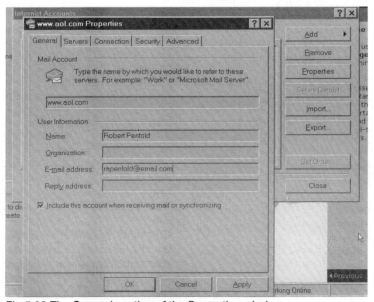

Fig.5.22 The General section of the Properties window

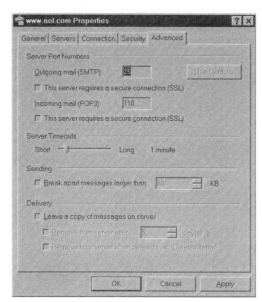

Fig.5.23 The settings available in the Advanced section

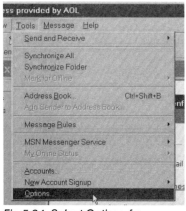

Fig.5.24 Select Options from the Tools menu

Outlook Express can give problems whereby it tries to dial up your Internet Service Provider every time it is launched, even if you wish to work offline. There is a similar problem where it tries to do the same thing even if you are already online. In both cases the most likely cause is that the options for the program are not set correctly. Launch the program and then select Options from the Tools menu (Figure 5.24). This produces a new window like the one in Figure 5.25, where the General tab must be selected. Note that you must be using a reasonably up-to-date version of the program in order to get the options offered in Figure 5.25.

The most important setting in the current context is the one in the dropdown menu in the Send/ Receive Messages section. This should be set to the Do not connect setting. When Outlook Express is launched, a message like the one of Figure 5.26 should appear, giving you the choice of connecting to the Internet or working offline. Any problems with the program trying to dial up your Internet service provider when you are already on line will probably

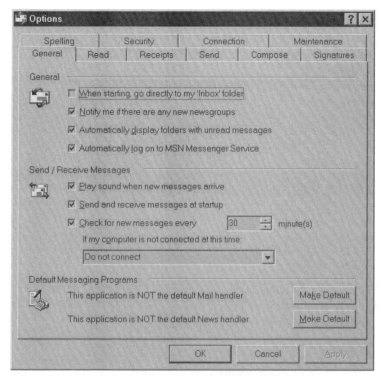

Fig.5.25 Select the General tab of the Options window

disappear as well. However, if problems persist you can try removing the tick from the "Send and receive messages at start up" checkbox.

Fig.5.26 The Outlook Express start-up message

No mail

If it is impossible to get your Email using Outlook Express, with an error message such as "Host not found" being produced instead, select Accounts from the Tools menu and then operate the Mail tab. This should give a window like the one in Figure 5.27. Are you using the right account, or one associated with a previous Internet service provider? The default

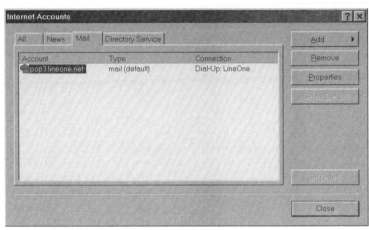

Fig.5.27 Check the settings in the Mail section of the Internet Accounts window

account can be changed by first selecting the entry for the one you wish to make the default account, then operating the Set as Default button.

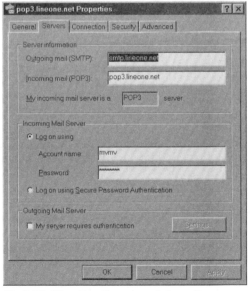

Fig.5.28 Checking the server information

Where there is an obvious account error, going through the installation process for your Internet service provider again might cure the problem.

Try operating the Properties button and then the Servers tab in the new window that appears (Figure 5.28). Is the server information correct? There are separate addresses for incoming and outgoing mail, so check the one for outgoing mail if this is also a problem. If these entries do not seem to tie in with your service provider, they should be able to supply the correct addresses.

Bounced mail

Perhaps the most common Email problem is mail that you send only to have it bounced back again. The most likely cause is an error in the address. Unless an Email has an address that is 100 percent correct down to the last full stop it can not be delivered. Always check this point very carefully before looking for errors elsewhere. Sometimes the error message produced by sending the Email gives a reason for its non-delivery, such as the recipient's inbox being full. Possibly the recipient's Email server is temporarily out of action. Sending the Email again later might prove to be more successful.

Send again

Sending the same Email again can be difficult with some Email programs, as can altering an incorrect address and trying to send the Email to the right address. It should not be necessary to do the whole thing from scratch though. If your Email software does not provide a better solution, the copy and paste facility of Windows should provide an easy means of copying text from the original Email to the new one. Select the text you wish to copy and then press the Control and C keys at the same time. Place the text cursor at the appropriate point in the new Email and then press the Control and V keys at the same time to paste the text into position.

Accessing Email

It can be difficult to access your Email if you use the Email account provided by your Internet service provider, and you need to access it via a PC other than your own. In order to access your Email account it might be necessary to set up the computer with your Internet account. This is clearly undesirable, and in many cases the owner of the PC simply would not allow it. The way around the problem is to use a web-based Email account. Fortunately, many Internet service providers now use this type of account, making it possible to access your Email via a computer that has an Internet connection. AOL for example, have the AOL Anywhere facility (Figure 5.29). In order to access your AOL Email account you simply type your screen name and password into the text boxes and operate the Go button.

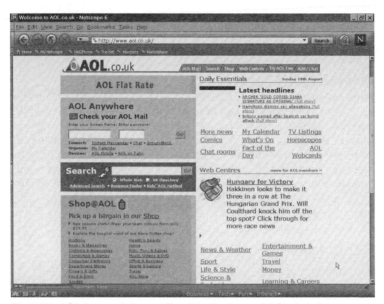

Fig.5.29 AOL has web-based Email in the form of AOL Antwhere

The usual solution if your Internet service provider does not have web-based Email is to open an account with one of the free Email companies such as Yahoo, Excite, or Microsoft (Hotmail). Apart from the fact that these provide a service that can be accessed from anywhere that an Internet connection is available, there are a couple of other advantages. One is simply that the Email address obtained from a web Email provider is usually quite short, whereas the Email addresses provided by Internet service providers are usually quite long. Another advantage is that an Email address provided by one of the web-based Email companies does not change if you switch to another Internet service provider. As many people change their Internet provider fairly frequently, this is a major advantage, since it avoids having to repeatedly tell all your contacts of an address change.

Working offline

One disadvantage of using a free web-based Email service is that most of these lack facilities for working offline. When using an Internet service that involves paying by the minute for access, composing Emails offline and sending them once online can save a lot of money over the years. Even if you have unmetered Internet access, you may still prefer to compose Emails offline so that the telephone line is not blocked unnecessarily. It is actually possible to compose Emails offline even if the Email service has no proper facilities for working this way.

First write your Email using any Windows word processor or text editor. A simple word processor called Wordpad is included as part of Windows and this is suitable. Then go online, access your Email account, and select the Compose option. Fill in the Address and Subject fields of the Email form, and then use the Windows Copy and Paste commands to copy the text from the word processor to the main body of the Email form. Finally, send the Email in the usual way.

Where several Emails are involved it is easier if your word processor can have several documents open at once. You can then quickly work your way through each one using the cut and paste process. It is otherwise a matter of saving the Emails to disc, and then loading them one by one so that they can be copied to Email forms using the copy and paste method.

Should you wish to extract the text from an Email that someone has sent to you, the copy and paste method can be used to copy the text from the Email to a word processor. It can then be saved to disc for viewing offline, merged into another document, or faxed to someone else if your PC has this facility. Once copied to the word processor it becomes standard text that can be manipulated in the standard ways.

Spell checking

This copy and paste method is useful if your Email service does not include a spelling checker facility and you wish to check Emails before sending them. The Email can be composed using a word processor that does include this facility. After the check has been completed and any necessary corrections have been made the text is copied and pasted to the Email form.

Do not overlook the built-in spelling checker of Microsoft Outlook Express. There is no facility to check spelling as you type, but completed documents can be checked. Select Spelling from the Tools menu to launch a conventional spell checking facility (Figure 5.30). There is also a spelling checker in AOL's Email system, and also in Yahoo's system, but it still seems to be something of a rarity with the free web-based Email systems.

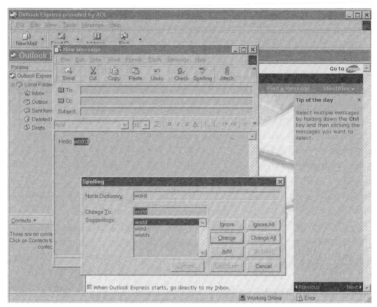

Fig.5.30 Do not overlook the spelling checker in Outlook Express

Spam

Spam is one of those "near miss" acronyms, and it sort of stands for spurious advertising material. It is the Email equivalent of conventional junk mail. Like normal junk mail, if you get large quantities it can take a long while to sort through all your mail to separate the junk from the important stuff. This is one of those things where prevention is better than cure, and it is advisable to take steps to minimise the amount of spam that you receive rather than relying on being able to automatically filter it out.

The more widely available your Email address, the more likely you are to get bombarded with spam. Placing your address in Email directories and on a web site makes it available to anyone, including the spammers. Unless you really need to make your Email address widely available, restrict its circulation to those you can trust not misuse it. Some web sites have free services that require you to register, and the registration process normally requires you to provide an Email address. You certainly need to check that the company is a bona fide operation before handing over your Email address or any other personal information. Also check their privacy policy, especially if it is a company you have not dealt with before.

The best ploy when an Email address is needed for registration is to open a dummy Email account with one of the free Email companies. You will have to provide personal details to the Email company in order to open an account, but this should be perfectly safe provided you use one of the large companies. Use this account only for registering with web sites. If it should fall into the wrong hands it will not matter too much, since the account receiving the spam will be one that you do not actually use.

Note that you will have to login to the dummy account every now and then in order to keep the account active. Most free Email accounts lapse if the account is not used for a period of about 28 to 60 days. Email going into your account is not usually sufficient to keep it within the provider's definition of active. You will need to login periodically to prevent it from being cancelled. If the account should lapse, most service providers have a facility that enables it to be reactivated, but it is easier to login from time to time and keep the account active.

Using the services of free sites that offer to remove your address from Email address from mailing lists is a slightly dubious course of action. What better way to obtain Email addresses than offer a service such as this? Even if the site is genuine, it is unlikely that their service will have any real effect on the amount of junk Email that you receive. Where a junk Email has an option to unsubscribe it is generally considered best not to do so. This may simply indicate to the spammer that your Email address is active, thus ensuring that you get a large number of junk Emails in the future. The best strategy is to dump junk Emails unopened. Do not reply to them and definitely do not open any attachments on junk Emails.

Spam filtering

Many Email service providers have facilities that attempt to prevent spam from reaching your inbox. Usually it is diverted to a separate folder, or there may be a facility to send it straight into the trashcan. Sending it to a separate folder allows you to check for any proper messages that have been misdirected into the trashcan. However, if you have a serious problem with spam it might be better to direct the junk Emails straight into the trashcan.

The main problem with large numbers of junk Emails is not having to check through them in search of "the real thing", but the fact that they

Fig.5.31 The Hotmail Options window

can easily use up all the server space allotted to your account. Many Email accounts come complete with one megabyte of storage space. Most Emails require only a few kilobytes of storage space, but with large amounts of spam this space can be used up, effectively blocking any proper Emails that are sent to you.

The filtering facilities vary from one service provider to another. Microsoft's Hotmail service has some of the best filtering facilities and this service is the one that will be considered here. After logging in select Options from the second menu bar down from the top of the window. This should produce a window like the one of Figure 5.31, and it is the facilities under the Mail Handling heading that are of interest here. The Junk Mail Filter is the first port of call, and this opens a page like the one shown in Figure 5.32. The radio buttons enable the filtering to be switched off or three levels of filtering to be selected (low, high and exclusive).

Ideally the highest degree of filtering should be used, which is the "exclusive" setting. Using this setting only mail from addresses in your address book will be placed in the inbox and all other mail goes to the junk mail folder. This is the most reliable method, but it will only work well if your address book is kept up to date. Also, it is of limited value if you are likely to receive legitimate Emails from senders not listed in your address book. The "high" option will result in most junk mail being filtered by the system, but some might still get through. Also, there can be

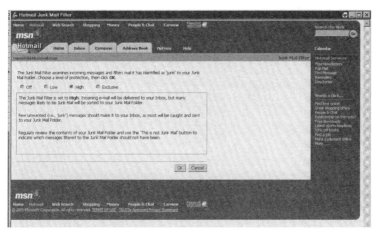

Fig.5.32 Three levels of junk mail filtering are available

mistakes with proper mail occasionally ending up in the junk mail folder. The low setting can be used if the high option produces too many misdirected Emails, but you may end up with a fair amount of spam in your inbox.

Blocking

Where there is a problem with junk Emails from just one source, or perhaps a few sources, the Block Sender option is the one to deal with it. This produces a page like the one in Figure 5.33. To add an address to the list it is typed into the textbox and then the Add button is operated. Any mail received from this address will then be discarded immediately, and it will not even appear in the Trashcan folder. To remove an address from the list simply left-click on its entry in the list to select it and then operate the Remove button. When you have finished adding or removing addresses operate the OK button.

The Custom Filtering option is a powerful one that can be useful at removing sources that consistently manage to get through the standard filtering. Many spammers send their mail from a variety of Email addresses, most of which are actually non-existent. This makes it difficult to block their mail, because each time you block one address they move on to another. However, you may find that there is a string of characters that is common to each address, or perhaps there is a common string of

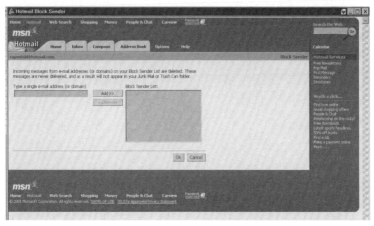

Fig.5.33 This page is used to block mail from specified addresses

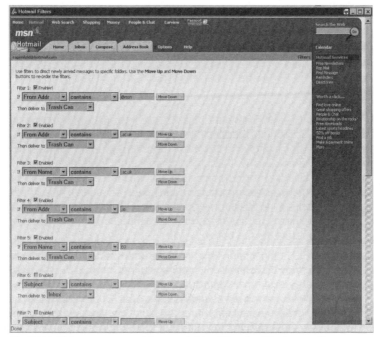

Fig.5.34 This screen provides useful facilities for filtering mail

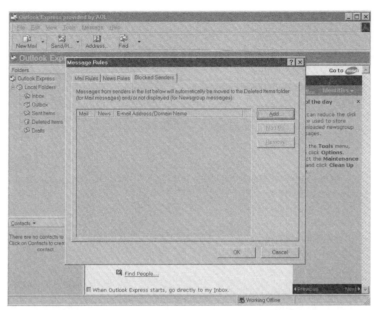

Fig.5.35 Mail from specified addresses can be blocked using Outlook Express

characters elsewhere, such as in the sender's name field. The Custom Filtering page (Figure 5.34) enables you to filter Emails that have a given string of characters in a selected part of the Email. The filtered Email is sent to the selected folder, which will usually be the Trashcan folder.

There are some further options available. One of these can be used to ensure that Emails from certain addresses are never filtered. Another option is whether to have junk mail deleted immediately or after a delay. With the right set-up it is usually possible to ensure that the junk Emails are efficiently filtered from the proper Emails.

If you are using Outlook Express do not overlook the program's built-in filtering facilities. For example, selected senders can be blocked by first selecting Message Rules from the Tools menu followed by Blocked senders List from the submenu. This produces a window like the one in Figure 5.35, and initially the list of blocked senders will obviously be blank. To add an address to the list left-click the Add button and then type the sender's Email address into the textbox of the window that pops up (Figure 5.36). Then operate the OK button to close the window, and

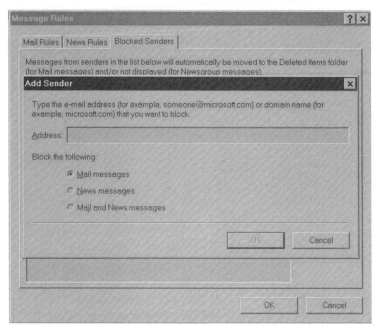

Fig.5.36 The address to be blocked is entered in the textbox

the address should then appear in the list. Repeat this procedure for any other addresses that you wish to block and then press the OK button to return to the main window of Outlook Express.

If you are getting huge numbers of junk Emails there may be no option but to "throw in the towel" and change to a new address. This usually only occurs where someone is making illicit use of your Email address. Typically, it would be used as an alias when sending out junk mail, and you end up with the thousands of complaints! Fortunately, this type of thing is very rare, and most spammers use a fictional Email address rather than one that exists.

Web-based Outlook

When using a web-based Email account you are supplied with at least basic Emailing facilities by the service provider. You may prefer to use Outlook express instead, but will find that it does not work with your web-based account. This is not usually due to any incompatibility

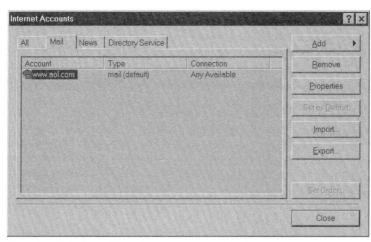

Fig.5.37 Select the Mail tab to start a new Email account

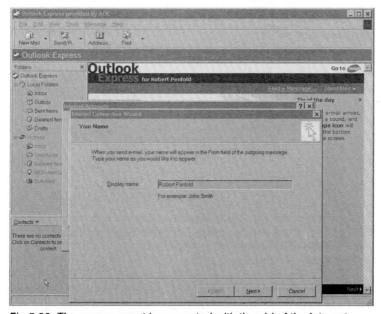

Fig.5.38 The new account is generated with the aid of the Internet Connection wizard

Fig.5.39 Enter the address of your Email account at this screen

between Outlook Express and the web-based Email account. The problem is simply that Outlook Express does not known about your new account until you create a new account within Outlook Express itself. This will work with most web-based Email accounts including those provided by Hotmail and Yahoo. I have never managed to get Outlook Express to work with AOL though.

To create a new account start Outlook Express and then select Accounts from the Tools menu. Operate the Mail tab in the new window that appears, and you should then have something like Figure 5.37. To create a new mail account left-click the Add button, select Mail from the pop-out menu, and the Internet Connection Wizard should then start (Figure 5.38). As when using any wizard, it is then just a matter of providing the requested information and moving on to the next screen. At the first screen you simply have to ensure that your name appears in the text box in the way you would like it to appear on your Emails. The next screen (Figure 5.39) is used to enter the address of your Email account. You have the option of using an existing web based Email account or creating a new Hotmail account. It will be assumed here that an existing account is to be used.

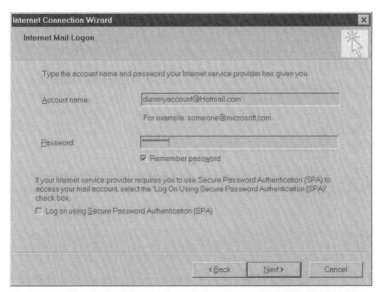

Fig.5.40 Your Email address and password are entered here

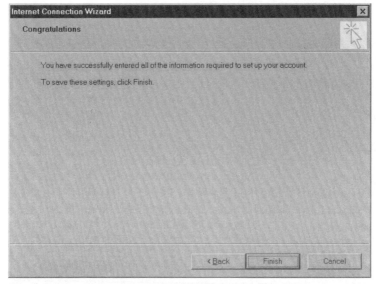

Fig.5.41 You will get this screen when the account has been created

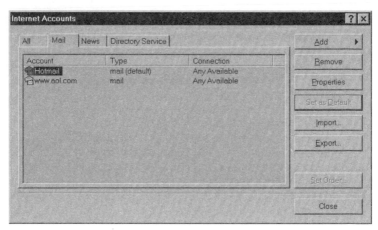

Fig.5.42 The new account can be set as the default account

At the next screen you have to provide your Email address and password (Figure 5.40), and then details of the Email server you are using are provided at the next stage. Simply accept the defaults if you are using a Hotmail account. For other service providers the appropriate details must be filled in, and these should be available from your service provider. Having completed this stage you should get the message screen of Figure 5.41 indicating that the new account has been created successfully. The new account should be included in the list of mail accounts (Figure 5.42). To set this as the default account, left-click on its entry to select it and then operate the Set as Default button.

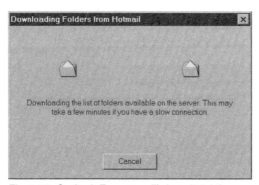

Fig.5.43 Outlook Express will download the folders for your account

Before the account can be used in earnest Outlook Express will have to download your Email folders from the server, and a message to this

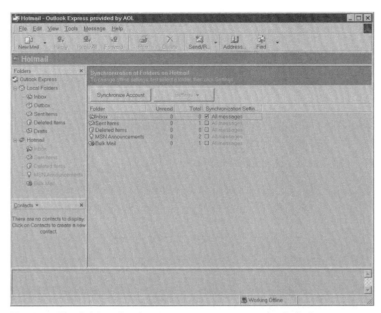

Fig.5.44 The folders for the new account are now included

effect will appear on the screen as it carries out the download process (Figure 5.43). You should then be in business, with the account and its folders accessible from Outlook Express (Figure 5.44). You can then read mail, compose mail, etc., in the normal way. In order to update the folders for future sessions with Outlook Express simply operate the Synchronise button.

Unwanted branding

Like Internet Explorer, Outlook Express tends to gain a brand name in the title bar when you sign on to an Internet service provider. This tends to annoy a great many people, and it is especially annoying when Outlook Express still shows the brand name of a company whose services you have not used for a year or two. Also like Internet Explorer, the brand name can be removed by editing the Registry directly or via a file. In this case we will use the file method of modification.

Start by opening Notepad, which is a very basic text editor supplied as part of Windows. To do this go to the Start menu and then select

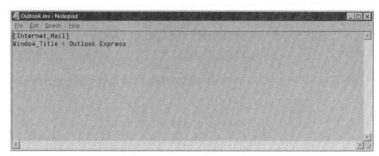

Fig.5.45 The short text file created in Notepad

Programs, Accessories, and Notepad. Now enter these two lines of text, exactly as they appear here:

```
[Internet_Mail]
Window_Title = Outlook Express
```

This should give you something that looks like Figure 5.45. Now select the Save As option from the File menu and save the file as "Outlook.ins".

*Fig.5.46 Operate the OK button when this
warning message appears*

The name of the file is not important and can be any valid name, but the extension must be "ins". This tells Windows that this is an Internet settings file so that it knows what to do when you run the file. It does not matter which folder you save the file to, but make it somewhere easy to find.

With the file saved to disc, exit Notepad and use Windows Explorer to locate the file. Then double-click on it, which will produce a warning message like the one in Figure 5.46. Left-click the OK button and the necessary changes will be made to the Internet settings. However, if you run Outlook Express you will find that the branding in the title bar is still present. This is due to the new settings not coming into effect until the computer is rebooted. After rebooting, Outlook Express should be returned to its non-branded status (Figure 5.47).

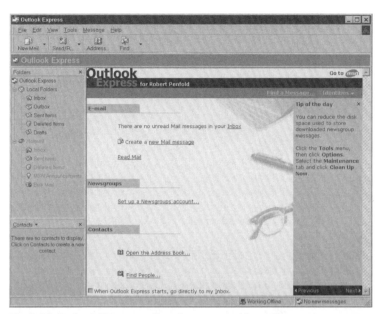

Fig.5.47 Outlook Express minus its unwanted branding

Address backup

If you have a new computer you have the problem of getting your existing Outlook Express address book transferred from the old PC to the new one. With only a few addresses it would not take too long to enter the data manually, but even with a few entries things are quicker and more reliable if

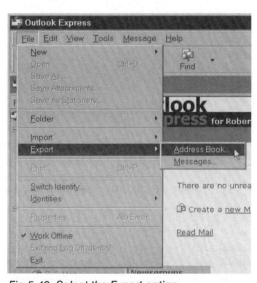

Fig.5.48 Select the Export option

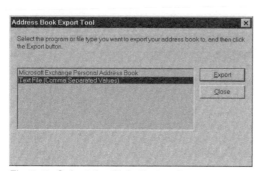

Fig.5.49 Select the Plain Text option

the address book is exported from one PC to the other. It is actually possible to import and export an address book, and it is not a bad idea to make a backup copy of the data. If your PC crashes and the data on the hard disc is lost, you can restore your backup copy of the address book which should be stored on a floppy disc, CD-RW, etc., and not on the hard disc.

To export the address book go to the File menu and select Export followed by Address Book from the submenu (Figure 5.48). A window like the one in Figure 5.49 should then appear. Two types of file are available, and the lower option (the plain text file) should be selected. This produces

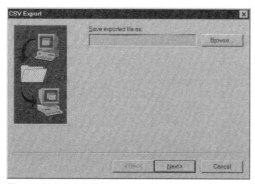

*Fig.5.50 It is best to use the Browse option
when you reach this window*

another window (Figure 5.50) where a filename for the backup copy can be entered into the textbox. However, I would suggest using the Browse button and the file browser that this brings up (Figure 5.51).

Choose the folder where you wish to save the file, type a suitable filename for the file, and choose

the "csv" option for the file type. Then operate the Save button to return to the previous window. Operate the Next button, which brings up a window like the one of Figure 5.52, where you can select the fields that will be exported. If in doubt select everything! Operate the Finish button and the backup copy will be saved to disc.

Fig.5.51 Choose csv as the file type

The importing process is the same whether you are restoring a backup copy after a system crash or putting an existing address book on a new computer. Go to the File menu and select Import, followed by the Other Address Book option. In the new window that appears (Figure 5.53)

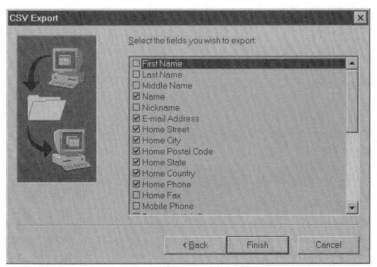

Fig.5.52 You can save selected fields or all of them

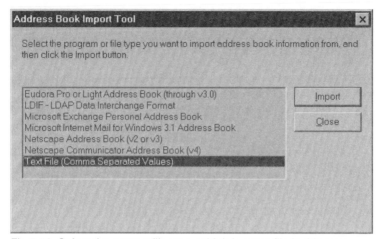

Fig.5.53 Select the correct file type, which is a text file in this case

select Text File from the list of importable file types. Then operate the Import button, which brings up a window like the one shown in Figure 5.54. Either type in the full name of the backup file including the path

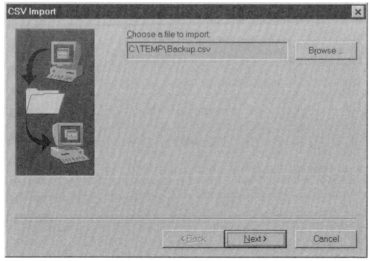

Fig.5.54 Type the full filename or use the browse feature to locate the correct file

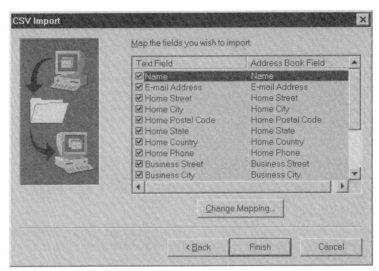

Fig.5.55 Select the fields that you wish to import. The default is for all available fields to be imported

and extension, or use the browser to locate and select it. Operate the Next button to bring up a window like the one of Figure 5.55, where you can select the fields that will be imported. Left-click the Finish button to complete the process and import the address book.

Points to remember

Large Email attachments can be compressed or split in order to get around size limitations. When sending a large number of small files as attachments it is generally better to combine them into one archive file. The recipient can split the archive into its constituent parts.

When sending large amount of data in attachments, bear in mind that there are usually strict limits on the amount of data that can be stored in an Email account. There is no point in sending more data than the recipient's Email account can handle.

If an Email is bounced back to you, check that the address on the Email is perfectly accurate. Did you put ".co.uk" instead of ".com" for example. If the address is correct there might just be a temporary problem in the system, so try again later.

It can sometimes be difficult to send an Email again when it has been bounced. Often the easiest way is to use copy and paste the main text to a new Email form, add the address and subject description, and then send what is effectively a new Email.

Use a web-based Email account if you need to access your Email from anywhere, and not just on your normal work and home PCs. Fortunately, most Internet service providers offer web based Email accounts, and there are free services from Hotmail, Yahoo, Excite, etc.

Some web-based Email systems include a spelling checker, and this feature is included in Outlook Express. Alternatively, generate the main text using a word processor, use the word processor's spelling checker, and then cut and paste the text into the Email form.

Outlook Express can be used with most web-based Email systems including Hotmail and Yahoo. However, a suitable account must be created in Outlook Express first.

It is better to restrict access to your Email address so as to minimise the amount of spam you receive, rather than rely on automatic filtering. The service and software you are using will probably provide useful filtering facilities, and programs designed specifically for this purpose can also provide these facilities.

Most Email service providers enable mail from certain addresses to be blocked, and this form of filtering is also included in Outlook Express.

Where an account is being bombarded with huge amounts of spam there is probably no realistic alternative to changing your Email address.

Annoying branding of Outlook Express can be removed by creating a small text file and then running it as if it was a program. This makes changes to the Registry incidentally.

It is a good idea to back up your address book to a floppy disc or CD-RW so that it can be restored if your PC goes badly wrong. An address book can also be transferred from one computer to another using the same facilities.

5 Email problems

Multimedia problems

Plug-ins

Multimedia is a slightly vague term that seems to mean different things to different people. Here we are only interested in multimedia as it applies to the Internet, which mainly means audio, animation, and videos. The most common problem with all of these is the required action failing to happen at all, although in some cases it may take place but in a totally scrambled form. You may also find that the audio track of a video plays perfectly, and everything would be fine if there were some pictures! Problems such as these are usually caused by a lack of a suitable plug-in to do the decoding, and there will often be an error message to this effect.

When dealing with multimedia it is important to realise that the browser does not usually deal with sound and movie files on its own. There are one or two exceptions such as GIF files, which can be used for still pictures or simple animations. Anything beyond a GIF file requires the browser to be given some outside assistance. In many cases the browser will not try to play the file at all, but will instead launch the default media player for the particular file type involved. In other cases the browser will use some additional help from a program that runs unseen in the background. This type of program has become known as a "plug-in". Matters are further complicated by the fact that the media player may need the assistance of a plug-in before it can handle a given file type. In other words the plug-in needs a plug-in before it can handle some files.

Up to date

The chances of playing media files successfully are greatly enhanced if you have the latest version of the Windows Media Player installed on your PC, together with recent versions of one or two others. Apart from

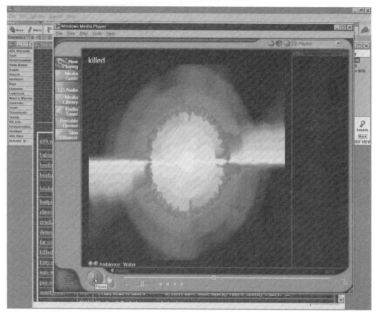

*Fig.6.1   The Windows Media Player has been automatically launched
       to play a file*

the fact that the newer versions generally have some extra features, they
also have wider file compatibility. No single media player covers all the
file types under the sun, so you will almost certainly need more than just
the Windows Media Player if you get deeply involved in Internet
multimedia. Any of the major software download sites such as
Download.com should have links to the latest versions of the popular
media players.

There are numerous types of multimedia file in common use these days,
and it is worth considering the popular types and their potential problems
individually.

WAV

This is a type of sound file that can be handled by the standard Windows
Media Player. Windows provides its built-in sounds such as the start up
jingle use WAV files. A WAV file is produced by converting sounds into a
series of numbers, and then converting the numbers back into their

corresponding sounds. In other words, it is a straightforward digital sound recording system, much like that used for audio CDs. WAV files can give very high audio quality, but it takes quite large amounts of data to produce long sounds. Consequently, WAV files are mainly used for things like short sound effects.

As with most multimedia files, left clicking on a link to the file will result in the appropriate media player being launched and the file will then be played (Figure 6.1). If you wish to have the file stored on disc for playback offline, right-click on the link and choose Save Target As from the popup menu (Figure 6.2).

Using a Netscape browser choose the Save Link As option. Either way, the usual file browser will appear and the file can then be saved to the selected disc and folder. This method works with any type of file incidentally. Of course, it will only work if the link is direct to the target file. It pays to check the

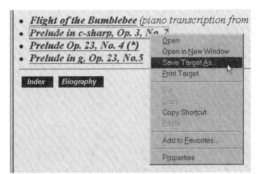

Fig.6.2 A file can be save to disc by right-clicking on its link

extension part of the filename before downloading the file. The link is to another web page if there is an "htm" or "html" extension. You must then go to that page and save the file from there.

Sound diagnosis

As WAV files are fundamental to Windows itself there is little likelihood of problems when playing them. When there is a lack of audio the first thing to check is the volume control setting. There is usually a volume control icon in the taskbar at the

Fig.6.3 The volume control icon is the one on the extreme left

bottom of the Windows desktop. This is the icon on the extreme left-hand side in Figure 6.3. Left clicking on this icon will produce a slider

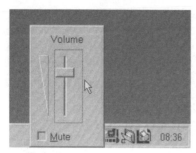

Fig.6.4 The popup volume control

control (Figure 6.4) that can be used to adjust the volume. In a fair proportion of cases where I am asked to assist with a PC that has "lost its voice" the problem is nothing more than this control being set at minimum. With some soundcards a more elaborate mixer panel is installed instead of or in addition to the basic volume control (Figure 6.5). Also, any media player will have a volume control somewhere in all the buttons and slider controls. Check every volume control you can find and ensure that none of them are set at zero.

If the controls are all set correctly and the speakers are switched on and wired up correctly, check that the sound card is properly installed. Go to the Windows Control Panel and double-click on the System icon to bring up the Device Manager window. Where there is a problem with the soundcard the Sound entry will already be expanded and there will be one or more of the dreaded yellow exclamation marks in evidence. You can double-click on the Sound icon to check the individual entries if this section is not already expanded. This should give something like Figure 6.6.

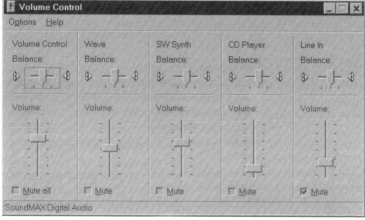

Fig.6.5 Most audio cards are equipped with a mixer

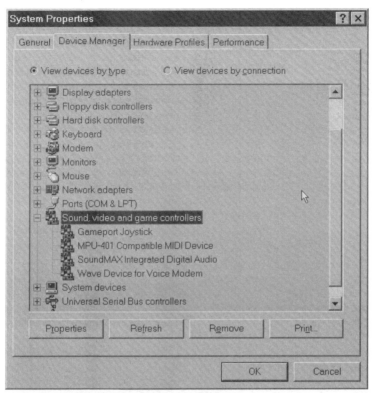

Fig.6.6 Soundcard entries in Device Manager

Soundcards are potentially confusing due to the number of entries they have in Device Manager. In this example there are four entries, although the bottom one is actually for the modem and is nothing to do with soundcard. The first entry is usually for the game port that is a feature of practically all soundcards. The next is for the MIDI driver, which enables the card to emulate a MIDI synthesiser. MIDI and MIDI files are covered later in this chapter. The next entry is for the wave synthesiser, which is the one that enables digital audio such as WAV files to be played. With some soundcards there are actually two entries for wave synthesis. This occurs where the card offers both basic wave synthesis and some more advanced version.

Soundcards have traditionally been very troublesome, but in fairness to the manufacturers of the current cards it has to be admitted that the modern cards are much easier to deal with. With a PC that uses an old soundcard that fits into an ISA expansion slot it is not too surprising if the card periodically "goes walkabout". Before doing anything drastic it is worth rebooting the computer to check that there is a genuine problem. Occasionally Windows fails to detect a device properly during the boot-up sequence, rendering the device non-operational. Rebooting should result in the soundcard being detected and normal operation being restored. If not, try removing the card and reinstalling it from scratch. Also check the manufacture's web site to see if updated versions of the device drivers are available. Reinstalling a modem and updating drivers was covered in chapter 2, and the process is essentially the same for a soundcard.

Speakers

Most computers use active loudspeakers, and "active" in this case simply means that there is a stereo amplifier built into one of the speaker units. These speakers are designed to operate with a low-level signal, which makes them easy to check. Disconnect the loudspeaker lead from the audio card and try touching the non-earth terminals of the plug via the blade of a small screwdriver. Figure 6.7 identifies the three terminals of the jack plug. Make sure that you are touching the blade

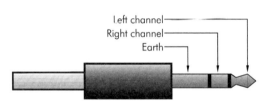

Fig.6.7 Terminal functions for a 3.5mm stereo jack plug

of the screwdriver and not just the insulated handle, because this test relies on mains "hum" and other electrical noise being picked up by your body. This signal should produce mains "hum" and other general noise from the loudspeakers provided the volume control is well advanced.

If you have an item of audio equipment that has a 3.5-millimetre stereo output socket, such as a personal stereo unit, use this as the audio source. Either way, a lack of sound from one or both of the loudspeakers indicates a fault in a cable or the loudspeaker units. If the loudspeakers are mains powered, as most are, check the fuse in the mains plug and ensure that everything is connected together properly.

MIDI

MIDI is probably the least understood of the audio file formats, even though it has been in existence for more than 20 years. MIDI stands for musical instruments digital interface, and it is really meant as a means of controlling electronic music instruments such as synthesisers, electronic pianos, and sound samplers. A MIDI file does not contain digitised sounds, but is just a set of instructions for an electronic musical instrument. The instructions are along the lines of switch this note on, turn that note off, and increase the volume on channel one.

The original MIDI specification did not include any sound assignments and a MIDI file played on one instrument could (and did) sound very different when played on another instrument. A track that was supposed to be produced using a synthesised piano sound could be played using a car horn sound instead! A standard set of MIDI sound assignments was added later though, and a MIDI file that uses these should sound similar when played on any instrument that meets the standard specification. Bear in mind though, that some methods of sound synthesis work better than others. A MIDI file that sounds great when played on one instrument might not sound as good when played via a budget model. The MIDI instrument sounds are quite poor on many older soundcards.

Virtually all PC soundcards have a combined game and MIDI port in the form of a 15-pin D connector on the mounting plate. This can be connected to MIDI equipped instruments using the appropriate cable, which is a special PC type and not a standard MIDI cable incidentally. However, this is not the normal way of playing MIDI files. Most people settle for playback via the PC's soundcard, and even the most basic soundcard should include the ability to mimic a MIDI instrument. As pointed out previously, with older and cheaper cards the sound quality is often something less than convincing, but many modern cards sound remarkably like the real thing.

Soundcards and PCs are often supplied with quite sophisticated programs for handling MIDI, but the Windows Media Player is all that is needed for basic playback of these files. This program is supplied with recent versions of Windows, and is included in a default installation. With older versions of Windows you will probably have to seek out a suitable version of the player at the Microsoft web site (Microsoft.com), or it can be found on many of the cover mounted discs supplied with computer magazines. It might be worthwhile seeking out the latest version of the player program even when using a relatively recent Windows installation. This program tends to gain new features with the passage of time, as well as better file compatibility. A lot of problems with multimedia are due to the use of old software that can not handle the latest file formats properly.

MIDI drivers

If MIDI files play perfectly apart from the fact there is no sound, or you simply get an error message when attempting to play any MIDI file, check that the soundcard is installed properly. The MIDI device drivers are not always included by default and the MIDI entry will be absent from device manager if they have not been installed. If necessary, go through the driver installation procedure again, making sure that the MIDI drivers are installed this time round. As always when there is a lack of audio, check that the active speakers are functioning correctly.

You do not have to use the sound card's built-in MIDI capabilities, and a suitable instrument coupled to the MIDI port should provide proper playback. A lack of playback when using a MIDI sequencer program is usually caused by the MIDI port being switched off in the software. The instruction manual for the program should explain how to switch on the MIDI port.

These days a large proportion of PCs have the sound facilities integrated with the motherboard rather than provided by an expansion card. The MIDI port is then part of the motherboard, and by default it is often deactivated. Some delving with the BIOS Setup program should enable the port to be switched on, and the manual for the computer or its motherboard should give some guidance here. Integrated audio can often be switched off altogether, either via the BIOS Setup program or a jumper connector on the motherboard. Where onboard audio fails to work it is worth checking that it is actually switched on.

MP3

MP3 is an abbreviation for MPEG 1 layer 3, and it is effectively the sound part of a movie file format that has been adapted for use on its own as a sound file format. Why did MP3 make such a stir when it was first introduced, especially amongst Web users? This comes down to its high audio quality combined with small file sizes. The method of storing sound used in WAV files, CDs and the like offers very high quality stereo sound, but with huge file sizes. A CD-R disc can accommodate 650 megabytes of data, which equates to about 74 minutes of normal CD sound. Downloading an hour of music in one of these non-compressed formats would typically take about 34 hours or so using a 56k modem with a reasonably good quality connection.

MP3 uses compression techniques that aim to give something close to full CD quality while reducing file sizes by a factor of 10 or more. An hour of audio will still take nearly three hours to download using a 56k modem and a "real world "telephone line, but this is a practical proposition, whereas 34 hours or so is not. There is some loss of audio quality with MP3, but the technology aims to remove the quiet bits that are not audible anyway due to the presence of louder sounds. It may not be to the liking of many audiophiles, but most users of MP3 are perfectly happy with the results.

MP3 to CD

MP3 is probably best known for its use with small personal stereo units. MP3 files are downloaded over the Internet and then loaded into the player's built-in memory. Of course, it is not necessary to have a separate MP3 player in order to listen to these files. Downloaded files can be played using the Windows Media Player program, and much other media player software. It is also possible to place these files onto a CD-R disc so that they can be played using most audio CD players. This is a common cause of problems though, and it will only work properly if it is done in the right way.

Many people produce a data CD containing the MP3 files and then try to play it in an audio CD player. This method will not work. There are some players that can handle normal audio discs and data discs containing MP3 files, but these are primarily intended for use with MP3 files and they are not ordinary CD players. Modern CD burning software such as Nero and Easy CD can produce audio discs from MP3 files, but it is not always possible with older versions of these and other programs. Unfortunately, the software provided with CD rewriters is not always the latest version, or anything like it, so you may need to upgrade in order to make it easy to produce audio CDs from MP3 files.

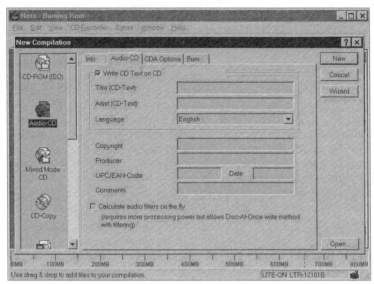

Fig.6.8 The opening screen of Nero Burning ROM V5.0

Burning MP3 CDs

Obviously the exact method of producing an audio disc from MP3s depends on the particular burning software you are using. For this example version 5.0 of the Nero Burning ROM software was used. This program has the option of using a wizard, but here we will use the fully manual approach. At the opening screen (Figure 6.8) left-click on the audio CD icon. A normal audio CD player can not use any form of data disc, so you must opt to produce an audio CD.

Next operate the New button, and the screen will change to something like Figure 6.9. The right-hand section of the screen is a file browser that is used to locate the MP3 files you wish to put onto the CD. The drag and drop method is used to place the selected files in the left-hand section of the window. In Figure 6.9 some files have already been dragged into the left-hand section of the window.

A bar and a scale at the bottom of the screen show how much data has been selected for inclusion on the disc, and this helps to avoid trying to get too much onto the disc. Bear in mind here that you are not placing the files onto the disc in MP3 format. The files are converted into ordinary digital audio that the CD player will be able to interpret correctly, and the

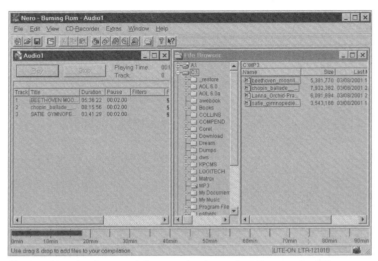

Fig.6.9 Use the drag and drop method to select the required files

files are effectively decompressed in the process. Although a CD may be able to accommodate 10 hours or more of audio in MP3 format, the normal 650-megabyte/ 74 minute limits apply when an audio disc is produced. The available space will fill up surprisingly rapidly.

When all the files have been added to the list, select the Write CD option from the File menu (Figure 6.10). A new window then appears (Figure 6.11) offering various options, but the defaults should suffice. Operate the Write button to start producing the disc, and a window like the one in Figure 6.12 will then appear, giving details of how things are progressing. If all goes well a message like the one in Figure

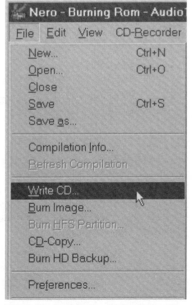

Fig.6.10 Select the Write CD option

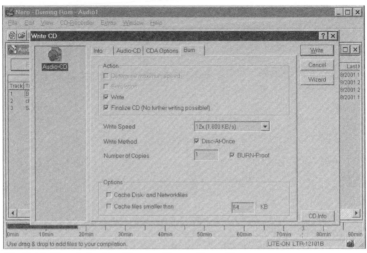

Fig.6.11 The default settings will usually suffice

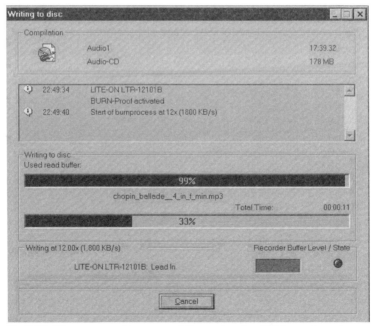

Fig.6.12 The program keeps you informed as the CD is produced

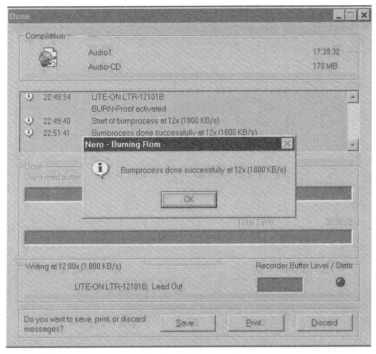

Fig.6.13 If all goes well you will get this on-screen message once the burning process has been completed

6.13 will appear, announcing that the disc has been created successfully. Left-click the OK button to remove the message, and a new message like the one in Figure 6.14 will replace it. Here you have the option of saving details of the disc so that it is easy to make another copy at a later time, or abandoning the details if you will definitely have no need to make another copy.

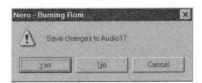

Fig.6.14 Details of the CD can be saved if you might need another copy, or discarded if no further copies will be required

Fig.6.15 Winamp with the two main windows in operation

Fig.6.16 The first step in the conversion process is to select Preferences

MP3 to WAV

Older CD burning software that can not make audio discs from MP3 files may well be able to use WAV files instead. This makes it possible to make audio CDs from MP3 files provided the MP3 files can be converted to WAV format first. There are numerous programs that can provide this conversion, and for this example the popular Winamp program will be used. Note that the process might be slightly different depending on the version in use. Version 2.7 of the program was used for this example. Start by launching the program and loading the MP3 files into the play list in the normal way. This will produce something like Figure 6.15, but the exact appearance will obviously depend on the sections of the program that are open.

Next go to the main menu by operating the small button in the top left-hand corner of the screen. Select Options and then Preferences from the submenu (Figure 6.16). Select the Output option in the left-hand

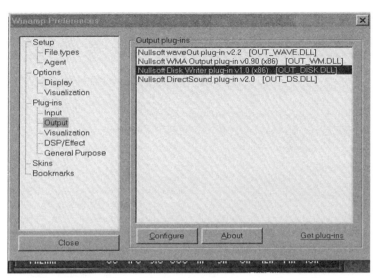

Fig.6.17 Select the Output folder in the left-hand section of the window
and then Nullsoft Disk Writer in the right-hand section

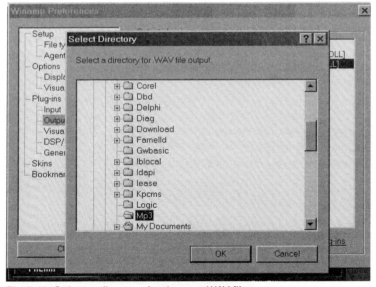

Fig.6.18 Select a directory for the new WAV file

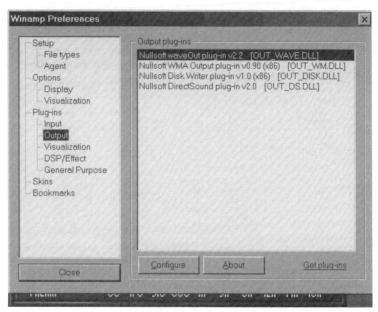

Fig.6.19 Return the Output folder to its original setting

section of the screen followed by the Nullsoft Disk Writer option in the right-hand section (Figure 6.17). Left-click the Configure button to bring up a simple file browser like the one in Figure 6.18. This is used to select a directory for the new WAV file.

Having selected the correct directory, operate the OK button and then the Close button to return to the main window. Use the Play button if the file does not play automatically. The playback speed will be much higher than normal and there will be no sound from the speakers. There will be a great deal of hard disc activity though, because the WAV file is being generated and written to the appropriate folder. Note that any changes to the frequency response added using the graphic equaliser will be applied to the WAV file.

The new file can be loaded into Winamp and tested, but first the output setting should be returned to normal. Once again, from the main menu select Options and then Preferences. Also as before, select Output in the left-hand section of the new window that appears. Next select the original setting in the right-hand section, which should have been the

Nullsoft wave Out option (Figure 6.19). Operate the Close button and any files loaded into Winamp should then play normally through the loudspeakers. Virtually any CD burning software should be able to produce an audio CD from the converted WAV files.

With the latest add-ons the Windows Media Player 7.x has a Copy to CD option available from the file

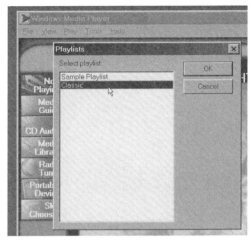

Fig.6.20 Select the playing list to be written to the CD

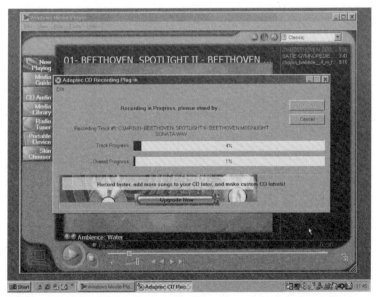

Fig.6.21 You are informed about the progress of the burning process

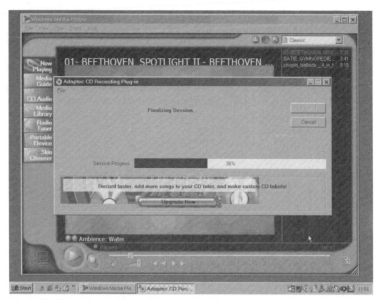

Fig.6.22 The disc is finalised once the files have been copied across to the CD

menu.   This enables audio files, including the MP3 variety, to be transferred to a CD in standard audio CD format. Obviously this option is only available with PCs that have a CD writer, and it will only work if you have a compatible CD writer. An error message appears if the program fails to find a compatible drive. An error message is also produced if you forget to place a blank CD-R in the CD writer.

Assuming all is well, selecting this option produces a menu of the available playing lists (Figure 6.20) so that the correct one can be selected. Where appropriate, the program converts each track into a WAV file and then writes the data to the CD. An information panel shows how things are progressing (Figure 6.21). Once all the tracks have been written to the disc there will be the usual finalising process and the information panel will again keep you informed of how things are progressing (Figure 6.22). When the disc has been finalised it is ready for testing in an audio CD player.

MPEG and AVI

MPEG and AVI are the most common video formats used on the Web, and both can include sound. Most media players, including the Windows Media Player, are quite happy playing either of these formats. There can still be problems when playing these files, and it is the AVI type that tends to be most troublesome. There should be no problem with straightforward MPEG or AVI files, but some files have additional encoding in order to reduce their size. These can only be played back if the player is equipped to carry out the additional decoding. It is unlikely that the player will have this decoding built-in, and it normally requires the use of a codec (coder-decoder).

The media player may well go in search of the correct codec automatically, and with luck the file will play once it has been installed. If not, any site supplying files that require a codec should have details of where to find either players that can decode the files or codecs that will work with the Windows Media Player. The Microsoft download site has add-ons for the Media Player, and it is advisable to check that you have the latest of these. Even if you have the latest version of the Media Player it is still advisable to download the latest add-ons, since some of these are strictly add-ons and are not incorporated into the main program.

There are numerous other file types in use, such as Windows own WMA audio and WMV video file formats, although most of them seem to be little used at present. The vast majority of formats will play properly using an up to date version of the Windows Media Player.

Streaming

Streaming audio and video via the Internet is something of a growth industry. With streaming of some material there is actually a file on a server that is being downloaded and played on your PC. A large percentage of streamed material is "live" though, and you have what are effectively radio and television stations broadcasting via the Internet. The range of material on offer is vast, and it would be wrong to dismiss streaming audio and video as small players catering for niche markets. Many large broadcasting organisations now put out their programs via the Internet as well as via normal broadcasting methods. In fact some short wave stations are getting out of traditional broadcasting altogether and using alternatives such as cable networks and the Internet.

Fig.6.23 RealPlayer 8 being used to view a web TV channel

The requirements for receiving streamed material vary considerably. Being realistic about it, there is no possibility of obtaining high quality television pictures via the Internet unless you have some form of broadband access. Even with broadband access the technical quality of the material may not be very good due to the limitations at the transmitting end of the system. Any form of streaming tends to eat up bandwidth, and some Internet service providers discourage or even ban its use over their systems. With a 56k connection it is possible to obtain reasonable audio quality, but any video content will be in the form of a small picture with rather crude movement. In fact the video part of the system sometimes consists of a series of still pictures rather than something that could genuinely be described as a video picture.

Some Internet broadcasts will work quite happily with the Windows Media Player, but many use a Real format and require the RealPlayer program. This is available from the large software download sites and from Real.com. RealPlayer Basic is free, and is sufficient for most requirements. There are "all singing-all dancing" versions available as normal commercial software. With RealPlayer installed the program

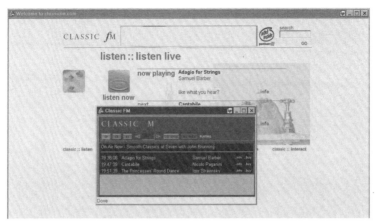

Fig.6.24 Classic FM being received via the downloaded player applet

should pop up when required and play Real Audio or Real Video data. Figure 6.23 shows RealPlayer 8 Basic in operation with Bloomberg TV (Bloomberg.co.uk). The moving pictures in the "television screen" defeated my screen dump programs, but this screen photograph gives a reasonable view of the player in action.

Special players are needed for some broadcasts, and these are normally small JavaScript programs (applets) that are downloaded automatically when you try to access the service. Figure 6.24 shows a player of this type being used with Classic FM. Any site that uses some form of streaming should be able to point you in the direction of a suitable player if something other than the Windows Media Player is required.

Stop...go

The usual problems with streaming are either intermittent operation or an error message with the player refusing to start playing the data stream at all. In both cases the problem is often a lack of bandwidth. For audio or video streaming it is essential to make sure that you have a reliable Internet connection that is as fast as possible. This was covered in detail in chapters 2 and 3 so it is not something that will be dealt with here.

The normal cause of the player refusing to start playing the data stream is that the download rate was poor when the connection to the streaming site was made. The player detects this slow rate and concludes that the

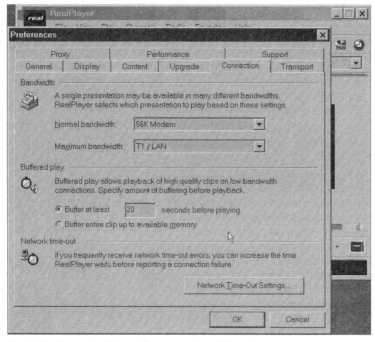

Fig.6.25 Changing the buffer size in RealPlayer 8

connection is not up to the task. If the problem is very intermittent it is likely that another attempt will be more fruitful. If the problem is severe there is little chance of obtaining satisfactory results even if a connection to the site is completed after several attempts.

Streaming is used in conjunction with buffering, which simply means that a certain amount of data is stored in the computer's memory before the player bursts into action. Usually about 10 to 30 seconds worth of data is stored in memory, and a "live" broadcast is actually delayed by this amount of time. The point of buffering is that there is some signal held in reserve if the download rate slows temporarily. The lack of data from the modem does not matter initially because the data in memory can be used to keep the player functioning normally. Of course, the data in the buffer will soon be used up if the problem persists, and there will be a break in the signal. If the slowdown is only temporary, the data in the buffer will be sufficient to smooth things over until a satisfactory download rate is restored. If the download rate is fast enough, the amount of data in the buffer will be restored to its normal level.

Where there is clearly a lack of speed the player may decide to switch to a lower data rate. This is usually sufficient to remove problems with an intermittent signal, but the audio bandwidth will be greatly reduced. This gives rather muffled sound quality with an obvious lack of high frequency content. With some systems the audio bandwidth is largely retained, but the amount of distortion increases very noticeably. Using a larger data buffer can be helpful as it enables longer slowdowns to be handled without any break in the signal. However, it means waiting longer for the player to start operating, and it will just delay the inevitable if the average download speed is simply not up to the task.

The size of the buffer used by RealPlayer when playing clips (but not "live" streaming) can be altered by selecting Preferences from the View menu, and then operating the Connection tab on the new window that appears (Figure 6.25). Using the radio buttons you can either opt to have the whole clip (memory permitting) downloaded before it is played, or a buffer size (in seconds) can be specified. It is worth checking that the setting for the normal bandwidth is correct. The usual range of modem speeds, etc., are available here.

If there are problems with distorted audio and (or) erratic video it is a good idea to left click the Performance tab and look at some of the available options (Figure 6.26). If your PC is rather sluggish in operation while RealPlayer is operating, perhaps making it difficult to control, the Playback Performance control can be moved to the left. This will not give the ultimate in performance from the player, but it should make the computer easier to use, with buttons, menus, etc., responding quickly and reliably. When using an older PC it is advisable not to have other software running at the same time as a media player. The media player will have the best chance of performing well if it is the only major software that is using up the PC's resources.

If there are problems with the audio playback try operating the Settings button in the section dealing with soundcard compatibility. Particularly with an older soundcard, it is worth switching from 16-bit to 8-bit operation by ticking the appropriate checkbox. Do not expect CD quality from 8-bit playback. On the other hand, fully working 8-bit playback is better than no playback at all or semi-operational playback. If there are problems with the picture playback try removing the tick from the checkbox in the video card compatibility section. The player program may be trying to use clever facilities of your graphics card that do not work reliably. A more simple approach to driving the video card might give slightly reduced performance but much better reliability.

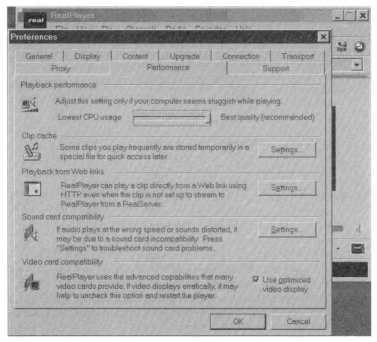

Fig.6.26 Moving the Playback performance control to the left can sometimes cure erratic performance

More buffering

The Windows Media Player can sometimes give very rough results if the Internet connection is a bit iffy. You often get rather short bursts of signal with a gap of a second or two in between each one. The default buffer length being quite short causes the problem. To set a longer buffer time select Options from the Tools menu and then operate the Performance tab in the new window that appears (Figure 6.27). Left-click the Buffer radio button and then type a new figure for the buffer time. A buffer length of about 20 seconds or so should give better results. Where the basic connection speed is not up to the task there will still be breaks in the program, but fewer and longer breaks generally give less garbled results.

While in this section of the Options window check that the connection speed is set correctly or that it is at the automatic setting. The automatic detection method is probably the best option, since this uses the actual

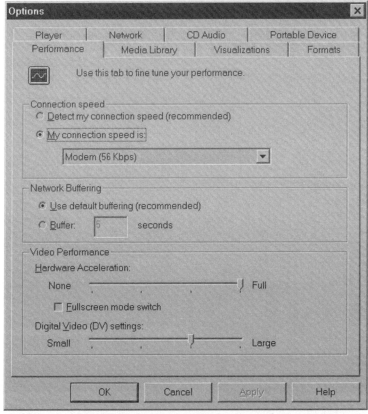

*Fig.6.27 The Perfomance options available in the Windows Media
Player include the ability to change the buffer size*

rather than theoretical connection speed to control the handling of
streamed media. Using less hardware acceleration might help problems
with erratic video. Four levels of acceleration from none to full are available
using one of the slider controls near the bottom of the window. The
optimum setting is the highest one that gives freedom from erratic
operation. When the desired changes have been made to the settings,
operate the Apply and OK buttons to make the changes take effect and
close the window.

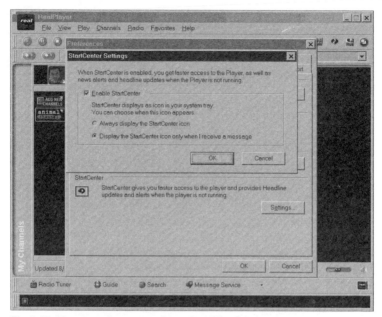

Fig.6.28 You can elect not to have RealPlayer 8 load automatically when Windows is booted

RealPlayer start-up

RealPlayer automatically loads as a background task when Windows has completed the boot process. This does not necessarily matter, but there can be compatibility problems with other software or you may simply prefer not to have it using the computer's resources. If you keep getting error messages that mention the RealPlayer program it is definitely a good idea stop it from running as a background task. It can be prevented from loading automatically by going to the Preferences window and selecting the General tab. In the StartCenter section of the window operate the Settings button (not the Settings button near the top of the window). This produces another window (Figure 6.28) where the automatic loading at start-up can be switched off by removing the tick in the checkbox.

Doing so results in the warning window of Figure 6.29 popping up. If the limitations this imposes are acceptable, and they are far from dire, operate the Yes button to close the window. Then operate the OK button to close

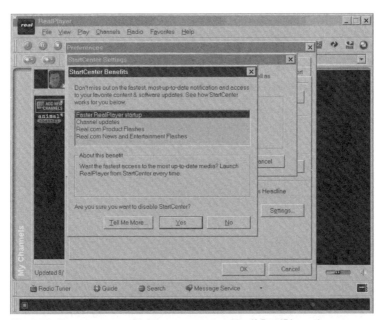

Fig.6.29 You are warned of the consequences if RealPlayer is not loaded when Windows boots

the StartCenter Settings window, and then the other OK button to close the Preferences window. The program will remain running in the background when it is closed, but it will not load automatically the next time the computer is booted.

No controls

Controls such as fast forward and rewind are sometimes present when playing a streamed signal. They are present when a file on a server is providing the streamed signal. If these controls are not present or are not functioning, it is unlikely that there is a fault with the player. The most likely explanation is that the signal is a "live" streaming type that you just have to take as it comes. Where the signal is provided by a file on a server it should be possible to save the file to disc by right clicking on the link and then using the Save Target As option from the popup menu. Of course, this is not possible with a signal that does not originate from a file. It might also be impossible with a file because the right mouse button has been deliberately disabled for that page in order to prevent material from being copied. This type of thing is annoying, but there are copyright restrictions on some web content. Incidentally, this disabling of the right mouse button can occur with images and other web content.

Which formats?

With so many media file types in use it can be difficult to know which one the Windows Media Player can handle. There is actually an easy way to find out which formats your version of the program can accommodate, and this is to select Options from the Tools menu and then operate the Formats tab of the new window that appears (Figure 6.30). This shows a menu of the available formats, and a brief description of the selected format is shown beneath the menu. Make sure that there is a tick in the checkbox for any format you wish to use.

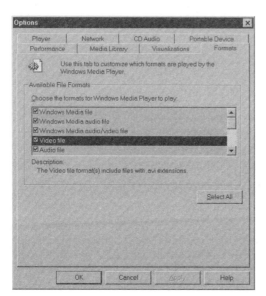

Fig.6.30 The list of compatible file formats

Statistics

With Windows Media Player it is possible to get some statistics on streaming media by selecting Statistics from the View menu. The initial window provides some basic statistics about download rates (Figure 6.31) and some further facts and figures are available if the Advanced tab is operated (Figure 6.32). These statistics are useful because they show whether or not the connection speed is adequate. If it is, the cause of any problems lies elsewhere.

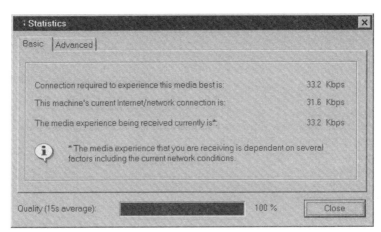

Fig.6.31 This window provides some basic download statistics

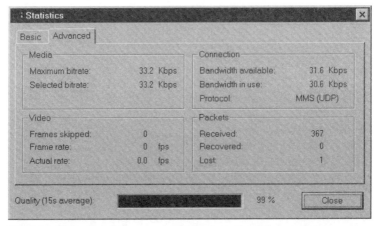

Fig.6.32 Further statistics are available from the Advanced page

Wrong player

When new software is installed on a PC it is quite usual for the new software to make itself the default program for any file types it can handle. Media player programs are certainly no exception to this, and if anything they are amongst the worst offenders. Of course, you will probably wish

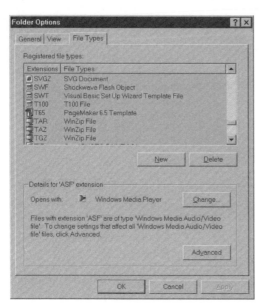

*Fig.6.33 The list of file associations in the
Folder Options window*

to use the new player for some types of file, but you may not wish to use it for all the file types that it can handle. File associations can be altered by first going to the Windows Control Panel and double clicking the Folder Options icon. Then operate the File Types tab in the window that pops up (Figure 6.33). The list shows all the registered file types, and the program associated with the selected file type is shown beneath the list.

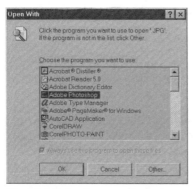

*Fig.6.34 Selecting a program to
open the selected file type*

In order to change a file association it is just a matter of selecting the file type in the list and then operating the Change button. A list of the installed programs then appears in a new window (Figure 6.34). Select the program you wish to use for the selected file type and then operate the OK button. If the program you wish to use is not in the list, left-click the Other button and then use the file browser that appears to locate the program file. This is only necessary for small stand-alone programs that do not require the usual Windows installation process. In practice it is unlikely that a media player would fall into this category.

On top

It can be handy to have a media player operating when a major piece of software is being used in full-screen mode. The problem is that the main item of software "covers" the player program as soon as you start using it and its window becomes the current one. It is easy to set the RealPlayer 8 so that it will always operate on top of other windows when it is playing. Go to the View menu and

Fig.6.35 The Player Options window

select the On Top While Playing option. To return to normal operation just select this option again.

A similar facility is available when using the Windows Media Player. Select Options from the Tools menu and then operate the Player tab of the new window that appears (Figure 6.35). In the Player Settings section there is a checkbox that can be ticked in order to make the player always appear on top of other windows when it is in compact mode. It would normally be used in this mode when operating in front of another program, since it would otherwise obscure too much of the main program window. Switch the player to the compact mode by selecting this option from the View menu. Note that, unlike RealPlayer 8, the Windows Media Player will remain on top whether or not it is playing.

Picture settings

Dark pictures that are difficult to see are a common problem when using media players. It is easy to overlook some useful controls of the Windows Media Player because they are not displayed by default. Controls for the brightness, contrast, etc., of movies can be switched

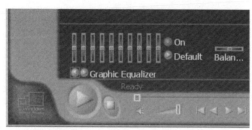

Fig.6.36 The Media Player's graphic equaliser controls

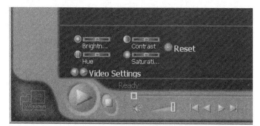

Fig.6.37 The video controls only work when a video is playing

on by going to the View menu and selecting Now Playing Tools, followed by Video Settings from the submenu. The video controls will then appear in the bottom left-hand corner of the media player's window (Figure 6.36). Note that the controls will only work while a video is playing, and not while it is paused. A graphic equaliser (Figure 6.37) is available from the submenu, and this is useful when playing audio files. A simple equaliser is also available from the View menu of RealPlayer 8. A more elaborate version is available if you upgrade to RealPlayer Plus.

Flash

Flash is a program that is used to produce animations, fancy buttons in menus, and provide interactive content in web sites. It is not restricted to web use, but this has become its primary application. There are now large numbers of web sites that use Flash animations, etc. In some cases you have the choice of using a Flash version of the site or one that is Flash free. Some browsers now have support for Flash built in or the Flash player is supplied with the browser. If you are using a modern version of windows and Internet Explorer it is unlikely that there will be any problem in using "Flashed" sites. If things simply grind to a halt when you enter a site that uses Flash animations, the most likely explanation is that your PC lacks the Flash plug-in. This can be downloaded free of charge from www.macromedia.com.

Point to remember

In order to play multimedia files a browser requires some form of plug-in, which is usually some form of player program. Some types of file, but particularly the AVI video variety, need a further plug-in to handle some of the decoding.

The chances of trouble free media playing are greatly enhanced by having the latest version of the Windows Media Player, plus all the latest add-ons for this program. These are all available from the download section of the Microsoft web site.

In order to handle a full range of media file types it is necessary to have more than one media player. As a minimum you will need the Windows Media Player and Real Player Basic.

If there is a total lack of audio when playing multimedia files, check that the soundcard is installed properly. Also check that the volume control or controls are not set at minimum. With an integrated audio system check that the audio circuits are switched on.

MIDI files do not contain digitised sounds, and they can only be played using a MIDI instrument. Virtually any PC sound system can mimic a MIDI instrument, but some sound better than others.

In order to produce a CD that can be played in an ordinary CD player you must produce an audio CD and not a data type that contains MP3 or WAV files.

Most CD-ROM burning software can produce audio discs direct from MP3 files, but with older programs the files must be converted to WAV format first. If you have the right hardware, Windows Media Player 7.x can produce audio CDs from MP3 files.

Some streamed audio and video can be handled using the Windows Media Player. In other cases it is necessary to use RealPlayer. The basic version of this program is sufficient, and it is available as a free download from Real.com and many software download sites.

An inadequate download rate is the most likely cause when streamed signals play intermittently. Adjusting the buffer size can help, but will not provide a cure if the average download speed is simply not up to the task.

Erratic operation of the Windows Media Player and RealPlayer programs can usually be corrected by altering some of the settings, such as the amount of hardware acceleration.

If the wrong player is used for a given file type, this can be corrected in the Windows file associations.

With an up to date browser and Windows installation there should be no difficulty in using "Flashed" sites. Download the Flash player from Macromedia.com if your PC grinds to a halt when confronted with a site that has Flash content.

Search
problems

Searching questions

Most web users spend a significant percentage of their time online using the services of search engines. With so many millions of pages on the Internet a conventional directory of sites is not really a realistic proposition, and it would be doing things the hard way anyway. The search method is a much more practical approach, and it is fine in theory. In practice things do not always go according to plan, and the most common problem is too many web pages that match your search string. Many years ago my sister enquired if the Internet would provide any information about the Metropolitan Opera House in New York. A quick search using a popular search engine produced about 140,000 matches! To see how things have progressed I tried the same thing again recently, and the number of matches had risen to well over 300,000! These days it is easy to end up with over a million matches.

A plethora of matches is not the only problem. Although information overload is a more common problem than a lack of matches, some searches do produce completely blank results from the search engine. Probably the most frustrating problem is when the search engine comes up with one or two pages that appear to be ideal, but when you try to load them they have disappeared without trace or the subject matter has changed. In this chapter we will look at possible ways of dealing with all these problems.

The right one

One of the most common mistakes when searching the Web is to assume that all search engines are much the same. They all trawl the Internet to produce a database of its content, and it would seem reasonable to assume that they would all produce much the same results. Using the

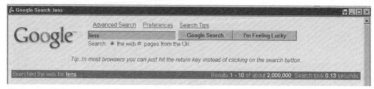

Fig.7.1 Using a single search word will often produce a huge number of matches

same search criteria with a selection of search engines would soon show that this is not actually true, and substantially different results would almost certainly be obtained. Each search engine has its own methods of searching the Internet for pages to include in the database, and they do not always have the same aims. If you require information on a company or product, Yahoo.com is a good place to start. It is less good if you are looking for information stored on a small and obscure web site, because that is not its primary function. A site like Excite.com or Lycos.com is a better choice for that type of thing.

You really need to try a range of search engines to see which one gives the best results with the type of information you normally require. If you need to search for two or three totally different types of information it may be best to use a different search engine for each type. Searching the Internet is certainly something where experience is a decided asset.

More is less

Many users of search engines make the mistake of thinking that adding more words into the search string helps the search engine to narrow things down and give fewer matches. Unfortunately, this is not necessarily what happens if you just type in the words with spaces in between. It does actually work with some search engines, and www.google.co.uk is one example where it will give the desired result. Figure 7.1 shows the result of searching for the word "lens", and it has produced so many matches that a precise figure is not given. The number is simply estimated at about 2,000,000.

Suppose that it is tests of camera lenses that are required. Adding extra words into the search string should narrow the search down. Figure 7.2 shows the result of using "camera lens tests" as the search string, and this has reduced the number of matches to a slightly more manageable 38,300.

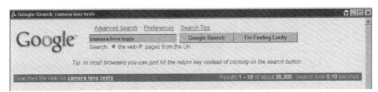

Fig.7.2 Using the Google.co.uk search engine, adding more words has gretly reduced the number of matches

The number of matches is still very high, but defining the search more precisely can reduce the number still further. Suppose that it is only Canon lenses that are of interest, and that it is only the auto-focus lenses and not the manual focus types that are of interest. Canon uses the EOS brand name for their auto-focus lenses, so adding this into the search string should remove many of the matches that are of no use. As can be seen from Figure 7.3, this has reduced the number of matches to a mere 1480!

The search could be defined even more accurately by adding in more words. If only zoom lenses were of interest, the word "zoom" could be added to the search string. However, it is not realistic to expect the

Fig.7.3 Adding more words gives a further reduction. There are now just 1480 matches!

search to produce just one or two web pages that are ideal for your purposes. This may sometimes happen, but in many cases there are a large number of pages covering the topic of interest. Rather than spending time trying to get the number of matches down to a very low number you might be better off looking through some of the pages for the information you require.

Fig.7.4 Some 51,000 or so matches have been produced

More is more

With many search engines adding more words into the search string does not reduce the number of matches, but actually has the opposite effect. Figure 7.4 shows the result of using "lens" as the search string at the Excite.com search engine, while Figure 7.5 shows the result of adding "camera" and "test" to the string. A not inconsiderable 51,000 or so matches in the first search have grown to over 1.3 million in the second! So what has gone wrong?   The Google search engine looks for pages that contain all the words you supply, but most search sites do not operate on this basis. Instead, any page that contains one of the words you supply will be considered a valid match. Hence the more words you supply in the search string, the greater the number of matches produced.

In order to define things more accurately with most search engines you must add either a plus sign (+) or the word "AND" ahead of each word. This tells the search program that it must look for pages that contain all the words and not just one of them. Repeating the search with the plus signs added reduces the number of matches to just 715 (Figure 7.6).

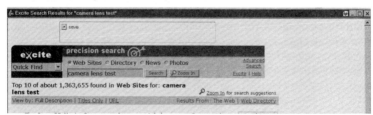

Fig.7.5 Adding more words has vastly increased the number of matches

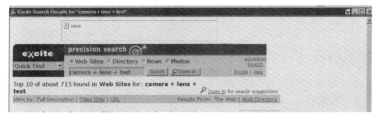

Fig.7.6 Adding the plus signs has had the desired effect

Omitting the plus signs is a common mistake, and many users end up using single word search strings in an attempt to keep the number of matches within reason. Using several words and the plus signs is clearly a much more effective way of searching the Internet. The number of matches is kept within reason and you tend to home in on a higher percentage of relevant sites.

Less is less

There is another useful trick that can help to remove matches that are of no real use. Suppose that in the lens test example you are only interested in sites that provide test results, but most of the sites suggested by the search engine have titles like "How to Test Your Camera Lens" and do not provide any lens tests. It is difficult to remove this type of site from the results by using more search words, since words in this type of site are likely to crop up in the sites of interest as well. The alternative method is to give the search program a word or words that can be used to eliminate pages from the results. In this case the word "how" could be used as the filter, with any page containing this word being removed from the list of matches.

A minus sign (-) or sometimes the word "NOT" is used in front of a word to indicate to the search engine that you are looking for pages that do not contain that word. Figure 7.7 shows the result of the lens test search using this refinement, and the number of matches has now been reduced to a very much more manageable figure of about 190. Obviously this method does risk filtering out relevant pages that just happen to have the word you are avoiding. This method is especially risky with a general word such as "how", which can occur in just about any page about any subject. If you can find a suitable word or words it is a method that will often provide good results. In this example there were probably a substantial number of relevant pages that were eliminated from the search

Fig.7.7 Using a minus sign has reduced the number of matches still further

result, but there were still plenty of pages remaining. Also, these pages contained a high percentage that was relevant, rather than just the odd page here and there that was of interest.

Advanced

Most search engines have a range of advanced options to help reduce the number of irrelevant pages still further. If you are only interested in UK sites and companies it is a good idea to go to the UK version of the search engine. Most of the large search companies have a general or US site with a .com address, plus other sites for specific countries. One of these is usually a UK web site having a .co.uk address. Fig.7.8 shows a menu available at the Excite.co.uk site, and this enables the search to

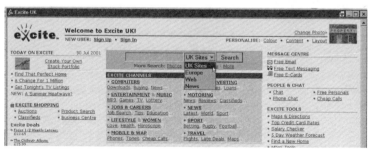

Fig.7.8 Excite.co.uk enables the search to be restricted to UK, European, or news sites

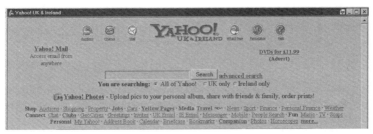

Fig.7.9   The UK version of the Yahoo site also enables restrictions to be placed on the search

be restricted to the UK, Europe, or to news sites. Of course, a full search of the Web is available as well. The UK version of the Yahoo site offers similar facilities (Figure 7.9). The radio buttons enable the search to be restricted to the UK or Ireland, or the whole of Yahoo can be searched.

If you are looking for (say) a shop in the UK that sells motorcycle spare parts, by restricting the search to the UK it is possible to immediately

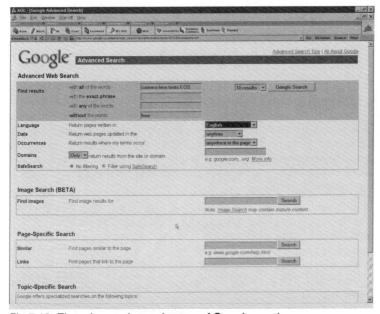

Fig.7.10 The advanced search page of Google.co.uk

filter out a vast number of sites that will be of no interest to you. The difference made by this type of filtering is usually vast. The number of matches will usually be reduced by well over 90 percent.

Some sites have a button that is operated in order to go into a special page that handles advanced searching. Figure 7.10 shows the advanced search facilities of the Google.co.uk search engine. Amongst other things this enables a search to be made for specified words, pages containing certain words to be filtered, and pages not in the specified language to be filtered.

Quotation marks

One of the most powerful facilities when using a search engine is to place the search string, or part of it, in quotation marks. A match will only be produced if the exact string of characters used within the quotation marks is found on a web page. Although this method normally works very well, you have to be careful when deciding on the search string. Searches are not normally case sensitive. A search string such as "babani + books" will produce a match with "Babani" and "Books" for example. Consequently, there is no need to worry about capitalising the first letter of a name, since a match will be produced either way. There can be a slight advantage in doing so when using some search engines, as this could result in the more relevant matches being presented in the first dozen or so matches rather than at somewhere around 8000 to 9000.

The situation is different when using double quotation marks, and the search string must precisely match the way that the string will appear on web pages. A search string like "babani books" will not match with "Babani Books" or "Babani books". This does make life a little difficult, because not everyone agrees about the way capital letters should be used. When searching for information on the well-known BBC music program you could use the search string "Top of the Pops".

This is the type of thing where the use of double quotation marks is usually very effective. The words "top", "of", "the" and "pops" could well turn up on every web page about pop music. The exact string "Top of the Pops" on the other hand, is unlikely to appear on any page that is not specifically mentioning the television program. However, if the person composing a web page decides to call the program "Top Of The Pops", "TOP OF THE POPS", or the trendy "top of the pops", you will not obtain a match.

Where there is a major problem with an excessive number of matches even after the usual multiword approaches have been tried, the use of double quotation marks to provide exact matching of a phrase will usually provide an answer. Be prepared to try a few variations on the phrase though, especially if the initial attempt produces few matches or none at all. Remember that it is possible to use an exact phrase match in conjunction with normal search words or other phrases. Supposing you were looking for information about Cliff Richard's appearances on Top of the Pops. Both of these search strings would be valid:

"Top of the Pops" + Cliff + Richard

"Top of the Pops" + "Cliff Richard"

On the face of it the second of these search strings is the better option, but the first is actually the more versatile in that it would catch any references that simply referred to Mr. Richard as "Cliff". Probably the most important thing when searching is to think things over before starting the search. With a careful choice of the search string you should soon home in on something useful.

Wildcards

Sometimes there can be search problems due to different spellings being used for the same thing or the same person. For example, names in Russian and many other languages are given their western spellings by converting them phonetically. In other words, the spelling is one that reflects the sound of the original name. The problem with this method is that the same name can be converted in two or more different ways, giving rise to alternative spellings for the same name. The Russian composer Tchaikovsky is also known in the west as Tchaikowsky for example. There can also be difficulties due to differences between American English and what for the lack of a better term we will call English English. For example, looking for the "XYZ Centre" will not produce a match for the "XYZ Center".

Some search engines allow the use of wildcards, and these will often permit a single search to accommodate two different spellings. Yahoo.com permits the asterisk (*) to be used as a wildcard. A match will then be produced with any letter at that position in the word. For example, "Tchaiko*sky" will match both "Tchaikovsky" and "Tchaikowsky", and "Cent**" will match both "Centre" and "Center".

Too much

Even with careful selection of the search string you may find that the search engines tend to produce large numbers of matches. There is no getting away from the fact that the Web contains massive amounts of information, with more pages being added every day. Particularly if you are searching for information on a popular subject, there could be many thousands of pages that are relevant to your search criteria. It could be that most of these contain the information you require, but it is likely that many will barely touch on your subject of interest.

The search engines try to rate pages in order of likely interest, and often provide each one with a score that indicates its likely relevance to your search criteria. Some advocate looking only at the first few pages of matches, and then trying again with a new search strategy if useful results are not obtained. I have often found it useful to dive into the middle of the list, or even have a look at matches near the bottom of the list that have very lowly scores. The search engines are based on some very clever programming techniques, but they can not mind-read. The search engine's rating system might have totally misjudged the type of thing you are after. There might just be some useful pages listed in the middle or even at the bottom of the list.

Missing links

A common mistake when looking through pages suggested by a search engine is to look only at the main content and ignore everything else. If a site covers the right subject area but does not have the exact information you require, it could still be useful. Many sites have some form of bulletin board facility where users can post information and ask questions. If the information you require is proving elusive it might be worthwhile posting a question to see if anyone can come up with the right answers. Requests for information often result in someone providing either the required information or a site that tells you what you need to know.

The most important thing to look for on "near miss" sites is a list of links to similar sites. Web sites often contain links to other sites of a similar nature, usually with a brief description of each one. These sites in turn will probably have links to yet more sites of possible interest. Having found a "near miss" site the best tactic is probably to follow the links from site to site, rather than going back to the search engine's list of pages, most of which are probably irrelevant.

Blank results

As already pointed out, the usual problem when searching the Internet is too many matches rather than too few. You will not always find a plethora of matches though. This is something where you have to be realistic in your expectations. Although there is a massive amount of information available on the Internet, there is no guarantee that you will always be able to locate the information you require. The more obscure the subject, the lower the chances of success. If you draw a blank using one search engine, try another or even several more if necessary. I sometimes have to search for technical information about computing and electronics. It is quite normal for the first, one, two, or even three search engines to produce nothing useful, before I finally "come up trumps".

A complete lack of response is often due to a spelling error. Remember that only an exact match will do when using double quotation marks. In a similar vein, if you are looking for pages that contain all the specified search words, a spelling error in one of the words will be sufficient to prevent any matches from being obtained. Particularly when dealing with names, double check that you are spelling everything correctly. The same applies if you obtain numerous matches that are nothing to do with the subject matter you are seeking, or a lot of the sites are in a foreign language. The misspelled word might not mean anything in English, but it could be quite common in German or Polish.

Shortcut

Many people make the mistake of using search engines when there is no real need to do so. If there is an obvious source of information always try that source first. For example, suppose you required some information on a Channel 4 program. You could use a search engine to find sites that cover that program, and you would probably find what you need before too long. On the other hand, you could simply go to the Channel 4 web site and look for information there. There is a good chance of finding the information you require straight away, or failing that you may find a useful link to another site. Try the obvious sites first and only resort to a search engine if it is really necessary to do so.

Search anyway

Very occasionally the opposite approach can be useful. Suppose you know the correct web address but you are not getting through to the site. Trying to access the site by first locating it using a search engine and then using the search engine's link is sometimes successful. One reason this will sometimes work is that the web site has moved, and the search engine is linking to the new address. Most web sites have a message on the old web site giving directions to the new one, or simply use some form of automatic redirection. Not all relocated sites have these facilities though, and they are unlikely to be maintained for long once a site has moved. Another reason that this method can work is that it takes you to the site via a different route. This route might bypass a blockage that is troubling the one direct to the site.

Missing pages

One of the most frustrating search problems is when you locate what looks like a very promising page using a search engine, but linking to that page produces some sort of error message rather than the page. There is a similar problem where the page appears, but it does not seem to have anything to do with the subject you are researching. When searching the Internet it is useful to bear in mind the general way in which the search engines function. Many seem to believe that the Web is scanned for suitable matches each time a search is made. However, this approach would take far too long. Instead, the search engines scan the Web and place so-called "snapshots" of each page into a huge database. Each time a search is carried out it is the pages in this database that are scanned and not the real thing on the Internet.

This method enables a massive number of pages to be searched in a few seconds, but it is "second-hand" data that is being scanned. Web pages are deleted or altered from time to time, and this can produce discrepancies between the content of the database and the actual pages available on the Internet. An error message could indicate that the page has been deleted, or it could just be that the server has gone down. It could also be due to a problem on the route between your computer and the target web site. Try operating the browser's Refresh button, and repeat this once or twice if necessary. If the page still fails to load, make a note of the web address and try again later.

Where a page has been changed or deleted it might be possible to obtain some of the information it contained. As pointed out previously, search

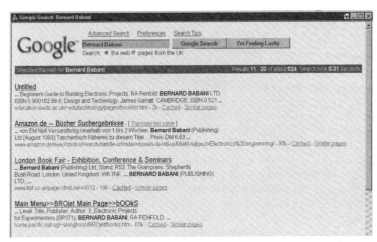

Fig.7.11 The cached link leads to a snapshot of the page, which should include all or most of the text

engines store a snapshot of each page, and in some cases it is possible to download this abbreviated version of the page. Figure 7.11 shows a section of some search results obtained using the Coogle.co.uk search engine, and for most of the entries there is a Cached option. Selecting this option results in the snapshot of the page being displayed and not the page at the actual web site. Figure 7.12 shows the "real thing", while Figure 7.13 shows the cached version of the same page. In general, the text from the original page will be totally or largely intact in the cached version, but any major graphic content is almost certain to be omitted as it is of no help when conducting searches.

Another useful ploy is to try using a shortened version of the web address provided by the search engine. Suppose that the address is:

www.thebestcamerawebsite.com/cameras/lenses/autofocus/tests

Even if this page no longer exists, the web site that used to contain it is still likely to be in business, and it might still contain useful information. One approach is to go to the home page web address, which is "www.thebestcamerasite.com" in this example. From here you might be able to follow links that lead to something useful, either on this site or another one. An alternative approach is to try the address with the last section removed, which means leaving out the "/tests" in this example. If this is not successful, remove another section, which would be "/autofocus" in this case. Once you are into the site, look for links that

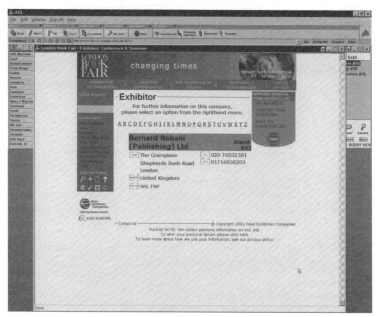

Fig.7.12 This is the real web page

will take you to something useful. These methods will not work in every case, but they often produce something helpful.

Turbo search

If you need to search regularly for hard to find information on the Web it can be very time consuming going from one search engine to another trying to find elusive snippets of information. There is a solution to the problem in the form of software that takes the provided search criteria and then uses it to search for results on a number of search engines. It then shows the consolidated results. The results do not pop up almost instantly in the same way that they do when utilising a single search engine, but the process is still very much faster than manual approach.

Web Ferret is one of the best known programs of this type, and there is a trial version that can be obtained from the larger software download sites. Figure 7.14 shows the main window where the search string is entered. The usual options are available here, such as searching for

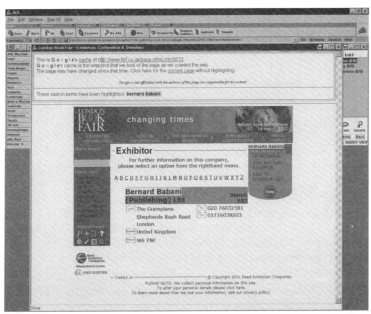

Fig.7.13 In this case the cached version of the page looks much like the original

matches for any keyword or all the keywords. Operating the Advanced tab provides further options (Figure 7.15). It is advisable to use the one that removes duplicate URLs.

Multiple matches for pages is a common problem when using search engines. It occurs where there are several places in a page that provide

Fig.7.14 The main window of the Web Ferret program

Fig.7.15 Further options are available under the Advanced tab

a match for the search criteria. Most search engines list a match for each occurrence of the search string in a page, and this is one of the reasons that so many matches are usually produced. When using software that provides the search by way of several search engines the problem is multiplied. Having duplicated URLs filtered out helps to keep things manageable.

Once everything has been set up correctly the Find Now button is operated and the searching begins. The window enlarges so that the results can be displayed (Figure 7.16). There is also the option of having

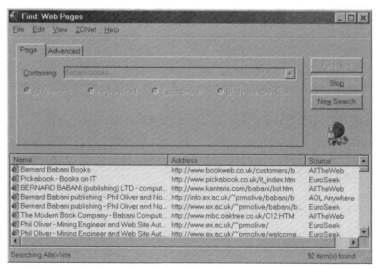

Fig.7.16 Web Ferret displaying a set of results

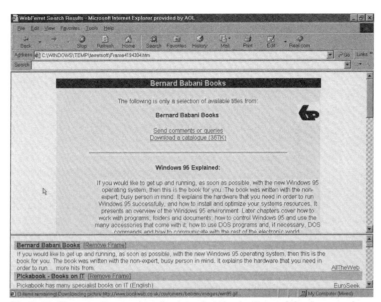

*Fig.7.17 The results can be displayed at the bottom of the browser's
window if preferred*

the results displayed in the lower section of the browser's window, as in
Figure 7.17. The main window is used to show the web pages selected
from the list of matches. If a large number of matches are being produced
or the search is taking a long time, operating the Stop button brings the
process to a halt.

Programs such as Web Ferret are very impressive in use, and are of real
benefit if you mostly search for obscure information that is normally time
consuming to track down. These programs are not really of much use
when searching for material that is on the Web in abundance. Using one
search engine will usually provide masses of matches, which usually
makes it pointless to use several search engines at once. You simply
multiply the information overload problem.

Red-faced matches

Most search engines will happily track down whatever material is required,
including pages that are pornographic, or sexual in nature. Unfortunately,
even quite innocent search strings can sometimes produce matches
with sites that have a strong sexual content. When searching for web

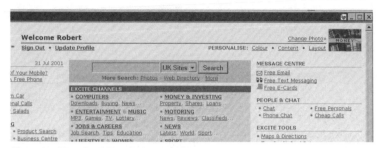

Fig.7.18 Use the More link to obtain moresearch options

sites supporting the Flash 5 graphics program I was not surprised that some of the matches were for sites having photographs of streakers in action. It was more surprising when a search for information on a graphics tablet called a Pen Partner produced a number of matches for pages giving details of a sex aid!

This can all be a bit unfortunate if you are showing your grandmother or the vicar's wife how to search the Web, and search for cheesecake recipes provides matches with some hardcore pornography sites. However, it is a problem that is easily avoided, since most search engines have a facility that tries to filter out matches with pages that have a strong sexual content. With the Excite.co.uk site for example, the word "More" under the Search button (Figure 7.18) is a link to a page where further search options are available. Two radio buttons (Figure 7.19) enable adult filtering to be

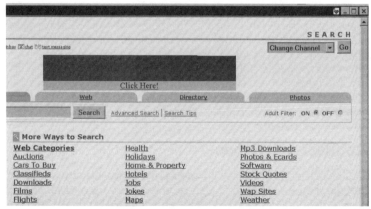

Fig.7.19 Adult filtering can be switched on and off using the buttons

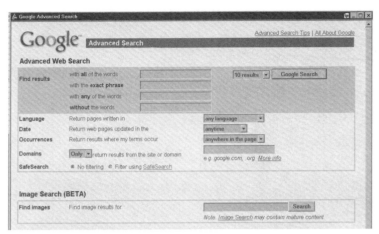

Fig.7.20 Google.co.uk also has the option of using adult filtering

switched on and off. There is a similar facility in the upper section of the Google.co.uk Advanced Search page (Figure 7.20), where radio buttons permit the SafeSearch adult filtering system to be turned on and off. If you look for similar facilities at any of the major search engines you will almost certainly find them.

It is only fair to point out that no adult filtering system can be guaranteed to be 100 percent effective, but a system of this type should filter the vast majority of potentially embarrassing search results. There is also a slight risk that this type of filtering will remove useful links. These systems operate by looking for "naughty" words in the scanned pages, and in some cases a page will be filtered if it contains a word that in turn contains a "naughty" word, even if the whole word is totally inoffensive. However, the number of matches removed in this way should be extremely small.

Easy searching

If you have real difficulty getting to grips with AND, NOT, etc., and nearly always end up with huge numbers of irrelevant matches, try using one of the modern search engines that try to make things easier. One of the best known of these is AskJeeves.co.uk, and this is the one that will be used for this example. I recently needed to know what a purchase order is. This is a good example of the type of thing that can be difficult to find using a normal search engine even if you are pretty expert at these things. The individual words "purchase" and "order" are likely to appear in a

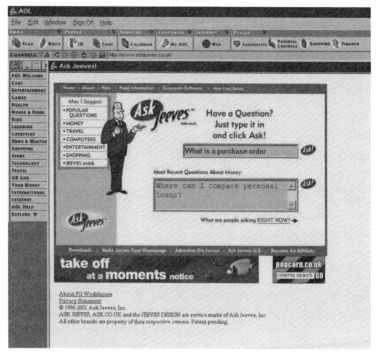

Fig.7.21 AskJeeves.co.uk uses natural language technology

vast number of web pages. Putting them together within double quotation marks reduces the number of matches, but tends to give numerous results about accounting software that are of no help at all.

With a natural language search engine such as AskJeeves.co.uk you simply type in a question as if you were asking a person for help. In this example I simply asked, "What is a purchase order" (Figure 7.21). The search engine looks at the phrase that you have typed in an attempt to find keywords that will help it to understand what you require. In most cases it will find more than one line of enquiry, and it will then give a list of alternatives in an attempt to narrow down the search. The initial result of this search is shown in Figure 7.22, and one of the things on offer is a definition of the financial term "purchase order". This is clearly what is required, and it linked to the definition I was seeking (Figure 7.23). There is no guarantee that this sort of instant result will always be produced, but a search engine of this type is well worth trying.

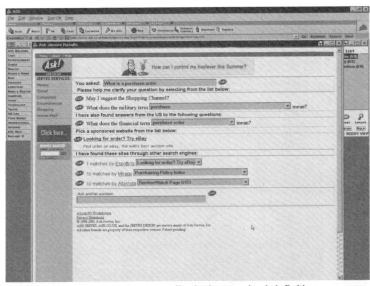

Fig.7.22 One of the options on offer is the required definition

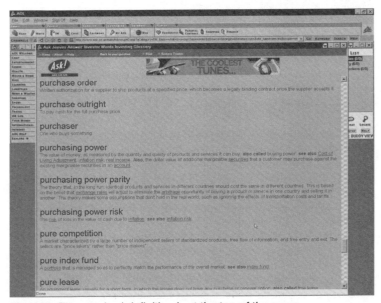

Fig.7.23 The required definition is at the top of the page

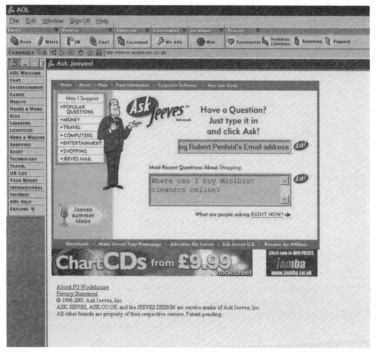

Fig.7.24 Using AskJeeves.co.uk to search for an Email address

Specialised searches

Going to a general search engine and typing in a few likely search words
is not always the best way of going about things. There are specialist
sites that deal with popular types of searches, and special facilities at
some of the main search engines that deal with this type of thing. One
obvious subject of this type is software. There are numerous sites that
deal specifically with software downloads, such as Download.com. As
explained in chapter two, there are even sites that deal specifically with
the search for software drivers. When you require a software download
it makes sense to try one of the specialist sites first. You will probably
find what you are after fairly rapidly, but you can always try a general
search if the software sites do not locate something suitable.

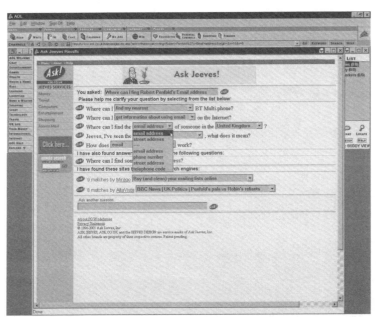

Fig.7.25 One of the options enables you to search for an Email address

People

Finding people is another specialist area where the general search method might not work very well. It works well if you are looking for information about someone who is even slightly famous (or infamous). There is bound to be some information about them on the world's web sites, and any good search engine should find those sites for you. It works less well when you are looking for a long lost relative, friend, or colleague. The search should find them provided they have a web site, which will presumably include their name. It will also find some information about them if their name appears on other web sites for some reason. With most people though, this method will not provide anything useful.

One way of searching for people is to go to the AskJeeves.co.uk site and type in a question along the lines "How do I find soandso's Email address?" (Figure 7.24). You will then be presented with a selection of questions to ask (Figure 7.25), and in this case we require the one that

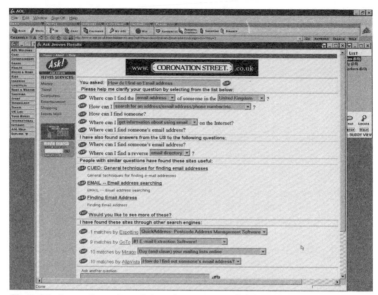

Fig.7.26 A number of useful options are available here

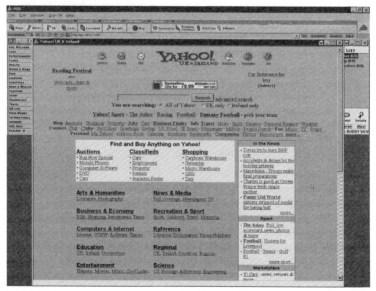

Fig.7.27 Yahoo.co.uk offers a People Search function

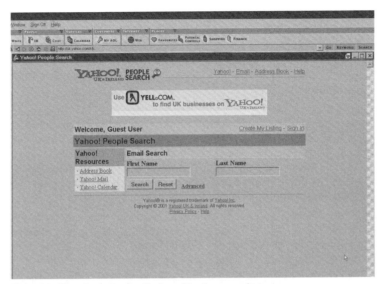

Fig.7.28 Simply enter the first and last names here

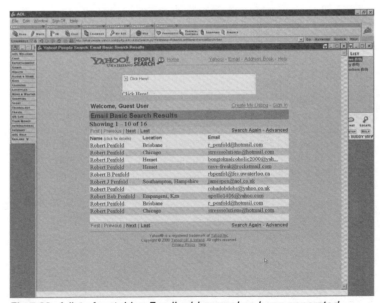

Fig.7.29 A list of matching Email addresses has been generated

enables a search to be made for the Email address of someone in the UK.   Note though, that the drop-down menu gives alternatives to searching for an Email address, such as looking for a street address or a telephone number.   Similarly, via another menu you can search for someone outside the UK.

An alternative approach with the AskJeeves web site is to ask a general question about finding an Email address, such as "How can I find someone?" This should produce a page something like the one in Figure 7.26.   One of the options is the same as before, but there are others that provide more information about the techniques that can be used to locate someone.   It also gives an option that helps you to find a reverse Email directory.   With a directory of this type you provide an Email address and it tries to find the name of the address's owner.

The Yahoo search engine includes a useful facility for locating people. Go to the home page at Yahoo.co.uk (Figure 7.27) and in amongst the numerous links you will find one called "People Search".   Left clicking on this link brings up the page shown in Figure 7.28.   Here you simply enter the first and last names into the textboxes and operate the Search button.   With luck this will produce a list of Email addresses (Figure 7.29) that includes the one for the person you are trying to locate.   Of course, if the person you seek has a very common name the list could be quite long.   It is actually easier to find someone with an unusual name, because you will only have one or two matches to check out.

Multimedia

There are plenty of other specialist search sites and facilities available. The MP3 sites such as MP3.com are probably the best known of these, and virtually all the large search engines have facilities for tracking down MP3 files.   Left clicking on the MP3 link of the Excite.co.uk site produces the page of Figure 7.30.   Here you can use the directory approach by first picking a category such as Pop, and then a subcategory such as 1960's pop, and so on until you find what you are looking for or run out of avenues to pursue.

Alternatively, a search string can be typed into the text box and the search facility should soon find something suitable, if it exists.   In an attempt to find Tchaikovsky's latest hits I typed "Tchaikovsky" into the textbox and received the results shown in Figure 7.31.   When searching for MP3 files you are spoilt for choice.   There are huge numbers of MP3 files and plenty of search engines to help you find them.   If a suitable file exists on the Internet you should be able to find it.

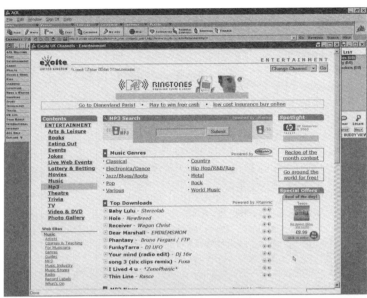

Fig.7.30   Using Excite.co.uk to search for MP3 files

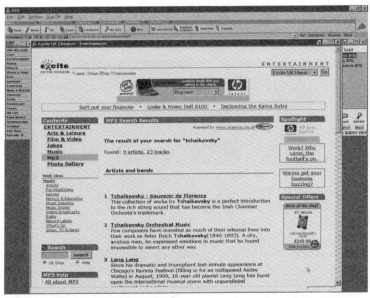

Fig.7.31   The results of the search

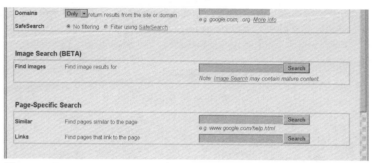

Fig.7.32 The advanced search facilities of Google.co.uk can be used to search for images

Images can be more difficult. A search engine should find information about any reasonably well known place or a person, but you may have to search through dozens of pages before you find a suitable photograph. There are online picture agencies, specialist sites for tracking down images and image search facilities at some of the large search engines.

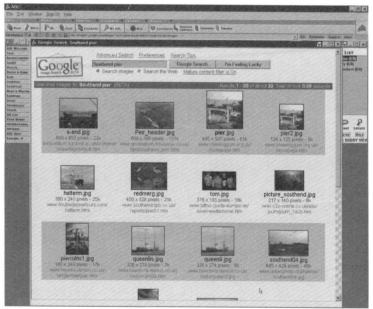

Fig.7.33 The search has provided some pictures of Southend Pier

Figure 7.32 shows part of the advanced search page of the Google.co.uk site, and this includes a section for image searches. The number of images available on the Web must be pretty staggering, and you will normally be able to find something suitable when a picture of a person, place, or an animal is required. Using Southend Pier as the search string the results shown in Figure 7.33 were produced, and these do indeed include pictures of the world's longest pleasure pier.

Cut off retreat

When using search engines you are quite likely to use links to other pages or even other sites when visiting some of the pages produced by a search. It is easy to end up well away from the listing at the search engine, which makes it time consuming to keep operating the Back button until you get back to the page with the search results. Also, some sites disable the Back button, presumably in an attempt to keep you at their web site. This blocks you from retracing your steps back to the search results. You then have to go back to the search engine and do the search again.

An easy solution to the problem is to right-click rather than left-click on links in the search page. This produces a popup menu like the one in Figure 7.34, and the Open in New Window option should be selected.

The result will probably look much the same as if the link had been left- clicked (Figure 7.35), but the new page will be in a new window. To prove this point the new window can be pulled out of the way to reveal the previous page (Figure 7.36). The point of the method is that you can go from one page to another for as long as you wish,

Fig.7.34 Right-click on the link and choose Open in New Window

but to instantly return to the search results it is merely necessary to close or minimise the second window. Also, if the back button is disabled you can still go straight back to the search results using this method.

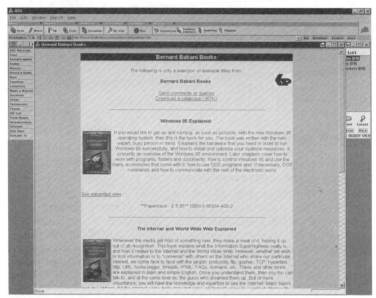

Fig.7.35 The new page seems to have opened in the normal way

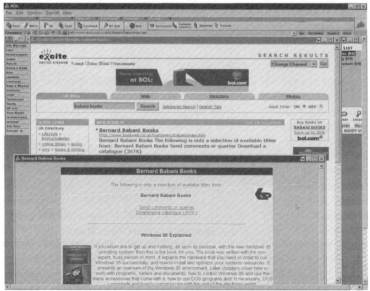

Fig.7.36 The original page is still there, ready and waiting

Points to remember

Search engines are not all the same, so try several different ones to see which engines are best at finding the types of information that you require. Results might be best using a different search engine for each type of information you require.

With most search engines it is essential to use AND (or +) in order to get the number of matches within reason. NOT (or -) can also be very useful in removing matches with pages that are actually irrelevant to your searches.

Try to use a number of words in the search string in order to focus the search as tightly as possible. Using one or two words and then wading through thousands of matches is not the way to obtain quick results.

Placing a phrase in double quotes is a powerful weapon in getting the number of matches down to a reasonable figure. However, bear in mind that the search usually becomes case sensitive when it is dealing with anything in double quotation marks. Unless you are careful the number of matches will be reduced to zero!

If you are directed to a page that is not quite what you are looking for, take a quick look around the site to see if there is anything more useful. There might also be links to other sites containing useful information.

Some search engines have a facility to look for sites that are similar sites found in the initial search. Using this facility might produce a list containing number of useful sites.

Where a complete blank is drawn, check that you are spelling all the search words correctly. Be especially careful when using phrases in double quotation marks. The web covers a vast range of subjects, but there are inevitably some subjects where there is little or no worthwhile information.

Where the first dozen or so pages suggested by the search engine are of no use, try jumping well down into the pages on offer to see if this produces better results. Search engines try to present you with the most useful pages at the top of the list, but they can get things wrong.

It would be a mistake to regard some of the more modern search engines as gimmicky. They are especially useful for those who find it difficult to master conventional search procedures. Even experienced users might find some types of search easier and quicker using a site such as AskJeeves.co.uk.

If the link to a page fails, operate the refresh button once or twice to make sure it is genuinely unavailable. Trying again later sometimes brings results. Where a page has been changed or deleted you may be able to glean some useful information from a cached version of the page if the search engine has one available.

In cases where the exact page you require has definitely been deleted, the site that contained the page may still contain some useful information or links to other sites that have the information you require.

A specialist search engine or a dedicated facility at a general search engine is usually the best way of finding people via the Internet. In fact specialist search engines and facilities represent the best way of finding software downloads, MP3 music files, song lyrics, images, and all sorts of things.

Security matters

What is a virus?

If you were to design a system that would make it easy for viruses and other computer "nasties" to spread as quickly and efficiently as possible, you would probably end up with something very similar to the Internet. Computer viruses can be spread in other ways, and it is important not to overlook this fact, but the Internet has become synonymous with computer viruses. There is actually a variety of program types that can attack a computer system and damage files on any accessible disc drive. These tend to be lumped together under the term "virus", but strictly speaking a virus is a parasitic program that can reproduce itself and spread across a system, or from one system to another.

A virus attaches itself to other programs, but it is not immediately apparent to the user that anything has happened. A virus can be benign, but usually it starts to do serious damage at some stage, and will often infect the boot sector of the hard disc, rendering the system unbootable. It can also affect the FAT (file allocation table) of a disc so that the computer can not find some of the files stored on the disc. The partition table can also be affected, so that the reported size of a disc does not match up with its true capacity. The disc might even be rendered totally inaccessible. The less subtle viruses take more direct action such as attempting to erase or overwrite everything on the hard disc, or erasing the system files while flashing an abusive message on the screen.

A virus can be spread from one computer to another via an infected file, which can enter the second computer via a disc, a modem, or over a network, which includes the Internet. In fact any means of transferring a file from one computer to another is a potential route for spreading viruses. A program is really only a virus if it attaches itself to other programs and replicates itself. A program is not a virus if it is put forward as a useful applications program but it actually starts damaging the system when it is run. This type of program is more correctly called a "Trojan Horse" or just a "Trojan". Either way, these programs can cause immense damage to the files on the disc, but there should be no risk of any hardware damage occurring.

Virus protection

This is a case where the old adage of "prevention is better than cure" certainly applies. There is probably a cure for every computer virus, but identifying and eradicating a viruses can take a great deal of time. Also, having removed the virus there is no guarantee that your all your files will still be intact. In fact there is a very good chance that some damage will have been done. In a worst case scenario there may be no choice but to reformat the hard disc and reinstall the operating system and all the applications software. This chapter deals with methods of recovering from a virus attack, but no excuse is made for also dealing with ways of avoiding infections in the first place. Everyone using the Internet needs to take precautions against viruses.

The ideal approach is to avoid doing anything that could introduce a virus into the system, but for most users this is not a practical proposition. These days computing is increasingly about communications between PCs and any swapping of data between PCs provides a route for the spread of viruses. It used to be said that PC viruses could only be spread via discs that contained programs, and that data discs posed no major threat. It is in fact possible for a virus to infect a PC from a data disc, but only if the disc is left in the drive and the computer tries to boot from it at switch-on.

These days there is another method for viruses to spread from data discs, and this is via macros contained within the data files. This type of virus can be spread via discs or via the Internet in data rather than program files. Obviously not all applications software supports macros, but it is as well to regard data discs and any downloaded files as potential virus carriers. Some of the most widespread and harmful viruses in recent times have been propagated via Emails containing macros infected with a virus. The "Lovebug" and "Kournikova" viruses are just two well-publicised examples of these macro viruses.

This is certainly a problem that needs to be taken very seriously. The rate at which some of these viruses spread was surprising, and was made possible by the automation features in some Internet software. Having invaded one PC, the Email then sent itself to every address in the computer's Email address book.

Given that it is not practical for most users to avoid any possible contact with computer viruses, the alternative is to rely on anti-virus software to deal with any viruses that do come along. Ideally one of the "big name" anti-virus programs should be installed on the system and it should

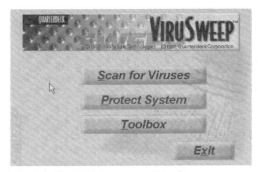

Fig.8.1 The initial screen of ViruSweep

then be kept up to date. This should ensure that any infected disc is soon spotted and dealt with, and that infected files on the Internet are

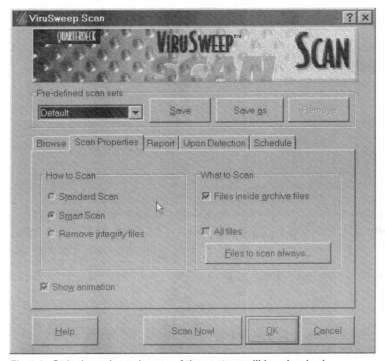

Fig.8.2 Only the selected parts of the system will be checked

Fig.8.3 This screen is used to select the type of scan that will be performed

kept at bay. Software of this type is designed for use before any problems occur, and it normally runs in the background, checking any potential sources of infection as they appear. There is usually a direct mode as well, which enables discs, memory, etc., to be checked for viruses.

Figure 8.1 shows the start up screen for the Quarterdeck ViruSweep program, and selecting the "Scan For Viruses" option takes the user into further screens that permit various options to be selected. The first screen (Figure 8.2) permits the user to select the parts of the system that will be checked. Viruses can exist in memory as well as in disc files, so checking the memory is normally an option. Further screens enable the type of scan to be selected (Figure 8.3), and the action to be taken if a virus is detected (Figure 8.4). Most anti-virus software has the option of removing a virus rather than simply indicating that it has been detected. Note though, that in some cases it might not be possible to automatically

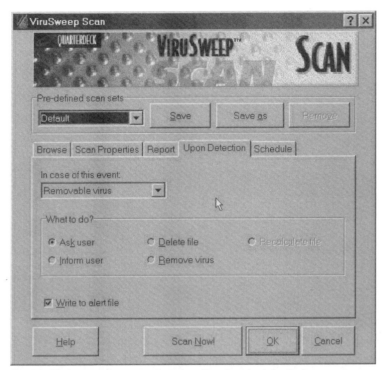

Fig.8.4 Various actions can be taken if a virus is detected

"kill" a virus. The program will then usually give details of how to manually remove the virus.

Things are likely to be very difficult if you do not use anti-virus software and your PC becomes infected. On the face of it, you can simply load an anti-virus program onto the hard disc and then use it to remove the virus. In practice it is definitely not advisable to try this method, and most software of this type will not load onto the hard disc if it detects that a virus is present. This may seem to greatly reduce the usefulness of the software, but there is a good reason for not loading any software onto an infected system. This is the risk of further spreading the virus by loading new software onto the computer. With a lot of new files loaded onto the hard disc there is plenty of opportunity for the virus to infect more files. Most viruses can actually be removed once they have infected a system, but it is not usually achieved by loading a major piece of anti-virus software onto the hard disc and using it to remove the virus.

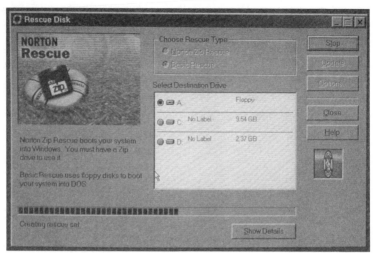

Fig.8.5 A set of five recovery discs are made when installing Norton Anti-virus 2000

Boot disc

The method offered by many anti-virus suites is to boot from a special floppy disc that contains anti-virus software. With this method there is no need to load any software onto the hard disc, and consequently there is no risk of the anti-virus software causing the virus to be spread further over the system. With the Norton Anti-virus 2000 program a boot disc plus four support discs are made during the installation process (Figure 8.5). If boot problems occur at a later date, the PC can be booted using the Norton boot disc, and with the aid of the other discs a comprehensive range of virus scans can be undertaken (Figure 8.6). In some cases the virus can be removed automatically, and it might also be possible to have any damage to the system files repaired automatically as well.

Diagnosis

Where a virus or similar program is the cause of a PC's problems it will usually become obvious quite early in the proceedings that a virus is to blame. The virus will proudly proclaim its presence with an onscreen message. In other cases it will not do so, making it difficult to determine whether the problem is due to a virus or a genuine problem with Windows

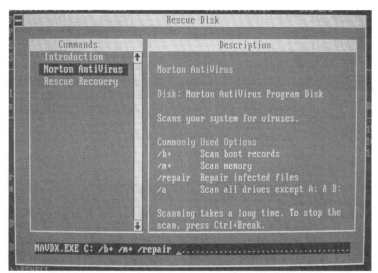

Fig.8.6 Scanning for viruses using the Norton Anti-virus 2000 recovery discs

or the PC's hardware. If there are repeated problems with the boot files becoming damaged or erased, it is very likely that a virus or similar program is responsible. A lot of inexplicable changes to the Windows Registry and other system or configuration files is also good grounds for suspicion.

There is plenty of anti-virus software available commercially, on the Internet at low cost or free, and it is often given away on the cover-mounted CD-ROMs supplied with computer magazines. If you suspect there may be a virus causing the problem it is best to use at least two and preferably three up to date anti-virus programs to check the PC's hard disc. Where applicable, download updates for the software so that you are using the most up to date versions that should detect any new viruses. There is no guarantee that the problem is not due to a secretive virus in the event that the programs fail to detect one. On the other hand, it becomes an outside chance and it is probably better to follow other avenues of investigation rather than pursue a virus that is probably not there.

It is only fair to point out that even if the anti-virus software does find a virus and kill it, you may still need to do some work in order to get the computer up and running again. The anti-virus program may be able to repair all the damage inflicted by the virus, but there is a fair chance that the damage will be too great for everything to be fixed. Anyway, with the virus killed off you are at least in a position to start repairing the damage and return things to normality.

Before continuing with this it is not a bad idea to give some thought to the way in which the virus found its way into your PC. There is otherwise a risk that it will soon return and undo the repairs you have made. If you had been using some discs from another computer prior to the problem occurring, check all those discs using the anti-virus programs. Have you downloaded any software from the Internet, or data files that could contain macros? The popular Word DOC and Adobe PDF formats can both contain macros.

Do not make the classic mistake of clearing a virus from you PC only to immediately return to the source and infect it again. Bear in mind that many viruses have a sort of gestation period, and that there can be a substantial gap between the virus program finding its way into your PC and the program actually starting to do its worst. Ideally you should check all discs that have been used with the PC in the previous few weeks or even months. This includes any discs that have been used to store downloaded programs, documents, etc.

Real-time

In order to be of maximum value in an Internet context an anti-virus program needs to operate in real-time. In other words it musty be running in the background all the time that the computer is operating, so that the program can make checks whenever you do anything that could introduce a virus into the system. It has to be pointed out that there is an overhead with this real-time checking. The anti-virus program will use up some of the computer's resources, which will slow things down slightly. The reduction in speed will normally be too small to be of significance, but it could be noticeable when using an older PC that has only a small amount of memory. The boot-up and shutdown times are likely to be slightly elongated as well.

Most anti-virus software either operates in real-time by default or gives you the choice of real-time operation during the installation process. With some anti-virus software you can switch the program to real-time operation via its menu system. Computer Associate's InoculateIeIT Personal Edition is one of the most popular free anti-virus programs (www.cai.com) and is a good choice if you are not prepared to pay for one of the "big name" programs. Updates are free to registered users incidentally.

This is an example of a program that enables real-time protection to be switched on via the menu system (Figure 8.7). You can also select the actions that will activate the monitoring process (Figure 8.8). When using anti-virus software to provide protection against attack via the Internet it is essential to read the "fine print" and ensure that real-time protection is being obtained. Without it the program is probably just lulling you into a false sense of security.

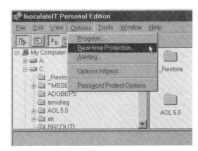

Fig.8.7 Switching on real-time protection in InoculateIT

Email protection

As far as I am aware, there is no risk in reading an Email message provided you are using up to date software. The real threat from Emails comes from attachments that are not what they are supposed to be. These

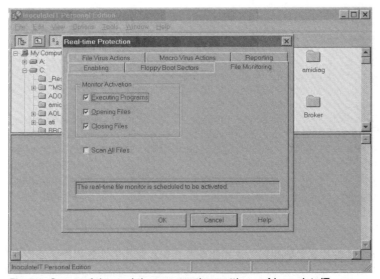

Fig.8.8 Some of the real-time protection settings of InoculateIT

Fig.8.9 First select Options

Email viruses utilise the automation features that are built into Microsoft Office and other programs. These facilities are intended to provide a means of doing clever things that make life easier for users, but they can also hand over control of the PC to a virus. If you do not need these facilities, disabling them is a simple but effective means of removing this threat to your PC. Microsoft has a useful download for Outlook 98 and 2000 that provides protection against viruses such as ILOVEYOU and Melissa. It disables the ability to download attachments that could contain a virus. The download and further information are available from this web page:

http://office.microsoft.com/downloads/2000/Out2ksec.aspx

Another tactic is to turn off the automatic running of scripts in Word, Access, and Excel. First select Options from the tools menu (Figure 8.9), and then operate the General tab in the window that appears (Figure 8.10). Make sure that the checkbox for Macro virus protection is ticked.

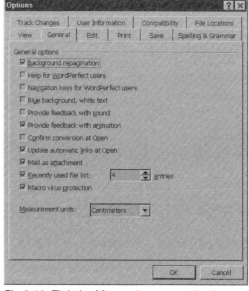

Fig.8.10 Tick the Macro virus protection box

It makes sense to have the security settings of Internet Explorer as high as possible, or failing that as high as possible without preventing the programs from providing the functions you require. To adjust these setting go to the Windows Control Panel and double-click on the Internet Options icon. Left-click on the Security tab in the window that appears, and it should then look something like Figure 8.11. Select the Internet icon in the top section of the window and then operate either the Default Level or Custom Level button. The latter produces a window like the one of Figure 8.12 where radio buttons provide control over individual functions. Here things such as Java and ActiveX scripting can be switched on and off.

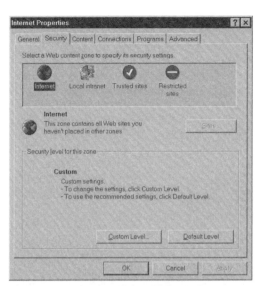

Fig.8.11 The Internet Properties window

The Default Level button is the better option if you do not wish to get that deeply involved. This produces a window like the one of Figure 8.13 where a four-position slider control is used to set the degree of security. This is set to Medium by default, and it is worth trying the High

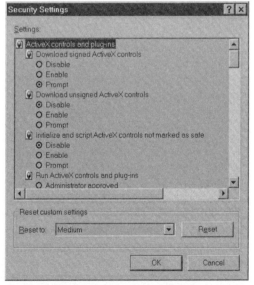

Fig.8.12 Radio buttons enable functions such as scripting to be switched on and off

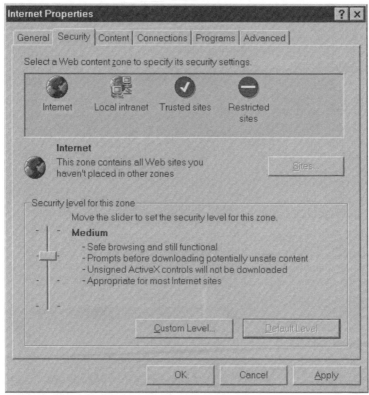

Fig.8.13 The slider control is used to set the required level of security

setting. If you can still surf the Web effectively, then leave it at this setting. If not, go back to the Control Panel and return the control to the Medium setting.

Email anti-virus

There are protection programs designed specifically to deal with Email viruses carried by scripts. Obviously this type of program has to run in real-time, and it produces a warning if it detects something suspicious happening. Figure 8.14 shows a warning message produced by Mail Watcher from Computer Associates, which detects attempts to access the Email system. Since many of the events detected by the program

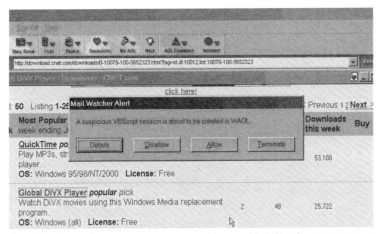

Fig.8.14 A warning message produced by the Mail Watcher program

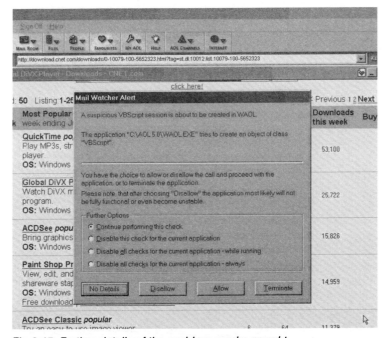

Fig.8.15 Further details of the problem can be sought

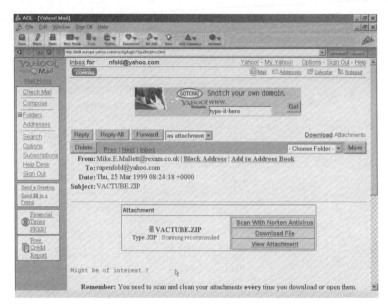

Fig.8.16 An Email being viewed via the Yahoo Email system

are perfectly legitimate it does not block them, but instead provides a simple control panel. The Terminate button is pressed if it is felt that the detected action is possibly a virus. Operating the Allow button enables things to proceed normally. Left-clicking the Details button opens a new window (Figure 8.15) that gives more details of the current operation and the options for dealing with it.

Some Email service providers have facilities for checking attachments prior to downloading them. Figure 8.16 shows an Email that is being viewed using the Yahoo.com Email service. This has a ZIP file attachment and one option for dealing with the attachment is to simply download it regardless of the risk. Another option is to scan it using the Norton Anti-virus program. The scanning process is very rapid because the file is being checked while it is still on the server. The Email, complete with its attachment, can be erased if a problem is discovered. In this way the file never reaches your PC and can not infect it. Usually everything will be all right and a reassuring message will appear (Figure 8.17).

A third option is available, and this enables the attachment to be viewed so that you can check that it is genuine and not an impostor. Obviously

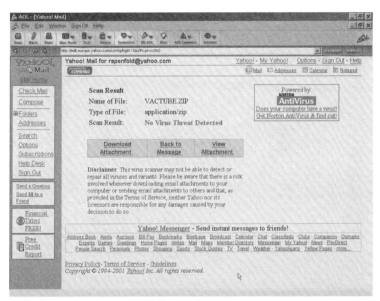

Fig.8.17 The attachment has been checked and is virus-free

this is not of much use with all types of file, but it is useful with something like a Word DOC file that could contain a macro virus. The system will accurately interpret the document so that it appears much the same as it would when viewed using Word itself (Figure 8.18). This method does not guarantee that the attachment is virus-free, but you can at least check that it is a proper document from someone you know.

If you need to work on the document in Word it must be downloaded, but this is not necessary if you only need to read its contents. Having viewed and read the contents the Email and attachment can be deleted. Another possibility is to cut and paste the text from the Email viewer to Word. Select the required text and press the Control and C keys to copy the text to the clipboard. Open Word and then press the Control and V keys to copy the text into Word from the clipboard. With this method any clever tricks in the original document will be lost, but so will any macro virus.

If you need to exchange formatted text documents via Email attachments it is worth considering the rich text format. Documents in this format can have the usual types of Windows formatting including alignment, different fonts, text colours, etc. It does not support any type of macro language, so files that use this format can not contain a macro virus. Plain text files

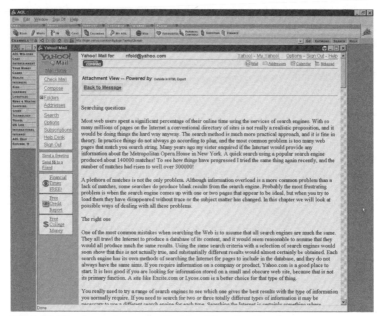

Fig.8.18 Viewing a document that is still on the Email server

are also safe, but have no formatting capability. Of course, these files are only safe when they are what they purport to be. Any data file needs to be checked for authenticity before you download it.

Firewall

Firewalls are mainly used with computers that have a broadband connection to the Internet. With a dialup connection your Internet service provider is part of the huge network that forms the Web, and your PC is tagged onto that network. With a broadband connection your PC is more directly connected to the Internet, and is part of the network. Also, the PC is connected to the Internet all the time it is switched on, and not just when you are actually using the Internet. This makes a PC that uses a broadband connection far more vulnerable to attack than one that has a dialup connection. A firewall is therefore considered essential when using a broadband connection, and it is often provided as part of the connection package.

A firewall can also be used with a dialup connection. If you spend a lot of time on the Internet it would be a wise precaution. The basic function provided by a firewall is to ensure that the applications only

Fig.8.19 *The starting window of the Zone Alarm firewall program*

access the Internet if you have given permission for them to do so. A firewall should block programs like secret Trojans and Spyware that tries to take information from your PC and send it to someone via the Internet. This information often includes things like keystrokes, which could divulge

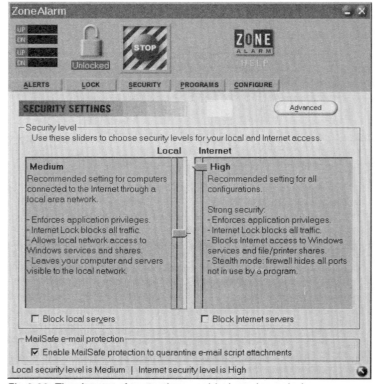

Fig.8.20 The degree of protection provided can be varied

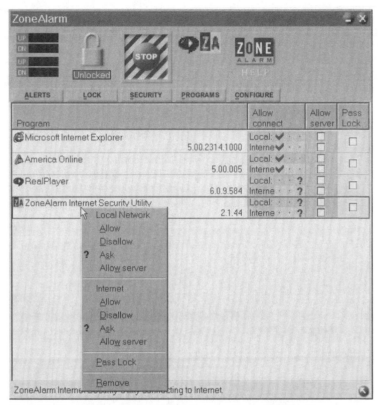

Fig.8.21 The access settings of programs can be changed

your passwords to whoever is spying on your computer system. These programs would not have your permission to access the Internet, and should be detected and blocked by the firewall.

There are plenty of firewall programs available, including some that are free for personal use. Be careful if you try to download a firewall, because disguising a secret Trojan as a firewall program is a popular way of getting these programs into PCs. Only download programs from large and well-established sites where the software on offer should have been thoroughly checked before it is posted on the sites. Alternatively, these programs appear from time to time on the "free" discs supplied with most computer magazines. All the software on these discs should have been thoroughly checked out.

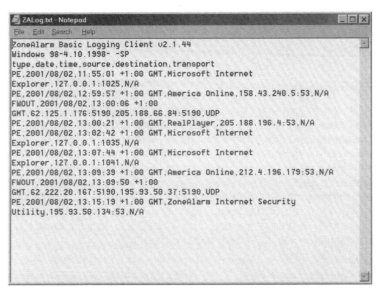

Fig.8.22 A log file produced by Zone Alarm

Zone Alarm from Zone Labs (www.zonelabs.com) is an example of a firewall program that is free for personal use. Running this program produces the small window of Figure 8.19, and operating the tabs enables various aspects of the program to be configured. In Figure 8.20 the Security tab has been operated, and this has slider controls that permit the degree of local and Internet protection to be altered. When a program tries to access the Internet for the first time you are asked whether or not it should be given permission to do so.

The Programs tab produces a list of these programs, and it is possible to change the current settings by right clicking on an entry to produce a popup menu (Figure 8.21). Operating the Alerts tab produces a list giving details of what has been going on recently. Popup alerts are available, but details can also be written to a log file (Figure 8.22). Fortunately, firewall programs usually carry very little overhead, so using one should not significantly slow down your PC.

Do not confuse firewall and anti-virus software. Anti-virus programs detect files that are infected and could damage your system. They will not detect someone trying to infiltrate your computer system via the Internet, although anti-virus software should detect files on your computer that would make the infiltration process easier. Firewall programs should detect anyone trying to infiltrate your computer system, but are not designed to detect and deal with infected files.

Hang-ups

Although it might seem like a good idea to have a number of anti-virus measures in operation on your PC, all simultaneously working away in the background, this is not a good idea. In general, only one real-time anti-virus program should be operating at any one time. It may be possible to have two anti-virus programs running provided they are guarding against different things. There is otherwise a strong likelihood that the two programs will fight it out for control of the computer, probably preventing it from working properly in the process. In fact with two real-time anti-virus programs installed on your PC it is likely that it will have the ultimate in security – it will fail to boot up!

Common sense

Your chances of avoiding problems with viruses are greatly reduced if some common sense is exercised. Using authentic commercial software and only downloading programs from the large and well-established software sites minimises the risks. Using ripped-off software and downloading programs from small sites of unknown pedigree is definitely living dangerously. If mysterious Emails appear in your inbox it is probably best to erase them, and it would be foolhardy to open the attachments of any unexpected Emails. Some companies and individuals have a policy of not opening Email attachments under any circumstances, which should be 100 percent effective in counteracting macro viruses.

An increasingly popular method of avoiding viruses via the Internet is to have a PC specifically for Internet use. This may seem rather extravagant, but many people buy a new PC when their previous one is still far from worn out. Surfing the web does not require the ultimate PC, so the old one should be perfectly adequate for the task. If you try this approach, as far as possible avoid swapping files between the Internet PC and the new one, so that any virus picked up by the Internet PC will not be transferred to the new one. Where (say) a program is downloaded for use on the new PC, thoroughly check the downloaded files using two or three virus checkers before transferring them to the new PC. If the old PC should be infected by a virus it should be relatively quick and easy to reformat the hard disc drive and reinstall the software, because there will be practically no applications software to reinstall.

Last resort

Preventing viruses from damaging your files is definitely better than letting the PC become infected and then removing the virus. This fact becomes more apparent if so many vital files are damaged that the computer is still unusable once the virus has been "killed". There is no absolute guarantee that it will be possible to completely remove a virus, although most of them do seem to be removable. In an extreme case there may be no option but to reinstall Windows.

Where there is some doubt as to whether or not the virus has been fully removed, the safest option is to reformat the hard disc and then reinstall Windows and all the applications software. In fact it is the only option. It is likely to be time consuming, but complete reinstallation should ensure virus-free operation. Also, most computers tend to slow down slightly over a period of time as the hard disc becomes cluttered with huge numbers of files, many of which are no longer necessary. Installing everything from scratch has the advantage of getting things back to an efficient set-up that should operate at peak efficiency.

Unless you have been unable to remove the virus, I would certainly recommend trying to fix Windows by reinstalling it on top of the broken version. If this fails to cure the problem it is time to install Windows from scratch The difference between the two types of installation is that when installing Windows from scratch it is necessary to wipe the hard disc clean first. When installing Windows over the existing version all the existing files on the hard disc are left in place. Simply run the Windows Setup program once the computer has booted into MS/DOS.

The basic installation process is much the same for Windows 95, 98, and ME. Although the description provided here is for an installation of Windows ME, the basic procedure is therefore much the same for Windows 95 and 98. Also, the process is much the same whether the operating system is installed from scratch or on top of an existing Windows installation. If Windows is already on the hard disc it will be detected by the Setup program, which will then reinstall it on top of the existing Windows installation, by default. Any Windows applications programs on the disc should remain properly installed with the new Windows installation. Programs will only have to be reinstalled if the original installations were badly damaged by the virus.

It is because Windows finds any existing installation and merges the new version into it that an installation from scratch is sometimes needed. Completely wiping the easiest way to ensure that there is no information left on the disc to lead the new installation astray. Completely wiping the disc will also remove any virus that can not be "killed" by other means. However, it also means that any data on the disc will be lost unless it is properly backed up. Of course, backing up the disc is not a safe option if it is still infected with a virus. Backing up and restoring files would almost certainly transfer the virus from the old installation to the new one.

Where appropriate you can try a middle course with the Windows directory structure being deleted, but everything else being left on the disc. With luck this will result in Windows being reinstalled successfully, and any problems in the old installation will not resurface. In practice there is no absolute guarantee of success though. Also, bear in mind that any Windows applications on the hard disc will not be installed in the new version of Windows. All the applications will therefore have to be reinstalled on top of the existing software. An advantage of this method is that any data files should be left intact, but note that configuration files for the applications programs will probably be overwritten when the programs are reinstalled.

Things can be taken a stage further, with the data files and any other important files being copied to a new folder. Everything else on the disc is then deleted and Windows is installed from scratch. Where there is no other means of backing up important files, this method has the advantage that the files should still be intact once Windows has been reinstalled, and there are no system files, etc., left on the disc that could have a detrimental effect on the new Windows installation. Backing up important files to another disc is still preferable, because the backup copies on the main disc will be lost if there is a disc fault or a major problem during the Windows reinstallation.

If you decide to delete certain directories rather than simply wiping the disc clean, it is best to do most of the deleting in Windows using Windows Explorer. Using Windows Explorer it is possible to "zap" complete directory structures almost instantly. Deleting large numbers of files and directories in MS/DOS tends to be a very long, slow, and drawn out process. If the computer will not boot into Windows normally, in most cases booting in Safe Mode will still be possible. Operate the F8 function key as Windows starts to boot and then select Safe Mode from the menu that appears (Figure 8.23).

The reinstallation process described here provides a true installation from scratch, with the hard disc being wiped clean. However, the initial part of the process is easily modified to accommodate one of the alternative methods outlined previously. The main installation then proceeds in more or less the same fashion.

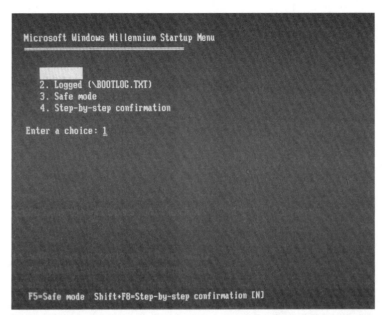

Fig.8.23 Safe Mode can be used if the computer will not otherwise boot into Windows

Booting up

The first task is to boot the computer from a Windows Startup disc. If you do not have a Startup disc, one can be made by selecting Settings from the Start menu, then Control Panel and Add/Remove Programs. Left-click on the Startup Disk tab, operate the Create Disk button, and then follow the onscreen prompts. With the Startup disc in drive A:, restart the computer and with luck it will boot using the Startup disc. The BIOS settings are unsuitable if the computer ignores this disc and tries to boot from the hard disc instead. In this event you must go into the BIOS and choose a boot-up option that has A: as the initial boot disc and drive C: as the second boot disc. Any subsequent boot options are irrelevant, because the PC will boot before it gets to them.

Once the PC starts to boot-up using the Startup disc you will be presented with a menu offering three or four choices. Select the one that boots the computer using CD-ROM support. This is important, because you can not run the Setup program on the Windows CD-ROM without the CD-

ROM support. The CD-ROM support works with the vast majority of CD-ROM drives, including virtually all types that use an IDE interface. However, it does not work with all drives. If it does not work with the CD-ROM drive of your computer you must make your own boot disc with CD-ROM drivers. To make a boot disc first boot the PC in MS/DOS mode. To do this you must operate function key F8 as the system starts to boot into Windows, and then select the appropriate option from the menu that appears. Once the computer has booted into MS/DOS put a blank disc in drive A: and issue this command:

format A: /s

This will format the disc and add the system files needed to make it bootable. In Windows ME there is no option to boot in MS/DOS mode, and your PC might not boot using drive C: anyway if a virus has damaged the system files. Instead the computer can be booted using a Startup disc, and then this command can be used:

format B: /s

In the unlikely event that your PC has a drive B:, this will format the disc in drive B: and place the system files onto it. If there is no drive B:, the operating system will use drive A: as both drive A: and drive B:, and you will have to do some disc swapping when indicated by the onscreen instructions. The CD-ROM and mouse drivers should then be installed onto the floppy disc. The PC should have been supplied with this driver software, together with instructions for using the installation programs. Once this has been done the PC should be rebooted, and it should then be possible to access the CD-ROM drive.

It is necessary to wipe everything from the hard disc if Windows and the applications programs are to be installed from scratch. The easiest way of achieving this is to reformat the hard disc. It will presumably be drive C: that will take the new installation, so this command would be used to format this disc:

format C:

It does not seem to be necessary to have the system files placed on the disc, and they are presumably added by the Windows Setup program during the installation process. The "/s" switch is therefore unnecessary, although adding it will not do any harm. Before formatting the disc the program will warn that all data on the disc will be lost. Where appropriate, make sure that all of the important data has been backed up properly before the disc is reformatted.

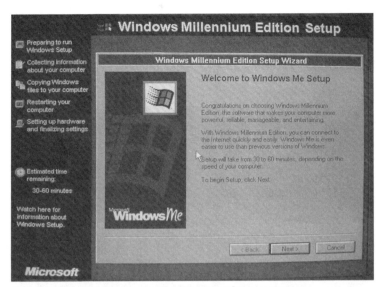

Fig.8.24 The initial screen of the Windows Setup program

Windows Setup

Once the mouse and CD-ROM drive have been installed it should be possible to run the Setup program on the Windows 95/98/ME installation disc. If the PC was booted using a Startup disc, this command is all that is needed:

setup

If the PC was booted using another boot-up disc the CD-ROM's drive letter must be specified in the command. For example, if the CD-ROM is drive D:, this command would be used:

D:\setup

After a welcome message on the screen the Scandisk utility will be run, and it will check for errors on the hard disc drives and any logical drives. Assuming all is well, a message will appear on the screen confirming that there were no errors. Press the "x" key to exit Scandisk and (if necessary) operate the Enter key to remove the onscreen message and go into the first screen of the Windows Setup program (Figure 8.24). It is then a matter of following the on-screen prompts to complete the Windows installation, providing the information that is requested, as described in the next section.

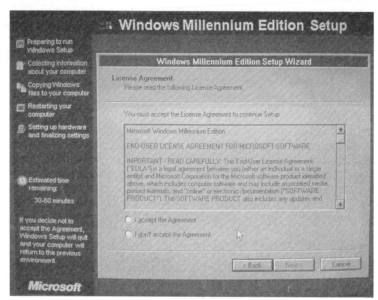

Fig.8.25 Windows can not be installed unless you agree to the terms
         and conditions

Note that you can install the upgrade version of Windows 95, 98 or ME
onto a "clean" hard disc, and that it is not essential to load your old
version of Windows first so that you have something to upgrade. However,
during the installation process you will probably be asked to prove that
you have a qualifying upgrade product by putting the Setup disc into the
floppy drive or CD-ROM drive, as appropriate. Do not throw away or
recycle your old Windows discs, as this could leave you unable to reinstall
the Windows upgrade.

Installation

First you have to agree to the licensing conditions (Figure 8.25), and it is
not possible to install Windows unless you do. At the next screen the
Windows Product Key has to be entered (Figure 8.26). This code number
will be found on the Windows certificate of authenticity and (or) on the
back of the CD's jewel case. Next you are asked to select the directory
into which Windows will be installed (Figure 8.27), but unless there is
good reason to do otherwise, simply accept the default (C:\Windows).
After some checking of the hard disc you are offered several installation

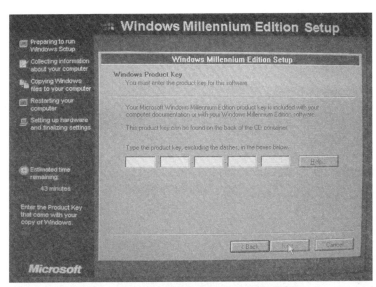

Fig.8.26 Enter your Windows serial number at this screen

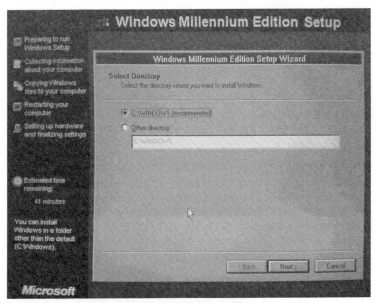

Fig.8.27 The default directory will usually suffice

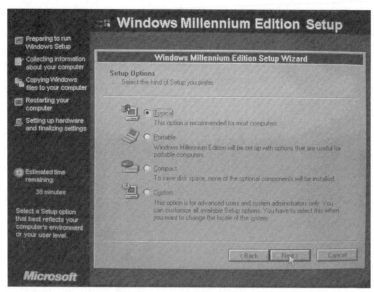

Fig.8.28 A typical installation is suitable for most purposes

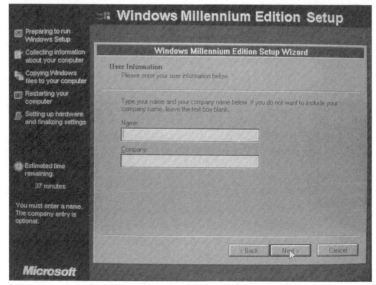

Fig.8.29 Private individuals can leave the Company field blank

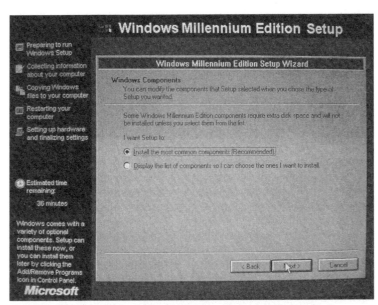

Fig.8.30 This window enables the information provided so far to be reviewed

options (Figure 8.28), but for most users the default option of a Typical installation will suffice.

Remember that you can add and delete Windows components once the operating system is installed, so you are not tied to the typical installation forever. The Custom option enables the user to select precisely the required components, but this can be time consuming and you need to know what you are doing. The Compact option is useful if hard disc space is limited. The Portable option is optimised for portable PCs, and is the obvious choice if you are installing the system on a computer of this type.

At the next screen you type your name and company name into the dialogue boxes (Figure 8.29). If an individual owns the PC the box for the company name can be left blank. The purpose of the next screen (Figure 8.30) is to give you a chance to check the information entered so far, and to provide an opportunity to change your mind before moving on to the actual installation process. Operating the Next button may bring up a network identification screen (Figure 8.31). Where appropriate, make sure that this contains the correct information. In most cases the PC will not be used on a network, and the default settings can be used.

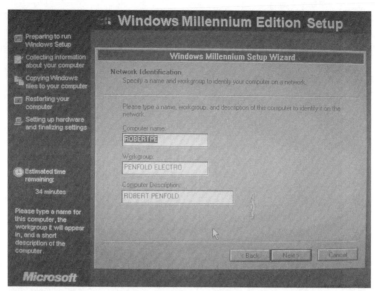

Fig.8.31 In most cases the default network settings can be accepted

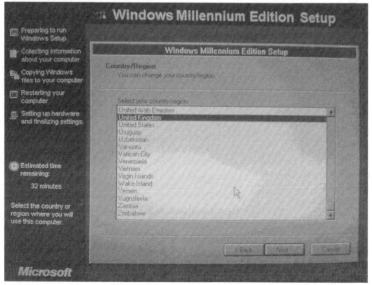

Fig.8.32 Here you simply select the appropriate country from the list

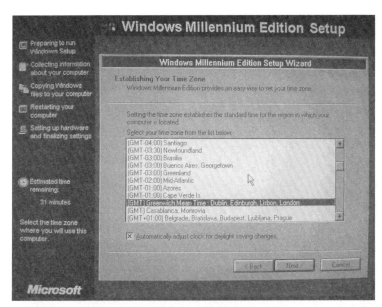

Fig.8.33 Next the correct time zone is selected.

Next the appropriate country has to be selected from a list (Figure 8.32), and then the required time zone is selected (Figure 8.33). This screen also provides the option of automatically implementing daylight saving changes. The next screen (Figure 8.34) enables a Windows Startup disc to be produced. If you already have one of these you may prefer to skip this section by operating the Cancel button and then the OK button. Unfortunately, floppy discs are not the most reliable of storage mediums. If you only have one Startup disc already, I would suggest that you go ahead and make another one so that you have a standby copy.

If you are using an upgrade version of Windows there will be an additional section in the setting up procedure where you have to prove that you have a qualifying product to upgrade from. The screen of Figure 8.35 will appear, so that you can point the Setup program towards the disc that contains the earlier version of Windows. To do this you will have to remove the upgrade disc from the CD-ROM drive and replace it with the disc for the previous version of Windows. Then either type the path to the CD-ROM drive in the text box (e.g. E:\) or operate the Browse button and point to the appropriate drive in standard Windows fashion. Note that this stage will be passed over if you are reinstalling an upgrade

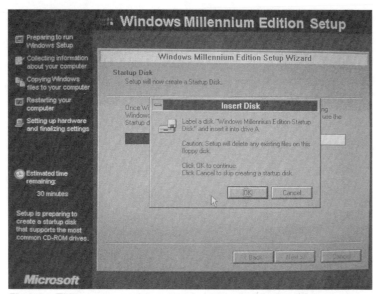

Fig.8.34 This screen enables you to produce a Windows Startup disc

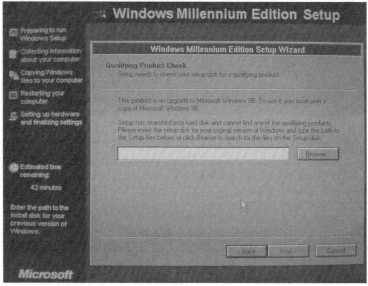

Fig.8.35 This screen appears if you are using a Windows upgrade

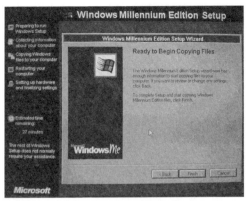

Fig.8.36 At last, the main installation screen has been reached!

version on top of an existing Windows installation. Windows will find the existing installation and will deduce from this that you are a bona fide user.

Having completed all this you will have finally progressed to the main installation screen (Figure 8.36), and from thereon installation is largely automatic. A screen showing how the installation is progressing will appear (Figure 8.37). The computer will reboot itself two or three times during the installation process, so if you opted to produce a Windows Startup disc during the

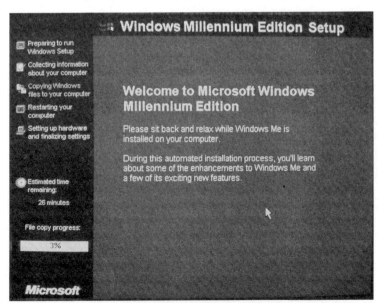

Fig.8.37 This screen shows how the installation is progressing

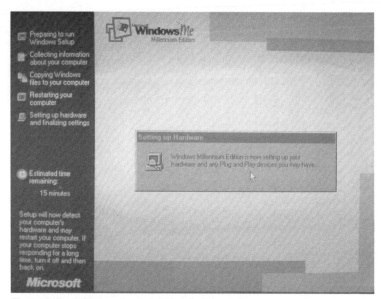

Fig.8.38 In the later stages of installation various messages pop up to tell you what the installation program is doing

initial set-up procedure remember to remove this from the floppy drive. Otherwise the computer might reboot from the floppy rather than the hard disc, which would interfere with the installation process.

In the later stages of the installation there will further screens telling you what the computer is doing, and giving an indication of how far things have progressed (Figure 8.38). No input is required from the user during all this, so you can let the computer get on with the installation. The one exception is that near the end of the installation process you will be asked to supply a user name

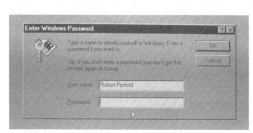

Fig.8.39 Just operate the OK button if you do not wish to use a password

and password (Figure 8.39). Simply leave the password text box blank if you do not require password protection. Eventually you should end up with a basic Windows installation, and the familiar initial screen (Figure 8.40).

Sometimes the Windows Setup program comes to a halt. Either the computer shows no signs of any disc activity for some time, or there may be repeated disc activity with the installation failing to make any progress. The usual

Fig.8.40 Eventually the PC boots into Windows

cure is to switch off the computer, wait a few seconds, and then switch on again. The Setup program will usually detect that there was a problem, and will avoid making the same mistake again. If the computer is switched on and off on several occasions, but the installation still fails to complete, it will be necessary to reboot using the Startup disc, wipe the hard disc clean, and try again.

Hardware drivers

There will probably still be a certain amount of work to be done in order to get all the hardware fully installed, the required screen resolution set, and so on. Windows 95/98/ME might have built-in support for all the hardware in your PC such as the sound and video cards, but this is unlikely. In order to get everything installed correctly you will probably require the installation discs provided with the various items of hardware used in the PC. These discs may be required during the installation of Windows 95/98/ME, or they may have to be used after the basic installation has been completed.

The instruction manuals provided with the hardware should explain the options available and provide precise installation instructions. These days even the motherboards seem to come complete with driver software for things such as special chipset features and the hard disc interface. It is once again a matter of reading the instruction manual to determine which drivers have to be installed, and how to go about it. Get all the hardware properly installed before you install the applications software.

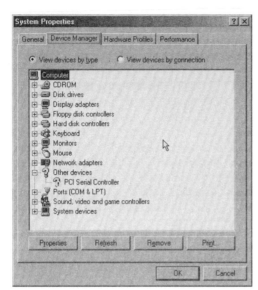

Get the drivers for the motherboard installed first, then the video card, and finally install the drivers for expansion cards such as the modem.

Once everything is supposedly installed correctly it is a good idea to go into the Control Panel program and double-click the System icon. Then select the Device Manager tab to bring up a window of the type shown in Figure 8.41. Look down the various entries to check for any problems. These

Fig.8.41 Check Device Manager for problems
with the hardware

are indicated by yellow exclamation marks, or possibly by yellow question marks. Certain items of hardware will not be picked up properly by Windows. It is no use relying on Plug and Play to install such devices for you, and they must be installed manually. Some types of modem fall into this category.

The question mark in Figure 8.41 is caused by a Windows modem that the system is unable to sort out on its own. As pointed out previously, many modems use relatively simple hardware plus software in the computer to provide the encoding and decoding. Unlike a conventional modem, a software modem does not interface to the computer via a true serial port. It is interfaced via a sort of pseudo serial port, and it is this factor that makes it difficult to correctly identify the hardware. There can sometimes be a similar problem with internal hardware modems.

If a problem is indicated, or an item of hardware is missing from the list, it will be necessary to load the drivers for the hardware concerned in order to get things working properly. This would be a good time to search the relevant web sites for updated driver software for the hardware in your PC. You may well find some newer and better drivers for the hardware in your PC. The hardware can be integrated into Windows

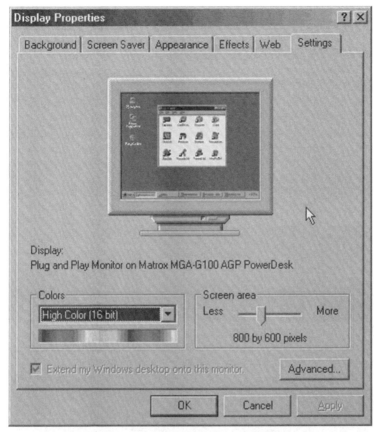

Fig.8.42 Setting the screen resolution and colour depth

using the Add New Hardware facility in the Control Panel. However, many items of PC hardware do not take the standard Windows route and have special installation programs instead. Read the installation manuals carefully and use the exact methods described therein.

Screen settings

Once the video card has been installed properly the required screen parameters can be set. To alter the screen resolution and colour depth, go to the Windows Control Panel and double-click on the Display icon.

Then left-click on the Settings tab to bring up a screen of the type shown in Figure 8.42. It is then just a matter of using the onscreen controls to set the required screen resolution and colour depth. To use the new settings left-click the Apply button. It may be necessary to let the computer reboot in order to use the new settings, but in most cases they can be applied without doing this. Instead Windows will apply the new settings for a few seconds so that you can see that all is well. Simply left-click on the Yes button to start using the new screen settings.

If there is a problem with the picture stability do nothing, and things should return to the original settings after a few seconds. This should not really happen if the monitor is installed correctly, because Windows will not try to use scan rates that are beyond the capabilities of the installed monitor. If a problem of this type should occur, check that the monitor is installed properly. In the Display window of Control Panel select Settings, Advanced, and then Monitor. This will bring up a screen like Figure 8.43, which shows the type of monitor that is installed. If the installed monitor is not the correct one, or is just one of the generic monitor types, left-click the Change button and select the correct one. If the picture is stable with the new settings but the size and position are completely wrong, there is probably no problem. It should be possible to position and size the picture correctly using the monitor's controls. Many graphics cards are supplied with utility software that helps to get the best possible display from the system, and it is worth trying any software of this type to see if it gives better results.

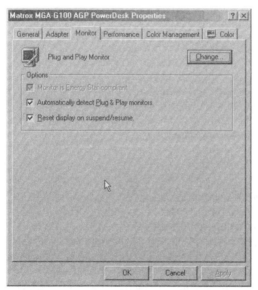

Fig.8.43 Checking installation of the monitor

Disc-free ME

It has been assumed in this chapter that you have a Windows installation CD-ROM. Some computers are supplied with Windows ME pre-installed, and they do not come complete with a Windows installation CD-ROM. Instead, the hard disc has two partitions with drive C: acting as the main disc and a much smaller drive D: containing the Windows files. There is usually a CD-ROM that can be used to recover the situation in the event of something like a hard disc failure or major corruption of the disc's contents. However, this is not an ordinary Windows installation disc. With a computer of this type it is necessary to resort to the instruction manual for details of reinstalling Windows.

Manufacturers are able to customise the installation software to suit their PCs and any software bundled with them. Consequently there are differences in the installation procedures, but there should be a quick and easy way of getting back to a basic Windows installation. In fact some manufacturers provide a quick means of getting back to the factory settings. In other words, the computer will have Windows installed and set up correctly for the hardware installed at the factory. Of course, if you have changed the hardware configuration of the PC, it will be necessary to install the drivers for the new items of hardware.

Secure site

Sites that take sensitive information such as credit card details normally use encryption so that your information is safe from hackers, but how do you know when you are using a

Fig.8.44 The padlock icon switched on in Internet Explorer

secure site. By default, Internet Explorer will tell you when you are entering and leaving a secure site. This can get a bit irritating, so most users switch off these messages. Even where they are still operational, it can

be difficult to keep track of things if the messages keep popping up. Fortunately it is very easy to determine whether or not a secure site is being accessed using Internet Explorer. A tiny padlock icon appears near the bottom right-hand corner of the

Fig.8.45 The padlock icon in Netscape Communicator

window when visiting a secure site (Figure 8.44). If this icon is absent, the site is not secure, even it contains claims to the contrary. Netscape browsers use a similar system, but the padlock icon (Figure 8.45) is normally the same colour as the background, and it turns yellow once into a secure site.

Covering tracks

A common problem with a shared computer is the lack of Internet privacy, with the History feature of Internet Explorer showing which sites you have visited, and even which pages of each site were opened. This is a problem that tends to be associated with visits to hardcore pornographic sites,

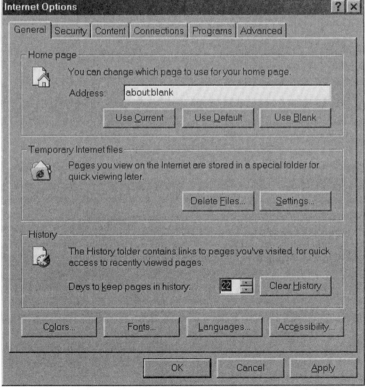

Fig.8.46 The Internet Options window controls the History settings

but most of us value our privacy and would prefer others not to have details of our surfing activities even if they are "squeaky clean". There are a number of programs available that can sweep away any records of your Internet visits, but it is not necessary to use one of these unless you are determined to remove every trace of your Internet activities.

For most purposes it is sufficient to delete all the entries in the History folder. In order to do this go to the Windows Control Panel and double-click on the Folder Options icon. This will produce the window of Figure 8.46. Left-click the Clear History button to delete all the entries in the History folder. The warning message of Figure 8.47 will appear, giving you an opportunity to change your mind. Bear in mind that there is a price to pay

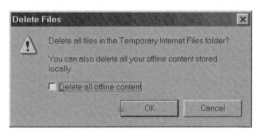

Fig.8.47 Operate the OK button to clear the History folder

for clearing the History folder. If you wish to return to a site and you have forgotten its name, the History folder will not be able to come to the rescue. Also, bear in mind that the History entries for other users will also be removed along with your own entries. Tick the checkbox if you wish to remove any pages made available for offline viewing. Again bear in mind that it is not just your own material that will be deleted, and any offline content will be removed.

Back at the Internet Options window you can operate the Delete Files button to remove the temporary Internet files. This further improves the degree of privacy, but may slow up access to sites that are revisited. Left-click the Apply and OK buttons and then try running Internet Explorer. Only the Today folder should remain in the History

Fig.8.48 Only an empty Today folder will remain

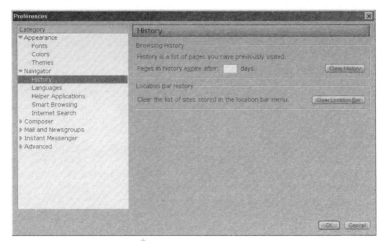

Fig.8.49 *The History folder of Netscape Communicator can also be cleared*

section of the window (Figure 8.48), and this should contain no entries. If the History folders are not cleared again, the weekly folders will reappear in the fullness of time. The deleted files do not appear in the Recycle Bin, so there is no need to empty the Recycle Bin in order to fully remove them from the system. However, this also means that once they are deleted there is no possibility of changing your mind.

Netscape browsers also have a History facility, and this can be cleared by launching the program and then selecting Preferences from the Edit menu. Left-click on the History entry in the left-hand section of the window, which should then look like Figure 8.49. Operate the Clear History button to delete the entries in the History folder. The Clear Location Bar button should be operated as well if you wish to remove the entries from the drop-down menu of the location (address) bar (Figure 8.50). Incidentally, with Internet Explorer this menu is automatically cleared when the History folders are cleared.

Fig.8.50 *The location bar can also be cleared*

Point to remember

A virus is a program that attaches itself to other files and spreads throughout a system, and from system to system if the opportunity arises. There are other types of file that can attack a computer system, including Trojans.

A good virus detection program should detect and deal with viruses, Trojans, etc., provided it is kept up to date. In order to be fully effective in an Internet context the anti-virus program must be capable of real-time operation.

A firewall program prevents others gaining access to and possibly even control of your PC via the Internet. Although mainly associated with always-on broadband Internet connections, a personal firewall is well worthwhile if you have a dialup connection, especially if you spend a lot of time online.

A firewall program is not designed to detect and deal with viruses, Trojans, etc., and it will not prevent you from downloading infected files. An anti-virus program will not stop someone from gaining access to your PC via the Internet. For full protection both types of program should be used.

Provided you are using up to date software there should be no risk of your PC being infected if you open and read an Email. Attachments are a different matter, and are now a common means of trying to spread viruses.

Where possible, check your Email attachments for viruses before downloading them to your PC. Never open Email attachments if the sender is unknown to you, or you are not expecting a file from that particular person. You can always Email the supposed sender of the file to check its authenticity.

Prevention is better than cure. It should be possible to remove a file that has infected your computer system, but it may do irreparable damage to the files on your hard disc first. In an extreme case the hard disc has to be reformatted and everything, including Windows then has to be reinstalled from scratch.

Data and configuration files are normally backed up to CD-RWs, etc., prior to reinstalling Windows from scratch, unless backup copies already exist. Making backup discs is a bit risky in cases where it has not been possible to fully remove a virus. Take due care not to re-infect the system from backup discs.

If infected files are detected on the hard disc drive, check any other discs that have been used with the PC in the previous few weeks or even months. A virus is easily spread to floppy discs, CD-RWs, etc., and it can be on the system for some time before it becomes apparent.

Programs that will remove records of where you have been on the Internet are available, but for most purposes it is merely necessary to clear the History folder. This facility is available with both Microsoft and Netscape browsers.

Index